GRANDMOTHER'S FOOTSTEPS

Jenny McCombe

June 2007

British Library Cataloguing In Publication Data
A Record of this Publication is available
from the British Library

ISBN 1846851262
978-1-84685-126-1

First Published March 2006 by

Exposure Publishing, an imprint of Diggory Press,
Three Rivers, Minions, Liskeard, Cornwall, PL14 5LE, UK
WWW.DIGGORYPRESS.COM

ACKNOWLEDGEMENTS

Welcome to the second book of my travelling adventures as an English grandma.

I acknowledge and thank the Surgeon who wished me luck on my 'cancer journey'. The Spot of Bosom Bother chapter is about this journey which I had not anticipated! The profit from your purchase of this book will go to Cancer Research – thank *you*!

I also acknowledge with thanks the friends who helped me with this book – especially Patti Keane who created the lovely covers. She, and several others, photocopied my letters and emails to their friends while I was travelling and encouraged me to write this second book. Thanks too, to Marge Sheldrake, for the photograph of me on the back cover

Most of all I send special thanks to the many amazing people I met along the way. Thanks to the families who 'put me up' and 'put up with me', thanks to Gap-Year friends for seeing me home in the small hours, to everyone who laughed at my jokes and to all those of you who have invited me back – see you soon!

CONTENTS

NEPAL

10.07.96

My first visit to Nepal was taken to obtain an extension to my Indian visa. I had been working in an orphanage in Tamil Nadu, Southern India, for six months, and I wanted to extend my stay there for another six. I am an English grandmother and this was my Big Adventure, following a (happy) divorce, after 39 years of marriage, children and grandchildren.

I was in the middle of a year's unpaid leave from work in England, and I loved the life in India and didn't want to leave. I had enjoyed such a colourful period getting to know the giggling, warm-hearted and appreciative children and staff in the large orphanage in a small village. I badly needed the extension to my visa, because I had promised to 'do' an English Christmas for the children.

17.07.96

On arrival in Kathmandu the Indian authorities were at first adamant that I couldn't have an extension to the Indian visa and that was that! This was in spite of showing my flight ticket home to England and a reference letter from my orphanage to prove I didn't intend staying longer than another six months.

Officials from the visa office told me to return in two days and apply again but I went back to the small hotel in Kathmandu and cried into my mushroom burger and dhal sauce, because the officials were not optimistic I would get the extension. I had to explain to the waiter why I was upset. He said, "If the Indians don't want you, why don't you care for our little boys?" and I thought 'Why not?' I could return to my Indians for a few weeks until my existing visa ran out and then explore Nepal on my way home to England.

I visited the Visa office daily. Someone told me you could sometimes get a Visitors' visa more easily than a Work visa, so I joined the queues of desperate tourists - Japanese, American, a few Europeans and all of us praying, begging or crying to the stern, miserable and unrelenting Indians. You had to talk through a grill in the wall outside the office, which was too high for most of us to talk normally and was in full sunlight whatever time of day we called. We had to answer questions like these:

"Why do you think you can treat India so cheaply, thinking you can come and go as you wish?
"Can't you read? It says write in black pen!"
"Stop that (crying) immediately!"
"Why are you travelling alone?"
"What is your husband thinking of, that he would allow you to travel singly?"

They asked a beautiful English girl in front of me in the queue why she wanted to come to India and she replied "I am on a mission from God". I was so proud of her, and it shut them up for a while - but she failed to get a visa.

While waiting for the Visa office to open one day, I found the Nepal Children's Orphanage, in Naxal, a rather run-down but beautiful building housing about 300 orphans. It was a short walk from the hotel and the somewhat arrogant, handsome boy in charge of it said they would be pleased to have me to help out in a few weeks' time. On the way home, in Mike's Breakfast - a cafe run by a very camp American - I met a stuffy British couple and lovely VSO Field Organiser, who told me where to look for digs, should I come back. Things seemed to be looking up. Mike's Breakfast was a bit beyond my price range but it was such an exotic spot that I returned whenever rupees allowed.

While negotiating with the Indians for my visa, I stayed in the 'Two-Seater' Rest House - in a nice small room with en-suite loo and shower - and only costing three pounds a night. I found that the blue knob over my bath meant Hot and if I let it run and wasted the cold water for five minutes, it was blissfully efficient. The first room I had been allocated was prettier but had a full sized tree growing in the middle of the bathroom and was so damp that mushrooms grew on my clothes within a day or two *and* it cost five pounds, so I didn't mind moving.

14.07.96
I had an acute shortage of funds by now, because my Visa card was being rejected by the Bank. All records had been destroyed in the IRA bombing of my Co-operative Bank office in Manchester! However, I decided to visit to Pokhara as a cheap time filler, and got a ticket and hoped for the best for money.

I discovered, on the morning of my departure, that there is a quarter of an hour time difference from Nepal to India. As this discovery coincided with the fact that my watch had suddenly gone rusty and stopped, I had a lot of scampering about to do to catch this bus. I found the bus stop without too much trouble and was just in time to catch the three year old Indian Duplicate, as they called the bus. (Means rusting heap I think!) Even at 5 a.m. there was a trader begging to sell me carpets! Whoever in the world would buy a carpet prior to a journey of this length?

I had a most wonderful six-hour scenic extravaganza - precipices and thousand foot drops on every winding hair-pin bend - with my teeth grinding and jaw clenched at the same time. I should have guessed from the mini-shrine on the dashboard, that help from The Gods would be needed.

The bus driver told me his life story, that bus drivers earn ten pounds a month, only crash when they are drunk or asleep, and three of them a year are just that. He also informed me that it is only eight U.S. dollars for a Chinese Walkman here, that only 7% of the Nepalese population are educated and *many* other unrelated facts.

From the lurching, smelly, speeding bus I saw terraced paddy fields below, shining like little mirrors set in grass. In the villages there were children carrying their siblings and babies hanging in slings or hammocks from rafters or trees everywhere - so many children! Many of the on-coming lorries had Christmas decorations all over their windscreens and bonnets. There was maize growing, drying, being barbecued without oil, or sold as popcorn. I thought the drying cobs, hung on the houses, were parrots' bodies at first. You suffered from the exhaust fumes everywhere - even at country stops. There were pomegranates, cucumbers and bananas being offered for sale, lifted up to us at the bus windows.

At one stop an American woman travelling by bus, the other way, told me that she was sickened by the poverty in India and Nepal and couldn't wait to "get the hell out of here". She considered English people to be better travellers than Americans because we like strange and peculiar experiences, while Americans prefer Holiday Inns and familiar surroundings. When I told her my tale of woe - no money since my Visa card had been cancelled - she immediately offered me dollars to be sure I'd get home! I declined and assured her I was getting to like a diet of bananas only and was optimistic of the Card people coming through with the goods soon! Her kindness confirmed my experience of the genuine friendliness and warmth of Americans and Canadians, wherever I meet them.

Nepalese women in Pokhara

Four boys of about 12 years got on the bus and began to beg and play homemade wooden fiddles and sing like mad. Other passengers didn't want me to give them anything because they said they were "rubbish", but I did. At another refreshment stop I saw a little girl scything grass with a great big scythe, and she couldn't have been more than five years old. All the children I saw en route were herding goats, collecting wood or straw or vegetables, and I only saw one 'crocodile' of immaculately uniformed children processing to a modern school building. All the workers in the fields wore Tibetan straw hats, which were a beautiful shape. I spent this day mentally with Dave - my nephew who teaches geography - because of the geological interest en route and a Dave look-alike on the bus, I expect). It often happens that I share my adventures with someone from home in my mind - I certainly take my family and friends with me when I travel and I rarely feel lonely or homesick.

An uneducated peasant on the bus asked me that day if Britain was a democracy or a monarchy, how much is a minibus in England, could he come and live in the orphanage with me, and what is the current rate of taxation in England!

Pokhara was a lovely little town with loads of snow visible on the Himalayas. The charge per night at the Pokhara Holiday Hotel was 300 IR per night. I must have counted my money in piles of Indian rupees and piles of Nepal rupees, a hundred times. My attempt at eating only a pomegranate for lunch, using scissors to cut it, caused me to stain my trousers in a horribly inappropriate place, so I pranced about in a fancy Laura Ashley dress to sightsee in Pokhara. The people I met didn't seem to mind. I was quickly befriended by Binni and Prem, two large ladies sitting on a mat in the middle of the road, smoking ciggies. They invited me home for black coffee with two ton of sugar in it and barbecued me a dry corn cob. I took photos but their address was very complicated and the post is unreliable so I doubt if I can send copies back to their house. Conversation was a bit 'sweaty' too but my grandchildren photos helped yet again. In the course of the tortuous conversation they said they were vegetarian and ONLY ate meat or goat......

During the afternoon a man attached himself to me as my Guide to the Museum. It was about two miles walk in 30 degrees as it turned out. He was called Dyamir and two British people and I enjoyed his tour and a cup of good coffee in the delightful museum. Just while talking to the British couple, the word Balti (an Indian cooking system which is new in England) came to me. I had been trying to think of the word for months. I also meant to ask them what deodorant is made of but I forgot. It is curious the questions that arise when you are away from home, isn't it?

I was buying a second-hand Jeffrey Archer and a map of Nepal from my limited resources when I met Julie from Ipswich - my home town! She is a mature Social Work Diploma student who knew everyone I knew at the Suffolk County Council offices. She had come to help people with learning difficulties in a Tibetan refugee camp and was a bit jet-lagged but was happy to have a San Miguel beer and a mushroom-burger with me. We watched a cow come into the restaurant garden and eat their best bushes. I moved to her Guest House, The Sherpa, for my final night in Pokhara - it was half the price of mine. Very early in the morning, Julie bought me a yak cheese roll from the German Bakery and left for work, and I got the bus back to Kathmandu. A student Brahmin boy sat next to me on the bus and he told me all about arranged marriages and how no cigarettes or beer are allowed in Nepal.

On reaching Kathmandu, I enjoyed a pot of tea in my room at the Two Seater Hotel and it was just like coming home. Again I counted my left-over money and calculated that the twelve hours travel there and back had cost two pounds eighty! I had one pound fifty pence left over. It was akin to lottery winning when the cashier in the Bank gave me a lovely wodge of rupees, having at last connected with my home bank.

Back to the Visa Office the next day, and I was allowed a personal appointment. I shamelessly ingratiated myself, even comparing grandchildren's' photos with the Visa Officer - who said I should come back at 4.30 p.m. and I might be lucky!

I got it! But only for three months, unhappily. Still I was pleased to be able to stay a little longer in India and felt more resigned to the situation, having decided on the new plan to come back to Kathmandu. On my return to the hotel a crazy rickshaw man tried to kill us both but I was so happy and relieved to have finished with officialdom that I didn't complain or shout at him. I staggered into my hotel room, calmed down after a shower, and did crossword puzzles and played tapes, had a sandwich and slept soundly. I returned to India the next day.

12.10.96
Three months later I am back in Kathmandu anticipating a new adventure, and having returned to Nepal, I must tell you: FOOD is the best thing to happen to me! After my months of predictably rather sparse and boring stuff in the Indian orphanage, I find the hundreds of cafes and restaurants serving food all day and late into the night, a wonderful dimension on life. The Nepalese people cater to every nation's tastes, the choice is incredible and the menu cards and notice-boards in English, hilarious!

'Tender hand steak, slaice steak, chicken sizlian, pouch egg, scrembled egg' etc. Sometimes I eat in the little hotel garden, with strange birds twittering and incense burning and English newspapers to hand, but every meal in a cafe is a different adventure in Kathmandu.

My first breakfast was wonderful and I knew that I would soon regain the weight lost in India. A typical breakfast menu, eaten in a hibiscus-and-bougainvillea-hung garden restaurant was two eggs, celery in baked potatoes, grilled tomatoes, two white toasts, wheat bread, jam or honey, tea or expresso coffee. Most of the cafes are courtyard gardens with exotic foliage and flowers and the humidity and noise of temple bells and even the traffic noise gave me such pleasure. I didn't even feel the need to *read* which I usually like to do if I am alone in a restaurant. (Tip from a lone granny: read a newspaper if you want to look available for chats, a book if you want to be alone.)

14.10.96

I started work at the NCO orphanage yesterday and I felt very lonely to start with, but now I have something definite to do, I don't mind having no English-speaking colleagues. There are Danish volunteers here but somehow I never meet them and this, compounded by the lack of information from the orphanage staff, makes it very different from my Indian experience.

The first suggested projects for me here are to re-open a Doll Exhibition and to start a Baby Clinic! There is an existing surgery for the orphans but they wanted to expand it to the community for giving injections and vaccinations to Kathmandu babies. I can't get an appointment to meet the doctor or nurse that are supposed to visit regularly - I am beginning to doubt their existence, actually.

I feel happier about the prospect of improving the Doll Exhibition, which is going mouldy in an attractive but shabby building. I think I could make it into an educational sort of doll museum and incorporate flags and maps of other countries and open it to the public, as well as to schools. First step is to get all the dolls out of their glass cabinet prisons and into the sunshine and dry them off before brushing with a toothbrush. Some of them are very beautiful and I will apply to the consulates and embassies in Kathmandu for any additional offerings they might like to give us.

Refectory make-over in Orphanage

12

7.10.96

I had seen an advertisement in a café, and so found my way to the ROKPA orphanage. This orphanage is financed by Swiss people and run by young, British volunteers. Jimpa, Kevin and Stephanie are working very hard here, and were very pleased to see the number of new recruits who had responded to the plea for help. There had been a bit of confusion about the administration at this orphanage and this lovely group was a bit depressed and uncertain about their roles and way forward. They told me that my advice following nine months' experience working in an Indian orphanage and my grandmotherly encouragement helped to restore their self-confidence.

There are only 25 children in this orphanage and they all attend a bilingual school, so it was lovely to be able to talk to them, unlike at the NCO orphanage. They are beautifully dressed by the Swiss, and somewhat precocious, compared with the NCO darlings.

One of the boys had fallen off a roof a month before, five storeys up, and lived. He only had a broken collarbone and teeth etc. but is hyperactive and the English volunteers admitted defeat with him and sent him to another school where he can board as well as be educated. They have also locked the roof off since then!

I decided to spend a couple of days per week at each of the orphanages. And it became apparent to me that my role whilst in Nepal was more as support worker for the staff and children rather than the primary carer that had been my position in the Indian orphanage. This gave me a lot more freedom to explore the country.

18.10.96

Because the refectory at ROKPA was fearfully squalid, we renovated it! The Swiss provided money for paint and some Australian backpackers volunteered to clean it down. After Fran, an Australian, and I had put white paint all over it, and painted the windows green, Californian Jennifer and the kids painted a Walt Disney Jungle Book theme on three walls. Jennifer is an arts graduate so she swings into gear with no trouble on the arty side, and to our amazement the kids and a 14-year old Tibetan refugee made a wonderful wall with chimp, snake, baboon, seagulls and other creatures. I was by now covered in green paint and, as I had forgotten my glasses, I fear the "finish" was not quite what it could be.

Jennifer knew all the words of West Side Story so we sang as we painted. She directed the artistic finishing touches, which were fantastic. We all enjoyed the transformation and Jennifer's Beatle tapes, which she also played and sang to, while skillfully directing the children. They were so proud of the colourful Jungle Book images they created.

The Swiss boy that was my assistant fell by the wayside due to the fumes from the paint. I can only assume that this is yet further proof that grandmothers have more stamina and resistance than these youngsters! Jennifer told me I was 'pro-active' at one point in the proceedings and I had to look that up. When I returned the compliment (well I hoped it was a compliment) by admiring her skills, she just flashed her wonderful American teeth and said, "Yes, I'm a rare bird!" I loved her enthusiasm and energy and we became firm friends.

I loved the 'before and after' effect of the painting and am continuing the transformation of the orphanage by cleaning and painting a room which is to become a library. The Swiss boy is called Roman. We all met up each morning and decided on a plan of action and the whole project seemed to be running very well.

On my way to work one day, I met Heather, a tiny blonde with long curly hair, who had been a Lanzaroti Scuba School owner. Despite the sexual harassment here, she is persevering and going everywhere on her own and loving the country. After her partner in Lanzaroti had left her for a younger woman, she had been to many different countries in her quest for a new lifestyle. She told me that she favoured Australia above all other countries, though she said they have the worst bed bugs she's encountered. Being a Jillaroo appealed to her - working on a cattle station! She had watched horns and bollocks being removed - it would certainly be a different career!

20.10.96
I felt so hot and sweaty in the market today that I couldn't count 20 times 20 rupees for some reed pipes I wanted for prizes for the boys at the orphanage. I walked about all day, taking in the sights and sounds - and there were plenty I must say. (I saw a chicken in a polythene bag under a man's arm, head sticking out, alive!) I got lost in the dark on the way home and kept turning up between the Cholera Hospital and the Eye Hospital. There were mud splashes up to my waist by now and creepy voices in the dark murmuring "Hello", "What's your name?", "Yes, Madam?", "Step inside!" No women anywhere I realised. They were all sitting safely in their homes, having a cup of tea I thought, and I wished I was. I bought Nepali newspapers to use for Christmas wrapping paper with thick golden string, and two cans of Carlsberg to sooth my shattered nerves. Eventually I was rescued by a lovely taxi-man and safely returned to my hotel.

I booked my flight to England today - for 21st December - and booked a typewriter for 50 rupees an hour, each day, to write up my diaries and thoughts on my adventures in India. I had letters from several friends telling that they had photo-copied my letters to their friends, and this was when my India book "Did I Tell You I Went to India?" was first mooted!

I am moving to a cheaper hotel, called Hotel Horizon, because it is such a gourmet's paradise here even by Western standards that I would like to spend the money saved - on FOOD! In Nepal I've decided there's better climate, food, hygiene (well a bit better – no, forget I said that bit), scenery, activities, cosmopolitan company and shopping, compared to India, but much more spitting and pollution than in ' my' bit of India.

My work here is completely different in that I don't get to know the children personally – I am more involved in decorating and renovating, and *very* involved with helping the young staff from the UK. I would have thought I would miss the rewards of teaching and playing with the children, but these new experiences are very satisfying.

Krishna, one of the residents in the Hotel, told me he was a naturopath and I would have loved to learn more about that job. He rather depressed me by saying that though he considered volunteers a very good thing for Nepal, he thought that their improvements were never maintained. He apologised for not speaking to me earlier but he thought I might be German!

At ROKPA the people are much more appreciative and encouraging than at NCO so, though it is 20 minutes rough ride and jolly hard work, I will keep going there, and still have time to eat lovely things and sit about and enjoy Nepal!

25.10.96
This is a fabulous place - I am so happy living here. There are people visiting from all over the world and wonderful things to do every day. There are courses on Buddhism, astrology, palmistry, yoga, reflexology, etc. An enjoyable aspect of these courses is the lunch break, al fresco and consistently delicious and shared with fascinating people from all over the world. My new found friend Jennifer and the other great woman from Australia - Fran - are good company and up for any of these diversions. I really hope they won't need me too badly at the orphanages because it will infringe on my social life!

I even love the *shopping* in Nepal! I found sequinned baseball and baker boy caps, rucksacks, Micky Mouse everything, mandarin jackets, tee-shirts with anything you want embroidered on them, scratchy but colourful jumpers, scratchy but fun socks, slippers and mittens, crocheted mules, cotton bedcovers with everything on them - particularly lovely elephants - and waistcoats of all sizes and colours.

I started yoga lessons but have got the same problems as I once had in pottery classes at home in the '70s. - I am in love with the teacher. He is Austrian and wants me to adore an Indian lady guru, but I'm afraid I am adoring him. When he said "Do you mind if I rest my hand on your head?" I nearly said something very inappropriate! The Indian lady is represented by a large photo draped in red and gold and she doesn't inspire any emotion at all.

26.10.96
The Poste Restante system works! I have collected a couple of letters from my mum and daughter, and I had to wade through hundreds of the box with my initials on, but of course it is worth it. I can't believe how many people

don't pick up their mail but I suppose they have to travel on before it arrives. The little Nepali man that sorts it here laughed when I shouted "YESSSS" when I found some for myself. I meant to rush to a café to open it, but I couldn't wait and sat on the Post Office steps to open it in the sun...

27.10.96
Today I had an interesting conversation with a guy outside a small temple at Kirtipur, which is 1400 metres above Kathmandu – a fairly easy walk from my hotel. We sat among yellow, white and red poinsettias and he told me of a marauding king that had come to this area in the olden days and cut off the nose and top lip of his enemies. It all seemed unlikely sitting in the sunshine, among ankle socks drying with the offerings of fruit on the shrine of this little temple. Hindus and Buddhists share some of the temples - wouldn't it be wonderful if more religions did this?

28.10.96
I have had varying success at the various Embassies in gaining 'stuff' for the Doll Exhibition. Every Embassy has a different 'ambience' and so far has been typical of the stereotypes. In the Russian Embassy there were acres of marble, and crazy-paving, and twenty feet high glazed areas and stern men with guns at the door. In a school a Russian lady head-teacher got a translator and told me that one of her colleagues would supply some Russian books. He did too - today - as did the American Embassy, who added maps and paper flags, and offered me coffee. The Sri Lankans gave a few leaflets and the oily Ambassador lusted after Fran and me, and ogled and questioned us and didn't listen when I told him what I wanted. The Danish were lovely in their very classical Danish way, and their waiting room was decorated stylishly. The Italians gave me wonderful posters that I want to keep for myself, and Jennifer was envious of them, too - she is an artist. The Nepalese in NCO had opened a parcel addressed personally to me from the Austrian Embassy and it contained the most beautiful doll in national dress. I was a bit miffed that they had opened it as they didn't keep the address of the donor so they wouldn't get a thank you letter from me.

30.10.96
I went with Fran to book a hair appointment yesterday and the salon was a hoot. There were Nepali customers sitting cross-legged and leaning backwards in the chairs to have their hair washed and a Western woman with green stuff in her hair, sitting bolt upright. A witchy-looking woman was having her chin waxed and very aristocratic foreigner waving green nails to dry whilst reclining on a chaise longue, completed the clientele!

On the day of our appointment Fran insisted that I must experience Head Massage. I was anointed with Oil on the bones of my forehead and shoulders and the massage was like a physical assault at first, but I gradually relaxed into it and felt enormous benefit. Fran said it was her "shout" (she paid), so that was very beneficial, too.

01.11.96

The clientele at the home of Llamo, a woman doctor in Kathmandu, must have felt *very* sick to undergo her 'treatment'. She was a small, squat Nepalese woman with turban and beads, and her unsavoury home was full of people wanting to be cured of smoking and mental and gynaecological problems to name but a few. Her method was to *bite* the person in an appropriate area. I watched as she bit a man on his chest and put straw on his stomach to extract a 'spirit'. She then sucked blood out of the hole in his chest and spat it into a bowl of something yukky, and declared him cured. There was a woman preceding him who must have given him some misgivings because she was rolling about in agony before he was worked on!

I had come with Roman who wished to give up smoking but I couldn't bear to watch his treatment. Though he looked pale when he came out, he was optimistic that whatever she had done, had done the trick. (However, next time I saw him he was puffing away - marijuana now!)

My 'conversations' with other folk awaiting treatment were confusing:

Me : "How far would it take me to walk to the nearby famous temple?"
He: "On foot?"
(He was wearing a tee-shirt with "Happy Birthday, Baby Jesus" writ large)......

Me : "Have you any dwarfs in Nepal?"
She: "No but my friend is only two feet tall."
(Funny question for me to ask, come to think of it! I don't know how the subject came up.)

Question to me: "Why, in the Kama Sutra are feet always in vaginas?"
Reply: "Dunno!"

I came home in a sort of daze at all that has happened today and forgot to buy some bread because in the shop my eye fell upon a whole cow's head with his fur still on. The top had been sliced off and it was sitting on the grocers' floor, by my feet

2.11.96

Today was somewhat different. Fran and I went to a very posh hotel where Fran's Nepali friend works. We had tea and Croque M'sieur (?) in the most beautiful gardens with the rich people of Kathmandu. Fran introduced me to her 'friend' called Pardon (or something) who has the flattest back to his head I have ever seen, like babies have when they are left in their cots a lot. Fran is staying for bed and breakfast at Pardon's house but they have fallen in love and he would like her to be his second wife, which is allowed apparently......!

I called in at the NCO to deliver a few more flags and posters that had been donated to the Exhibition, and was a bit dismayed to find all the glazed cupboard doors had been closed again. Having spent days removing the

17

mould from the dolls with a toothbrush, because they had been incarcerated in the humid cupboards, I had hoped to persuade the staff to risk burglars (the rooms are very severely padlocked) and leave the dolls in fresher air, but I had obviously failed.

4.11.96
Fran presented me with a condom this morning on the way to work. She announced that it is National Condom Day However, she replaced it in her pocket when I giggled and handed it back. Then, when a beggar on crutches asked her for money, she said no, walked on a bit, then put her hand in her pocket and accidentally bought out the condom. The beggar saw this, dropped his crutches and ran after her to collect it.....

An enticing advertisement for Ecological Treks, invited me to join a dozen or so other visitors to experience climbing a portion of the Himalayas and the receptionist in the agency promised me that a *gentle* pace meant I would be welcome.

I decided to go on the trek in a couple of weeks' time, when the planned work at ROKPA was completed. The prospect of the trek was exciting and much as I loved working with the children and my new friends, I was becoming aware of the time slipping past. The thought of awaking to the sight of the Himalayas, whetted my appetite for an entirely new experience.

5.11.96
A Meditation Lecture, held in The Nepalese Kitchen, was given by three British Buddhists today. One was a deep-voiced actor type, one a white ankle-socked-tennis-playing bald man and one a lovely, humorous Yorkshire man. They had worked in Britain, Nepal and Australia, lecturing in Meditation.

They told of Bharavana, meaning the cultivation and development of concentration, awareness, compassion and positive emotions. Lotus position here means stretching your arms above your head, which creates a symbol of our potential to reach above the layers of muck/obstacles and emerge as beautiful flowers.

Dyarna means absorption or being totally engaged. Evil will always fragment but good is a coming together of energies.
Vipassana is the true meaning of life - the reality in three areas of one's life. which are: earning your living, family and friends, and your leisure time. Sanatha are positive emotions, a clear mind and Samachi is the fixative of awareness.

All this was explained in a very down-to-earth way and questions were welcomed. A Swede, who had tried to meditate for ages and failed, was told that coffee precluded concentration, which explained one aspect that had impeded *my* efforts; a guru advised loosening one's belt to achieve true comfort in the lotus position, and this was another angle I hadn't thought of.

All in all, it certainly gave me a lot to think about and whetted my appetite for:

6.11.96

Buddhism Today was another meditation session. I went with Fran this time, to the Yogic Institute and our lecturer was Judy Something or Other. She lectured all day in a very pleasant, understandable way. Lunch was provided in the garden. Judy says that Buddhism means taking refuge in an internal focus. You decide where you are placing your trust and Buddha recommends a mid-path between life styles. The talk today was promoting his advice to us to have compassion at all times. The compassion in you is like the oil from a sesame seed - it needs pummeling to get it out and flowing. A Buddha nature is awareness, light and potential and overcoming poor accumulations of your past.

Suffering has to be faced up to and recognised as the other face of happiness. More next week: Death and Rebirth being the topic!

I enjoyed this verse which was printed in the foyer of the Meditation centre:

"Now is not good for the Christians' health to hustle the Aryan brown
For the Christian rules and the Aryan smiles and he weareth the Christian down
And the end of the fight is tombstone white with the name of the late deceased
And the epitaph dream "A fool lies here, who tried to hustle the East".
Rudyard Kipling

9.11.96
Trekking in the Annapurnas
I reckon I qualify for the Duke of Edinburgh Gold Award, the Gurkas, the Outward Bound Diploma - everything! I'm just back from my nine days trekking in the Annapurna mountains and I don't know where I hurt most. I crossed and waded through rapids, climbed through clouds and over rope bridges and my *bod* ......the toll it took! It was a marvellous experience though, and the weather, food and company were all first class. If I hadn't tried so desperately to hide the fact that I was a granny and not a Youth trainer like the others, I would have taken it a little slower and not fallen over so much......

I set off by bus again for the six hours from KTD to Pokhara and a lovely Deepok accompanied me and got me coffee at all the stops. He is a porter and comes as part of the deal when you pay for the trek. He is 22 years old, has treacly deep brown eyes and is justly proud of his education and his spoken English.

We flew from Pokhara to Jomsom and he hadn't flown before, so I made him swap seats with me in this tiny little plane so that he could see out of the only window. I read the sick bag in the back seat, as that was all I could see. We landed on what looked like a runway the size of a dining room table. The plane bucked and dropped and boy! - did you know that you were flying in the mountains. It was terrific!

We then met up with four other Brits that made our party - sisters Heather and Lorraine, and their friends, Martin and Mark. They were friends from a Walking Club in England and members of a team that train youngsters for the Duke of Edinburgh Award. They were horribly fit and young but they, and the Guide Durga, and our two porters, Deepok and Ramasol, took great care of me and called me Amah, (Mum) for the duration of the holiday. They kept assuring me that much older people than me coped with the trekking.

I kept up with them, but it was the hardest physical challenge I have ever endured - miles and miles of walking up high stone steps, right up the sides of the mountains, or slithering down gravelly drops or leaping down deep steps. We walked for miles in the deepest valley in the world, so named because the mountains each side were the sixth and eighth highest in the world. There was this wonderful scenery everywhere but the party travelled at such speed I missed much of it, trying to keep on my feet!

We walked through a valley in a sandstorm at one point and my old sun hat saved the day again - tied on by the scarf belonging to my salwar kameez - a sort of Indian pyjama suit that was also perfect for the expedition: a long loose top over drawstring trousers. I think I was probably more comfortable than the other jeans-and-baseball-capped travellers. My Italian straw hat was bought (at huge expense) for my daughter's wedding but it was The Best Thing for India and Nepal and justified the original price.

We waded across incredibly strong rapids, holding hands, and if Lorraine hadn't been such a strong girl, I would've had a dunking, or a drowning, even. Then we crossed a river on a rope bridge that was made of string - honestly! Even that was better than the two pine trees strapped together - so slender and long, and slung across a raging river - which we had to negotiate as well. A bridge had been swept away and we clambered over the two slim pines which were the make-do replacement bridge, singing my theme song throughout this Himalayan adventure - "If TheyCould See Me Now!" It was never more apt than on this bridge, swaying over the racing water below.

We joked about the Big Ups planned for the next day, or the Big Downs which were worse! I sprouted blisters, sprains, grazed limbs and even blisters on my hands and knees. Most of these injuries were sustained secretly where possible but at one point I got desperate enough to ask if I might hire a horse. (I had seen a couple of enormous German ladies using one and I thought it would be fun to share with the others, as well as give me a bit of a rest.) However, it nearly proved my undoing. First of all the man hired to drive it, helped me up into the saddle and put his hand in a very inappropriate place for a granny (or anyone, come to think of it.) Then the horse refused at every incline and fell on his knees at one point and I'm not even fat these days. To my horror he nudged a small woman, sitting on a wall and she nearly fell down the precipice behind her. At another point, if I hadn't raised my left leg to an incredible height, the horse would definitely have caused it to be amputated against a flinty wall. Oh, it was awful. The poor thing fell on his knees again when Durga was trying to show me how nice a horse he really was. In the end I sent him home and wasted the fifteen pounds it had cost. I took to the road walking again.

I then met an American who had fallen behind her husband and was hurrying to catch him up. I asked her to explain to my friends ahead, that my horse had fallen down and my guide had now got toothache, had overdosed on paracetamol and kept wanting to go to sleep! Eventually Durga and I sprinted along to catch up with the others and I had glimpses of the most wonderful sights, but only glimpses because when you trek with these guys, you hurtle....

After we caught up with the party, we agreed to go to bathe in some hot springs on the roadside. I can't tell you how wonderful this hot water was, and how it helped all my 'sore bits'. I went in - fully clothed of course, to preserve the niceties, and talked to a Belgian psychotherapist and admired the beautiful physique of an Australian bather.

It was at about this point that my boots *burst!* They were completely unstitched and there was no way they could be repaired so I had to continue the trek in some 'health shop' clogs! All my party were appalled and I had to pretend that I always love walking in clogs. I plodded along and tried not to be too obvious about the tipping over, lurching up and down the mountains and smiling reassuringly whenever anyone looked round sympathetically. When I fell against Durga at one point he yelled out in surprise and said he thought I was a cow falling from the pasture on our right.......

The tea-houses where we stayed each night were very basic but clean and cheerful and the food was wonderful. They cater for visitors from all over the world and so you could have pasta, crepes, Tibetan bread, moussaka, lasagne, Quaker Oats, all topped off with pots of green tea. It was absolutely imperative to come in after a days' walking and eat these feasts to keep up your energy levels. Once or twice it was really cold at night and they shoved a little barbecue-type stove under the table and table cloth - full alight! The tables are steel lined to take the heat and it was so cosy and nice. We played cards and drank lemon tea and fell into bed at 8 or 8.30 p.m. as if it was midnight.

The foreigners we met were equally fascinating. I overheard two more Swedes discussing the availability of drugs and the fact that most Swedish youth roll special tobacco into wads and eat it just like the Indians and Nepalese eat pan.

Another interesting 'overhear' was Claudia (23) from Germany who had come on her own because her partner was ill, but she had quickly been 'adopted' by a jolly party of German men aged about 50 who ensured she wasn't lonely!

Another American woman told me that her psychiatrist sister thinks our short-term memory loss these days is not early Alzheimer's - it is brain over-stimulation. She considers it a twentieth century complaint, and inevitable because of the facts that we are bombarded with, and expect our brains to retain. The losing of words is our way of coping - we just recall what we want to. I like this theory, don't you?

One morning I woke at about five and there was a rat somewhere very close, squeaking and scrabbling. I got fairly calmly out of my sleeping bag and then screeched into the kitchen where the hostess made me a cup of tea and I sat at the kitchen table and went back to sleep with my head among the sauce bottles....

We passed through hundreds of little villages, mostly financed by tourists from all over the world. We had tantalising glimpses through the doors of sunlit or lamp lit interiors, of mothers oiling their babies in the sunshine and fathers rolling on the floor with their toddlers; one man was having his head shaved and the luxuriant brown curls fell to the earth floor of his house. Outside bright blue birds sang, and exotic flowers grew in small gardens. Families were meeting and having meals together. There was a special festival - Dossain - one day and all the women were wearing red and gold and the children had new clothes for the special day, however poor they were. The numerous dogs and cats were absolutely horribly mangy but the calves, cows, goats and sheep were carefully tended and looked fit. They gave a biblical feel to the small villages. The chickens also looked healthy and colourful, when compared with the dogs and cats.

We slept at the highest point of our trek and got up early to see the sun rise over Everest before we began our descent. It was here that I left my sun-hat! I hung it on the back of the door and came away without it but I feel it was an appropriate place to leave it, if I had to part with it, after all our adventures together! This hat had been wonderful going up the mountain - a sunshield, head protector and also, pulled down, it stopped me getting dismayed at what lay ahead - nearly always a Big Up! It didn't owe me anything since India, either. The children there fought to carry and wear it, but they twice passed their head lice on to me in this way.

We got a bus at some point for the rest of the journey and it was once more one of those journeys where you think the bones of your bottom will come through the skin. I was very happy to sit down though and easing my clogs off and tucking my feet up was blissful. I sat next to Dormouse (Ramasol's nickname because he kept falling asleep like the one in 'Alice'). He kept falling asleep on ME and then waking to inspect his nose pickings - VERY basic, the Nepalese men.

I was sad to leave everyone because there was that camaraderie you get when you endure together. Our adage had been what doesn't kill you, makes you stronger. Also it was good to share funny happenings. The only thing I find about travelling alone is that I miss that exchange of a smile, or big laugh, which beats a 'solo' giggle.

18.11.96
I was pleased to be given my same room at Hotel Horizon - (Two Pounds a Night - inclusive of Large Pot of Tea with Separate Milk Twice Daily) and they greeted me like a long-lost friend. They had kept my luggage safely in their storeroom and took all my laundry and returned it beautifully clean and ironed. I am now down to my 1974 weight. (I have to be dragged past full-length mirrors because I can't believe my eyes, I am so sylph-like.) Mind you I have perhaps three layers of bags beneath the eyes, and that greenish pallor that you get when there is high humidity, but I would heartily recommend the trekking adventure for weight reduction.

My Large Pot of Tea, requested when I had resettled myself in my little room, was delivered as Pot of Coffee. I drank it and then - still awake at 3 a.m. because of it, I decided to 'dilute' it with a Toblerone, half a pound of Bombay Mix and three bananas! Slept like a baby after that!......

19.11.96
I returned to the NCO orphanage today but it is still very difficult to work productively because all the staff seem to go on leave all the time and none of them speak English so can't help us to help them in some ways. I had eagerly looked forward to creating the new Baby Clinic but the promised medical staff never did meet up with me and my lists and diagrams and research were wasted, but the Doll Exhibition has taken shape and, as it turned out, is just the right amount of 'work' for me to handle.

I rushed to the Poste Restante today and there, right on the top of the pile was a letter from my daughter, Jane, about grandchildren Holly and William and their delight with a Rosy-Cheeked Bee and tasselled hat respectively, which I had posted before the trek. How I love post when I am away and how loyally my friends and family supply it.

I've turned down an invitation to "Cultivate Compassion" tomorrow at the Yoga Institute, because Durga has asked me to his house for lunch and my fellow trekkers want to know why he wears a headscarf and baseball hat all the time! This is probably our last opportunity to find out....

20.11.96
Lunch with Durga and Sita
I had a lovely time but it was certainly a lunch with a difference. First of all Durga came to collect me an hour *after* the arranged time. Though this is typical here, when he admitted he hadn't been home all the night before because he had been at a party, I became a bit anxious. Then he admitted he

hadn't told his wife he was bringing me to lunch. However, she smiled happily when we met and didn't even appear to be ever so cross with him. She was incredibly beautiful. Their flat was two rooms in a decrepit alley but was full of love and happiness - they kept exchanging loving glances and both adored a thirteen month old baby son, carried most of the time on her back in a woollen scarf. None of the rest of the family who called in to meet me, could pass the baby without kissing him or pulling his cheek out about a yard and letting go - Nepali version of baby-cheek-squeezing. He *was* adorable and had a little topknot of curly black hair and great big treacly eyes.

Durga commenced to 'do' his whole toilet - because he had been out all night I suppose - including his toenails. He also managed to help Sita cook the meal and show me their kitchen, which had a shrine in it. The kitchen was meticulously clean and there was much hand-washing all the time. They were delighted when I took their photos in the kitchen and I felt very welcome — even though I had heard that neither dogs nor foreigners are allowed in Indian or Nepalese kitchens!

They made lunch of daal-baat - which is rice and a separate dish of mildly curried beans and peas, and is the favoured dish of all Nepalese. This light curry was followed by at least a half a pint of hot chocolate. To my huge embarrassment they served my meal to me on their double bed. They must've eaten their meal one at a time in the kitchen. A huge T.V. belted out a Hindi film all the time I was there, with, as usual, much dancing about on hill tops and stabbing each other on the bus going home, and then crying and then giving loving glances again. Films are always extremely action-packed in India and Nepal.

This family rent their 'flat', and have another house in the country where they actually live. Their ten year old son - by Durga's previous marriage - was like a little Sultan and this is the normal way apparently. The boy children are adored from birth on.

Sita did bring up the matter of last night's party and said why didn't Durga telephone her but he just smiled and tucked a roll of notes in her sari, earned as Guide on our trek, and she just smiled back......

As for my investigations, I can only think the different head covers worn by Durga were to protect his somewhat bald head from the sun so I reported this to Heather and they were envious of my interesting and colourful experience.

21.11.96
I am down to three lots of fading bruises, two scabs, one elastic bandage and two plasters now - following the trekking, so I have been going around to collect items to add to the Exhibition.

They varied from posters and flags to a beautiful Austrian doll and almost doubled the effect of the exhibition. The children love it but the staff are *proud* of it and several of them brought their families to admire it.

We moved Jennifer into new digs yesterday – just up the road from my orphanage. Jennifer made us a house-warming cup of tea but thought you put the tea leaves in the kettle. I am now able to meet Jennifer as well as Fran for breakfast in wonderful 'Mike's Breakfast' from time to time. His exotic garden has lily ponds, poinsettia 'trees', begonias and other lovely plants. They play classical music and have exhibitions of pottery and tapestry and paintings. The cost for a full English breakfast is only about one pound and the menu includes homemade apricot jam and toast and other English delicacies! There are refills of coffee for ever, too. It is just far enough out of KMD to be less polluted and the temperature at the moment is perfect, so there are no bugs either.

The lack of organisation at the NCO orphanage depresses us at all at times but we are hanging on. We are constantly touched and humbled by the poverty levels here in Nepal. Yesterday two nice Nepali men brought in a little boy about two years old, clutching a paper bag with a bun it. He had tears on his face and wore a purple pixie hood. "No mother and no father" they said. He will be kept here and his photograph shown in the newspaper for three weeks before he is officially an inmate.

There seems to be quite a steady flow of foreigners adopting babies from NCO and I observed many couples who were staying in local hotels while they 'bonded' with their chosen children.

I did wonder whether the poverty levels and the hesitation on the part of local people to adopt, would justify removing these babies and toddlers from their native country and the possibility of their meeting up with their extended families, even if their parents were dead. I had been so happy to watch Indian would-be parents, collect the Indian babies from 'my' orphanage, but this didn't happen much in Nepal.

The foreign adoption process here seemed to be trouble-free and I got choked up just seeing the happy people walking in the grounds with adorable babies in their arms. There were, of course, problems sometimes and a Swiss couple talked to me of their exhaustion, getting through the bureaucracy to claim 'their' baby. I don't think, to be honest, it is as bad here as anywhere else. It must be so frustrating to be told the baby is yours, and then have delays while the papers are sanctioned. I love being 'in' on the actual collection day, when the parents have had two or three weeks, bonding, and then may take the baby home with them.

22.11.96
Bi Tikka - the Celebration of Siblings
Fran's new Nepalese family (she has moved digs) invited us to this special event which was like a sibling version of Mothers' Day. All the brothers and

25

sisters were painting coloured splodges on each others' foreheads as we arrived. I had seen this done in previous festivals - bright pink rice in a rice pudding consistency is literally dolloped onto their foreheads. We were also garlanded with everlasting purple flowers - it is said if we wear these particular flowers a certain God couldn't 'go against' or harm us.

The day started with hot, spicy fish cutlets, and bottles of beer (divine decadence!) All the women were honouring their brothers like mad and giving them gifts. Only from time to time did the men return the honour to their sisters! Everyone was dressed in their colourful best clothes and we sat about in gardens which were incredibly dusty but full of arum lilies, marigolds and lush greenery. The view from the rooftop over the Kathmandu valley was wonderful and not too polluted this morning.

A circle of oil and water was run around the older men to prevent the devil harming them. Gifts were handed to brothers and sisters and big straw trays handed round with Betel, popcorn, cashews, pistachios, coconut pieces, huge circular doughnuts, bananas, oranges and apples, dried fruit and nuts laid out on them. Neighbours and hoards of relatives came and pleaded to be photographed with us.

In the evening we returned to the family's downstairs rooms and watched T.V. It was a Hindi film whose star had just died in real life in childbirth. She really was the male star's wife. The film was the usual mixture of singing and dancing over hilltops, holding hands, and gentle but torrid love scenes with elderly-looking stars and always the finale of a bloodbath of stabbings on the bus going home.......

Jen (U.S.), Fran (Australia) and Jenny (U.K.) on Bi Tikka Day
(Celebration of Siblings)

An 87 year old granny and I were given the only seats in the room, "because we were grannies". I was a bit upset about this, secretly, but in the end I nodded off during the film and decided it was worth being old to be allowed to be so impolite! My fellow-granny apparently got up in the night, not knowing the time I guess, and offered Fran some orange and purple knitted socks because the weather had turned COLD!

We had a marvellous day and night - it was terrific to be in a Nepalese family.

Even more about Jennifer: She is in love with Janak, a young hotel manager in KMD and it is so fascinating seeing her overlook all the cultural differences because he is so lovely to her and she loves him so much. I feel about a hundred years old. She reckons she has to teach him to KISS because he has not had any experience - he's 26 and Nepalese girls are not allowed to 'go out' with boys. She and Fran - who now lives with her Nepali love - insist that Nepali and Indian men have something special about them, but I have seen no further than their hawking and spitting and scrotal scratching so far…..

23.11.96
Life here continues to be a series of incidences of interest: I met a man with a bear on a rope today! In the orphanage I overheard one of the children explaining to a friend that he had a blind neighbour. He couldn't think of the word for blind and said "His eyes are broken…."

I tried not to look - from my viewpoint in a roof top café - while three children were playing with two metre fluorescent tubes on a rubbish truck below……

The dogs here are absolutely awful. Moth-eaten at best and downright diseased most of the time. In spite of their appearance, the other day was Dogs' Day. They all had flowers around their necks and blobs of coloured paint on their foreheads! A cow was being beaten by a market stall holder. They are never abused generally but this one was seen with a huge bunch of white carrots in his mouth, which he'd pinched from the stall.

FOOD!
I am still experiencing gastronomic delights here in Kathmandu: a Capuccino and cinnamon bun costs 5p, cream cheese balls rolled in finely chopped green pepper and chives plus brown home-made bread and heart shaped portions of yak butter,(delicious), costs one pound and there is more than enough for two. Chura is beaten rice with soy beans and is almost free of charge.

Nepalese Kitchen Buffet is a café providing curried beans, curried chicken, curried vegetables, rice, dhal sauce and Ratzi (local brandy) with yoghurt and cinnamon, dried fruit, nuts and cherries - all for £1.50 and you could keep eating all night if you desired………….

I did once have a Less than Lovely Breakfast, which was such a rare occurrence that I will tell you about it. It was in a previously unknown café which had both Christmas and Bi Tikka decorations still up and a huge Shrine in middle of a tacky looking room. All the staff - about seven of them which is the usual number - stood about sniffing and coughing in their anoraks and the cheese omelette and coffee, when it eventually arrived, could've been anything. This disaster only seemed to highlight the high standard elsewhere.

Belinda, Vicky and Julia - a very British trio, had supper at the Nepalese Kitchen with us. We waited ages to get served which is very unusual so when I asked about the delay, the waiter said: "Suddenly you will get" - and we did!

Fran's Nepalese Gran was heard to put a curse on whomever it was that had taken cashew nuts from her room! She said she wanted the culprit to be paralysed! Fran was intending to go home limping tonight!

24.11.96
I bought some cane bookshelves for the orphanage today. They only cost about two pounds and I carried them easily on my head even though they were six foot by four! It is lovely that it doesn't invoke stares here because everyone carries everything. I have met people carrying wardrobes, fridges, settees — you name it. I had trouble walking up one alleyway one day when it was obstructed by a motorbike overtaking a man with a BATH on his head! - honestly!

Tonight I had a "Date"! In my innocence, I believed a chap when he asked to meet me for supper to discuss some cushions he said he could get me, free of charge, for the orphanage library. I should have guessed - he wanted to try the cushions out with me. He told me he had spent three wonderful months in Australia when tourist friends he met here had had a whip-round for his fare. He couldn't get over how hard, and for such long hours, Australians worked. He said they never had a day off to sit and talk with their friends! He taught me to say "How is It Hanging?" which I have now learned is a rudish Aussie greeting of men to each other. He then started on about sex again and I waxed eloquent about him being 'like my son' but he said: "Even sons need a warm place and some love to be given" and at this point I decided the cushions weren't worth the hassle......

25.11.96
All Aboard for Nagarkot
A trip with Fran to view Everest at Sunrise and Sunset started at 6 a.m. at the bus stop in KMD. I had to persuade the man selling carpets, yet again, that I didn't need one, but I bought some Tiger Balm from him, which I wished I had bought for the trekking. The bus arrived but there were no seats booked for us, as had been promised, so we were thrown off! However, a man came along with three spare seats in his Land Rover and we were charged less than the bus fare. After a pleasant journey to a mountain top,

we walked about admiring winter jasmine which was three times the size of the English variety, lilies, cacti, pine trees, and eucalyptus. It only cost three pounds a night for the room for two people and we could see Everest from the bedroom window. We met an author called Tony and his wife Hannah, who was Korean photographer.They told us their life story, and then we moved on to talk to a couple of Irish girls from Wexford who were staying in a nearby chalet. They told us that Ireland is a great place "to come *from........*"

There was a temple at the top of 'our' mountain with a view of the sunset which was even more beautiful than the sunrise. I am, however, still the only person I know that has seen these events, apart from Fran, of course. It is usually too misty and people are disappointed. The stars and moon were indescribably clear and beautiful, too.

27.11.96

On my return to Kathmandu I witnessed the visit of the German President to the King and Queen of Nepal. The visitors were escorted by a Nepalese pipe and drum military band of both men and women, who wore white uniforms with tartan scarves that looked like curtain material. The horses and carriages had men running beside the horses waving white yak hair and the horses had what looked like wide bands of toilet rolls on their backs behind the riders. The bespectacled German President and his white-haired wife looked serious and the crowd waiting was hushed. The whole occasion was very formal – the Nepalese being a quiet people. I stood with a man with a live chicken under his arm but had to give a stern look to another man that would've knocked me down to get in a space which was a better viewpoint - women are nothing here. There were hundreds of police motorbikes and army personnel about and I was reminded of the special building for Victims of Violence I had seen here, which, it is said, houses people beaten up and tortured by the Nepalese police and army.

28.11.96

A prison visit.

In answer to an appeal in a café in KMD, I went to visit a prison inmate. The request for visitors that spoke English to go 'with a smile' intrigued me. I found the prison without much trouble but had to spend about twenty minutes waiting outside with some women. They were cheery and enthusiastic about the canisters which they were selling and spraying everywhere. They had to mime to explain which was insect repellent, which was perfume, and which cough medicine.

The guard at the prison door told me, with tears in his eyes, of the children in jail because their sole parents were prisoners. The guard said he had 23 in the jail at the moment, and they were underfed and uneducated, and couldn't I do something about it. Unhappily, I didn't have the time or opportunity to help these children but I still think of them to this day.

I was taken to a room like a passage with a grill window in it, and Cedric Edwards arrived. He was a lovely, smiley, Barbadian, about 28 years old, who had been imprisoned without being charged, for nineteen months! He only had time to tell me that his case is 'postponed' by the judge every time it comes up. He managed to tell me he needs a warm jumper - the nights are freezing in my hotel, so the prison must be awful. Anything else I could afford would be welcome. He said he was charged with cashing someone else's travellers' cheques but has got proof of his innocence and still can't get a proper hearing. His parents have visited and eight tourists went to Court to try to help last time. He has to wait another month for another hearing. He had to go away in the middle of telling me this as the 15 minutes were up.

A Polish teacher was sitting beside Cedric, yelling to be heard above the din by a Dutchman who was also visiting as a result of the café advertisement. We had both visited with fruit and vegetables and books and jumpers. The prisoners cook their own food and appeared to be fit and fat enough on it.

29.11.96
Thanksgiving Supper.
Thanksgiving Supper at Mike's Breakfast meant pumpkin pie, nutmoast! Gironde wine (five pounds a bottle), sweet potatoes and Jennifer talking about sexual matters very loudly. Two lovely American boys called Jake and Farmer, who sat with us round a half barrel filled with sweet smelling wood, burning merrily, were part of a large party of Americans making a very American atmosphere.

30.11.96
Chitwan Game Park
Fran and Jennifer and I set off in a coach and counted six trucks or coaches which had crashed or were in the gutter on the route, but the spectacular scenery took our minds off that problem. I recommend a salami roll and cold frankfurter from the Austrian deli as being the best 'coach trip' breakfast you can have. They stayed me on an extremely 'whirly' journey and I didn't feel ill at all. The trip was as full of intriguing sights and incidents. While passing the Hotel Monalisha we watched a man swap a bundle of spring onions for an ashtray. We saw a man with a cart attached to his bike, which held a megaphone and battery operated tape-recorder, giving details of a sale in the village.

We went straight to the Hotel and out again to the elephant breeding ground. Apart from being appalled at their short chains, we were delighted with elephants. They are lovely animals: so soft-eyed and patient and even the babies were enormous.

We ate chicken spring rolls and drank Tuborg beer in a lovely dining room and learned that we were the first ever customers to the Game Park. Sharad and two other Nepali men escorted or guided us all weekend, even though we weren't part of their hotel 'package'. An Englishman called out from the dining room doorway "I've got diarrhoea so I'm not coming on the jungle walk!" This prompted Jennifer to launch into her 'troubles' in that area - very nice with your supper, I thought…..

A canoe ride up a river was just like being in Butley Creek, Suffolk, with pied, giant and grey hornbills, magpies, little ring plovers, kingfishers, heron, martins, swallows, egrets, sand martins, teal, ruddy shelducks, black headed gull, long tailed tree pie (?) which is a papaya eater, bull bulls, storks and many pea-fowls. Phew! I was amazed by the song of the kingfisher. Our guide said he knew of 450 species of birds in Nepal and had 'ticked' 340 of them himself. There are more species than anywhere else in the world, and 10% of the world's birds are in Nepal, he said.

Chitwan Game Park

Jennifer, Herbert the Austrian, Deepok and a Driver and I went for a two or three hour ride on Lakshmi. She was a lovely pink and grey elephant with huge ears and when it was my turn I was given a seat facing her rear with the best view for photographs of her tail and my own feet, but the wonderful, silent, swaying journey through the jungle was memorable. The smell of the leaves being crushed by the elephants, the trumpeting of one elephant to another, the banyan trees, jacaranda trees, and orchids growing in trees made the experience one I'll never forget.

The huge elephant footprints in the mud were joined by tiger prints and fresh tiger and rhino poo piles and these were the only proof of other animals, as we didn't see anything else except a wild rooster and a huge spider!

Jennifer didn't sleep because my snoring kept her awake, but everything else about the weekend was wonderful. We had tea brought to our room whenever we wanted. We could see the Annapurna range from our bedroom window - wonderful when moonlit!

We saw Tharu dancing in a nearby hall one night. About a dozen men wore football tops, football socks and skirts which fitted up their bottom cracks and barely covered their boxer shorts. They had either one big stick or two smaller ones, which were bigger than Morris men sticks. They did intricate and wonderful things with these sticks in a circle while a bored man in a dirty anorak in the middle did wonderful things with his drum. Another man wandered about in the middle with an expression that said "What did I come here for?" The dancing was intensely exciting, though. It was so aggressive and war-like. Then a wonderful boy came on dressed as a peacock and leaned over to place flowers in Jennifer's hair and made a hole in her head, she said, afterwards. We were invited to join in the dancing but we were the only tourists so we didn't like to. The dancers were totally un-self-conscious in their 'nappies' and it was exhilarating to watch them. We were given feathered bandoliers to accompany them at one time, too.

Supper in another Guest House which caters for foreigners offered us Bangh Lassi. Lassi is yoghurt drink usually made with bananas or other fruit, but Bangh is Hash! We declined!

4.12.96
On a jungle walk at Chitwan the guide told us of the two sorts of crocodile in the river: one endangered and now protected and one normal one which is two metres long. The protected one has increased to about one thousand in number now. In the morning at 7 a.m. the small jungle children were put out to play with the fires in front of their wattle and daub type huts which had finger marks, hand-marks, geese etc. painted on their clay exteriors. Lots of the women smoked. None of them seemed to speak English but one said what a pretty old lady I was! Jennifer speaks a little Nepalese and translated this with a big grin.

I met an Englishman, Alex, on the canoe ride. He was 18 years old, pale, bespectacled and was cycling round India and Nepal on his own! He was an academic type and enjoyed having his lunch with us beside the river. He told of the loss of some of his luggage from his bike in Delhi, but how much freer he felt without it!

On the walk through the jungle we had such dire warnings of what to do in the event of meeting an attacking rhino, or an angry leopard, that he thought he'd like a stick. I stripped some leaves off one and he joked that he never thought he'd be helped by a granny in these circumstances - he thought we all went to Bognor Regis for our holidays....

Our guide explained about keeping together at all costs if we 'come across a tiger or something.' He had had three friends who had 'expired', being killed by leopard and rhino because the members of the expedition had separated.... He also warned us to avoid Burning Bush leaves, which hurt. They are used in prisons to torture murderers apparently! Alex and two other nice Brits swam back over the river after the walk. We carried their gear and I wished I had had a suit with me, but I couldn't swim in my salwar because I wanted to lunch in it in the restaurant by the river.

6.12.96

Back in KMD a married couple - American Janet and Nepalese Ram - offered a Nepali Cookery Day for 500Rs. We sat on cushions and drank cinnamon tea and ate Chura, which is beaten rice with chick peas and spices, in their kitchen which had no fitted units or furniture. The floor was marble and I had removed my shoes at the door with everyone else but my feet went dead with cold within minutes so I asked to have them back.

The only kitchen fixture was a stainless-steel topped table. We learned to deal with dahl, spices, rice, veg. curry, dahl bat, tomato pickle, mo-mos (little dough parcels with veg. in) and ate all these things at intervals in the dining room. We sat on the cushions again and ate from brass plates and drank home made beer (warm) in wooden 'vases' called Tomba, through wooden straws.

All these proceedings were interrupted when I asked Fran's advice about something hurting my eyelid. She announced that it was a leech, which must have been in there since the jungle walk. It was still wriggling when she extracted it with tweezers and I was *very brave* throughout - in my opinion! She muttered something about eggs still being in there which didn't give me a warm feeling, but we went back to the cooking and finished the day discussing mixed marriages with the English, Japanese and New Zealand people on the Course. The hosts taxied us back to KMD and we all hope to go again some day.

A tiny woman, about fifteen years old I think, was begging with her baby outside my hotel. When I told her about the orphanage she declined my invitation to see it, saying she earned about 40 rupees with the baby and without it she would not get enough to live on *and* she would have to part with the baby.

9.12.96
Pasuparti
These are areas called Ghats for burning people who have expired. Fran and I spent Saturday morning together with three families who put their loved ones on a pile of seasoned tree trunks and cremated them. Their remains were then put in the river beside which we sat. The jewels, clothes etc. that go in with them are picked up by beggars within sight of the funeral. The men closest to the deceased have their heads shaved, while sitting with their backs to the deceased and we watched this also. We could see the limbs that stuck out of the fire and saw a bladder or something, burst and a seemingly endless spray of liquid arch up into the air.

American tourists were filming all this – to my dismay – and it was only later that I learned from a Nepali woman that this would not have been seen as intrusive at all.

The rivers flow into the Ganges, which is significant to them. Edmund Hilary apparently once drank some of the Ganges to illustrate a point. He didn't get sick but it looked extremely horrible

Conch shells are blown preceding the procession and during the burning. Apparently they are found underground in Nepal, as is coral, and prove it was at sea level once. There were more than usual human faeces everywhere in the 'village' and rats decomposing and the dogs were the worst I've ever seen. There were also horrible monkeys as well as a few nice baby ones. The largest Hindu temple is here. We weren't allowed in, as Christians, but could see a huge golden bull's rear end through the gate.

11.12.96
Tibetan Café
I enjoyed supper here with two Australian boys and an English "Gap" girl. I loved the Aussies because they were so keen for me to visit Australia, and encouraged me with instructions such as "You want to hit the bitumin at Darwin and go about 500ks towards Adelaide". I was so enraptured with the idea that I scarcely noticed my mushroom burger with garlic and cheese sauce and salad. (I lie! It was scrumptious). They said I could forget hopes of work as a barmaid because my boobs weren't big enough….. Ah well!

13.12.96
On my second visit to Cedric in prison, he told me of his surprise at my visit and indeed at the number of people who troubled to visit him because he himself would never have done it. He gave me a handful of 'friendship' bracelets he had made for Holly!

Postscript 28.2.97
I received a letter from Cedric when he returned to India. He thanked me for visiting him and told me that he had eventually been acquitted of the charge.

19.12.96
Final Days
I am typing this last chapter on a hired typewriter in Kathmandu! I found an upstairs garret in a typewriting school where I could rent a typewriter, which was circa 1850, but the 'ambience' in the studio is wonderful. There are rows of elderly Olivettis and Underwoods, mounds of carbon paper and stencils and the strongest smell of ink and the most ancient Roneo printer I've ever seen. I love working here, under the elderly fans, and it is very nostalgic to thump away on the keys and crash the carriage back again as I used to in the 'fifties'.

I had a very tearful 'session' with Jennifer and we vowed to be friends for ever and ever. She is very much In Love with her Nepali boyfriend and assures me they will invite me to the wedding in Kathmandu! I will never forget her energy and enthusiasm for travelling and I so admire her knowledge of the *words* to songs and ability to keep the tune!

Fran is also my role model as regards sorting the good aspects from the bad in foreign parts and I wouldn't be at all surprised to get another wedding invitation from her! She is going back to Australia soon but vows to keep in touch and I believe her.

I am desperately looking forward to seeing my family again and it is helping me to separate from this exciting country. I can't believe I have been able to do so many unusual things – riding on elephants, trekking up mountains, meeting local people and eating the widest variety of food I've ever seen. My lack of visa for India really put the icing on my cake because it allowed me to have three months here. Serendipity or what!

The orphanage people in both orphanages were very pleasant and appreciative when they said goodbye, but thankfully they are more used to volunteers coming and going and didn't wail and cry as they did when I left India so I coped much better!

20.12.96
Penultimate breakfast
White scarves are traditionally given as presents to departing friends and I had one from the Hotel Horizon men, another from Fran and another from Cedric, the prisoner!

21.12.96
I ate my last breakfast in the garden café where I had been so many times with Fran. The gardener had been sacked - I wonder why? I ate scrambled egg - cooked to my specification and on one side of me a lady with a hat like white blancmange tucked in to her food and on the other was a woman with what looked like thatch on top of a crash helmet!

I bought a Parker Pen and some samosas with the remainder of my rupees in Kathmandu airport. Before boarding I talked with an English girl whose memorable travelling tip is: always empty your hot water bottle to reduce your weight allowance....

The strong smell of feet sitting next to me in my window seat took nothing away from the sight of the Himalayas on one side of the plane, and the red sunset on the other...

We were given cough sweets to clear our sinuses for landing at Moscow. From the plane I could see clouds, snow, icicles, silver birches and cars driving on the right hand side of road. I had to have a tea bag of my own, and beg hot water (which was given free), because I had no change to buy anything else. Russian men and women staff were boozing and smoking at 1.56 a.m. when we landed. Many of the staff were asleep in rows on cardboard throughout the airport. Nepali passengers were shivering and shaking with cold. I noticed that Russian women look like men, and are unsmiling. I slept upright and fitfully for a few hours and when I did wake up, there to my astonishment was a little cat, nestling in the crook of my arm in my warm woolly coat. After a nasty breakfast of frankfurters, brown rice and white bread with processed sliced cheese and hot chocolate, we took off for Dubai and then arrived HOME in the UK at 10.50 a.m.

I heaved my luggage home and have never had such wonderful presents for my family - I heartily recommend Nepal for Christmas shopping, or any shopping – even if, like me, you don't really 'do' shopping!

HONG KONG WITH MOLTO

June 2000.
"Can you be Molto's mum for twelve weeks?"
This was the invitation that I eagerly accepted and it promoted my first adventure of the new millennium. I was to travel to Hong Kong and use my grandmotherly skills to care for a highly emotional Dalmatian for six months. These English 'parents' wanted to go to Australia, but their darling dog would not cope with the Hong Kong kennels for three months, so they asked me to look after him in the manner to which he had become accustomed. I cannot say that I am dog mad but really feel the same about them as I do children – it depends on their personalities doesn't it?

21st June 2000
My flight from London to Bahrein was 3,168 miles, it was 62F at Heathrow and the flight would take 6 hours 10 minutes. Having written these details down, I tucked into spicy curry while we flew over Alexandiopolis, and drank from my own metal cup (huge), filled with tea by an agreeable hostess over Tripoli. A gangster look-alike slept next to me all the way, but I never mind if I am being ignored - just having little snacks, my big cups of tea and delicious alcoholic drinks brought to me, *and* a long read is my idea of heaven.

We landed in Bahrein for a couple of hours A man was playing a grand piano in the airport foyer and there were crowds of women in purdah and Indians in saris. I enjoyed iced tea in this fascinating atmosphere and had a good long chat with a solicitor/anthropologist, who looked about 12 years old. He spoke fluent Welsh as well as his other qualifications. A little later on I made such an impact on a Pakistani woman with whom I set the world right that she kissed me good-bye! We flew on via Bangkok and never saw our luggage at all until the carousel in Hong Kong.

It was 35C when we landed in Hong Kong and terribly humid as well, but I was too excited to mind. A charming American man guided me to the space-age train, which takes passengers from the airport to Hong Kong Central. Molto's owner, Jane, was there to meet me and it was only a short distance by taxi to their flat in Conduit road, Central Hong Kong. I was pleased to find that there was Internet access and the World Service on the radio in the flat, and Jane assured me there was a huge second-hand paperback supply at the YWCA where she worked. With these facilities and my mountain of teabags, I was ready for anything.

Molto, Italian for *many* and describing his black spots, was *enormous* and very excitable. My first impression was that he lived like a battery hen in the flat, which was eight storeys up. I went for a walk with Jane and Adrian, 'his parents', to see where he was allowed to poo and they explained the system for scooping and disposing. My overriding feeling was of sympathy for this wonderful dog that could never be let off the lead for a proper run. My parents had a Dalmatian when they lived in Northern Ireland, and his life on the miles of empty beach seemed idyllic by comparison. However, there was I and there was he, we would have to make the best of it and were to become firm friends. He certainly didn't *look* unhappy about his life in Hong Kong.

Everywhere I looked that first morning I saw sky-scraping blocks of offices and flats and all the residents live what seems like miles up in the sky. My travels have taken me to a many great cities but here in Hong Kong I was hugely impressed with the dizzying architecture and wonderful use of glass and steel.

22nd June, 2000
Day two, and I was taken to a neighbours' baby's birthday party. The Swiss parents talked calmly about the burglar who had fallen eight storeys to his death after attempting for a second time to break into their flat! We ate quiche, fresh fruit, and gooey cake and drank white wine and the couple told me of the shortage of grandmothers in Hong Kong and how welcome I was going to be.

On this same day Jane took me to mainland Kowloon (HK being an island) on the Star Ferry. It was fantastic to actually swish over the short stretch of water that I had seen so many times in films. We wandered about the quay and admired the huge cruisers berthed there and the fabulous Concert Hall across the water, which I thought similar to the Sydney Opera house.

We later ate Adrian's speciality – Green Noodles and Chicken, and they went off to Australia, leaving me in sole charge of their 'baby'. I was awake all night but I am sure it was through excitement and not jet lag or anxiety. Molto slept in his bed and didn't seem to miss them – yet!

23rd June 2000
Well it is the first day alone with Molto, but I had to leave him sulking and go on my own to find the YWCA. He is not allowed on public transport and wouldn't manage the crowds apparently. Jane says I will be sure to find English and Chinese friends at the YWCA and I will register for as many courses and lessons as I can afford.

I took a bus from just outside the apartment block and then walked through the Botanical Gardens, Zoo and Aviary, which are on each side of a main road in Central HK. There were black jaguars at the entrance and exotic species of birds and animals inside – all in excellent condition and housed in natural cages and pens. I was fascinated with the cranes. I had read that they copulate just for fun and kill their young if they are not speedily removed at birth. I scrutinised the pair of cranes that have bred there for the last twelve years, using this regime, and couldn't help being intrigued with this method of birth control!

Hundreds of white cockatoos looked lovely in the lush greenery but I read that they are damaging the trees, and are considered a pest. I saw a white-faced Saki bird which is being conserved but I don't know why – yuk, it was horrible. There had been three ancient tortoises living in the zoo, but two were stolen recently. A passing Chinese woman was proud of her English and was the first of hundreds of people who asked to practice with me while I was in Hong Kong. She told me that the mother porcupine which we were admiring, lays an egg and puts it in her pouch until it hatches and then she feeds it in there – wouldn't that be a nice way to start life? I also saw crested gibbons, orange flamingos, thumb-nail sized frogs and huge snails.

After this lovely look round I spent a pleasant hour or so with Jane's friend Tracey, who is Queen Bee at the YWCA or 'the Y' as it is known. I will definitely enroll for some classes, though I declined today's offering of 'Belly Dancing', for the time being.

After leaving I got confused and took the tram to the West instead of the East but it didn't seem to matter as it went along tracks that brought me back to where I'd started and gave me the most exciting first views of Hong Kong. The trams are packed with people, but are inexpensive and don't get held up much, so I could see why they were popular. I loved the *look* of them - mine today was PINK!

Molto   **Molto sulking when denied 'walkies'**

27th June 2000

This morning I set the alarm clock so that I could get up and walk Molto before it got hot. We walked half way to the famous hill called The Peak, overlooking HK, but it was too far for him – he became out of breath and was panting and unhappy. Jane had warned me that big dogs are prone to heart attacks in the heat so I took him home. He did three poos and it was absolutely yucky collecting them up but he was so happy to be outside that it was worth it.

I then had a domestic day pottering about and telephoned to book some courses at the YWCA. I called 'Mums R Us' – an au pair agency - but they had no work for me as I didn't have a work permit. I haven't much money as the cost of living is high here, but I think I would feel a bit guilty working as an au pair anyway, because of the thousands of Filipino au pairs who need the money more urgently.

My Lonely Planet book is coming into its own in helping me find my way about, but I am having trouble reading the small print in it, even with my glasses on, which is a bit worrying. Is it because I have reached the Big Sixty?

28th June, 2000
I took the star Ferry to Tsai Tui, which is the first really Chinese area opposite Hong Kong and I had to do a marathon walk to get home but I met and talked to an Australian mum and her two daughters and vowed to decrease my tea consumption on her advice. "Your teeth and insides are very, very brown" they said!

I had a meal in a Greasy Spoon (?Greasy Chopstick) Cafe later – filleted fish on elderly noodles with spinach and green tea. I then bought two plants for Jane and planted them on her windowsill.

29th June, 2000
Today I treated myself to a Starbucks coffee. Everyone says it is The Best. I thought it was like diesel oil – expensive too – but the U.S. ambience in the café was good and Grace, the manager for a week, was so nice that I nearly wrote a letter to the owners to tell them so.

I sat with a German man and a Chinese girl and when I offered to take their picture together the German politely said he wouldn't be able to explain his camera function to me! Since I had completely lost the TV picture on two stations that morning, he was definitely being intuitive about my relationship with modern machinery. I had been admiring another very loving and glamorous couple, sitting on the other side of me but was rather disappointed when I overheard her going into details about her daughter's very runny, huge cold-sore.

I posted letters home to mum and dad and stickers to grandchildren Holly and William. There are wonderful stalls here selling the sort of colourful junk that I love sending to them when I am away. I like to think that by sending parcels, they won't forget me. I enclosed a message to William to tell him about Sue Mi (a solicitor's wife) and Ah Choo (a dentist's sign)!

29ᵗʰ June, 2000

The Hillside Escalator Link is the longest escalator in the world and begins near 'my' flat. It was going *down* on the Sunday I found it but met me coming *up* today. I wondered if it was doing ups and downs on alternate days until someone told me that it runs downhill during the morning rush-hour and uphill for the rest of the day. 200,000 people use it *daily!* It is outdoor, silent, and surprisingly uncrowded, comprising 20 escalators. They snake from where I live at Mid-Levels down to Central, descending steeply for 800 metres. A curved glass roof shelters it, open at the sides so it is airy and light. It is nice to stare into the windows of the apartment blocks and shops en route and there are loads of places to hop off and investigate the markets and antique shops.

Sacred Circle

I saw an advert in the "Y" for a gathering of people of different religions, who meet every now and again to talk about feelings and futures and 'life' generally. Having been brought up as a Presbyterian, and now lapsed, I have always been interested in exploring other faiths. The hosts for the first evening I went to were Yvonne and Martin, definitely missionary types, from Britain. Martin was a little cynical, Yvonne a little intense, especially about health problems which she seems to have a lot of, but they were warmly welcoming and I loved being in their beautiful flat which overlooked Hong Kong Harbour.

A Chinese surgeon called Peter 'kicked off' the discussion by describing his feeling of security when he 'hides behind' his surgical mask, gloves, aprons, and hats. David, an Australian, admitted to feeling completely different about life, since shaving off his beard and cutting off his ponytail. He was baldish, with a nice face, and was happy about my observation - that it was just part of his maturing – that he now felt secure enough not to hide behind his hairy image.

Jan was a German Sight Restorer! He believes he can restore your vision by taking you back psychologically, to when you had good vision. (I was quite taken with this idea).

There were two 'psychic' women from NZ, one of whom wished we would all contribute to her dream. I readily confessed to my dream of getting my book about my year in an Indian orphanage published. This lady's dream was to be rich, have a huge luxurious house and a car with a driver. We all put our thoughts into her wish and into those of several others so I shall 'watch their space' as they say.

The whole evening was fascinating – a bit intellectual for me at times – I even had to ask the chap next to me what the topic title meant at one point. As I left, he assured me that the cumulative 'will' of the company would contribute to my successful mission to find a publisher.

Their flat overlooked the harbour and as all the lights came on, and the candles flickered all around the room, I was entranced by the wonderful atmosphere. Tea was provided at the end but I had to rush off early to return to Molto. We were still bonding and I didn't want him to lose confidence in me. Tracey and her friends gave me a lift home that night. They then invited me to swim, have cups of tea, walk to the Peak and generally join in their lives, while I am here. I felt really welcomed by them and looked forward to being involved in the social life of Hong Kong.

2nd July, 2000
It is velly, velly hot today and velly, velly wet!
I have been here over a week now and it is certainly a very different adventure to anything that I have done before. Molto and I have bonded so well I can't even put the kettle on or go to the loo without finding him beside me, nuzzling. We watch Wimbledon together, get absolutely soaked out walking together and eat together, but so far I have been able to sleep on my own! He doesn't seem to mind that I call him "Susie" (our dog at home) or "Sam" (my parents' dog) and say "Good Girl" as many times as "Good Boy".

3rd July, 2000
I have put my newly acquired Feng Shui skills into practice in Jane's flat, moved some of the furniture and also re-potted some of her plants. I hope she won't mind. Feng shui is much discussed at the YWCA and I hope to go on a course to learn more before I go home.

Molto and I continue to watch Wimbledon on TV. He sits beside me on the settee and every now and again almost speaks with his pleading eyes, asking me to take him for yet another walk. If I say NO very firmly, he turns his back on me and sulks! This is the first time I have ever been able to watch Wimbledon live. I have always had small children about, or have been in full time work. I loved seeing it as it happened and of course hearing all the English gossip from the commentators and spotting the odd celebrity. Watching the Agassi/Martin match, whilst scoffing watermelon, was absolute bliss.

4th July, 2000
I had a small problem at the entrance to the tram this morning. I got the spiky barrier – like we have in the public loos in England - stuck up the leg of my shorts. I escaped and sat on the wooden benches on the top deck and toured Hong Kong. A ride only costs 2$ and you can stay on as long as you like.

I saw hundreds of Filipino girls today. They work here in Hong Kong and meet on Sundays, that being their one day off. They congregate in the centre of Hong Kong and massage each other, look at photos, picnic, play cards and read each other's fortunes. I was told that they live on their employers' balconies in some instances, or in what are virtually cupboards, sending their wages home to support parents or their own babies. Yet the Filipino maid that cleans for Jane told me that they prefer to work in Hong Kong than anywhere else in the world, with about 190,000 Filipino women working in Hong Kong today.

My tram went to Wan Chai and en route I saw "Rome wasn't built in a day either, so be patient" written on a huge sign on a building site. I bought a beach-ball for grandson William and chocolate for me. I *didn't* buy a Daily Mail – because it was $6, so an American told me. However, I enjoyed coffee and a free fill-up in McDonalds. After all I have said about McDonalds, I now admit that their coffee is consistently good and their loos are the cleanest in Hong Kong, *and* they are air-conditioned.

From the tram I spotted a workman in the road who had his safety helmet on *over* his sunhat! I saw the Hong Kong State Theatre, North Point Station, The Kodak Building and Kornhill Plaza. Overall I was not disappointed as the buildings were clearly architecturally and historically interesting in themselves and it was almost thrilling to actually view them from the tram.

Is the hanging-down root tree, I see everywhere, a BanYan I wondered? I was also intrigued by the bus ticket bought at a kiosk that can be 'screened' through my purse. You press it to a little lit-up panel on entering the bus or train and it even tells you how much money is left on the ticket.

The Peak
5th July, 2000
Today I left Molto for a few hours and took the tram to the Cable Car station, which runs to the Peak and is a copy of a cable car made over a hundred years ago. It was packed with Japanese tourists and jolly to be on. The Peak Tower and Galleria are huge architectural monstrosities built for tourists but the shops inside were air-conditioned and spacious. I found a coffee lounge and free newspapers, Internet access and delicious coffee. The views from inside or outside on the terrace are spectacular. One can see all over Hong Kong and the liners in the harbour. The houses on the Peak, despite being unimpressive architecturally, routinely sell for millions of dollars. A group of Chinese schoolgirls conducting a survey outside the Galleria were thrilled when we swapped e-mail addresses and amused me by *whispering* to each other in Mandarin, in case I should hear what they were saying. (My three weeks' Mandarin tuition in Beijing was absolutely no help here!) I bought myself bookmarks, pens and postcards and promised to return to these shops.

Finally I hurried home to Molto. After his walk we watched more Wimbledon. (I think he's really getting into 'Bonk Bonk'), and then we went to bed early so that I would be ready for an eight o'clock meeting in the morning with a new friend, Mandy.

6th July, 2000
Mandy is a very friendly, Scots business woman married to a charming Manchester-born Chinese, Jim, who works incredibly hard, as most people

seem to here. Jane had introduced us before she left for Australia and I felt as if I had always known her and Jim, from day one.

They belong to a Cricket Club which also provides tennis courts and a swimming pool. Whilst Mandy played tennis, I lay by a deep blue pool and talked to everyone. I realised that I hadn't talked to anyone in depth for what seemed like ages One of Mandy's friends, a New Zealand immigrant with three boys, talked at length on many unrelated topics- faiths and beliefs, Chi Gong, Nei Gong and Fallon Gong, how lottery ticket results are shown on mobile phones in Hong Kong and how much Chris Patten was loved by the Chinese. I learned that Mandarin, Canton and English are taught in all the schools, but not so much English as formerly, now that Hong Kong has been handed back to China. We talked a lot about eyesight – there are many more short-sighted Chinese children than you see in England, maybe due to their having to write intricate Chinese characters, for genetic reasons, or early eyestrain because they start studying much earlier than we do.

Mandy says I can join them all next Thursday for lunch – and, if I can get Molto 'emptied' by someone else - has invited me to her birthday celebration on a Chinese Junk (yes, a real one!) the following Sunday. It sounds like a most Special Day Out. I enquire nervously about cost, but it seems 200 HKD (just under £20) will be the only bill, for lunch on shore.

On our return from lunch, Grace, the Chinese security lady in Mandy's block, again told me "You be Careful" as I left for home. I don't know if it is the crime rate here, my age or my knackered appearance that makes her so anxious about me, but she says it every time she sees me!

I've worked it out that I shall possibly need to take Molto for 420 walks for wees in ten weeks. Today my most embarrassing moment occurred whilst Molto was 'performing'. We were observed by an airline-pilot-type and his chic Hong Kong girl-friend at the bus stop. They watched fascinated as I scrambled to collect poos that were rolling off downhill…....

7th July, 2000
Lamma Island Hike
I met Tracey, leader at the YWCA, and eight other members, at the Outlying Islands Pier No.5. We took the ferry to Yung Shue Wan and walked around the island, to Sok Kwu Wan. Lamma Fortune Seafood Restaurant provided us with a scrumptious lunch – vegetable spring rolls, prawns in ginger and spices, sweet and sour pork, fried diced chicken with cashews, steamed whole fish (snapper or gli wong), steamed rice, fried eggy rice and pak choi (a popular green vegetable like cabbage).I shared a bottle of Carlsberg with Alison who had been a Tring pharmaceutical rep. at some time and I talked to a tall, vital American woman about 'bulking the carbs'. She has invited me to the Marriot Hotel on any Thursday between 10 and 12, for an American Womens' Association Meeting, where Ex-Pats get the chance to talk and help each other.

I loved the lush scenery and vegetation on this island. It is famous for ex-pat hippies but I only saw one drunken Englishman with two of the most horrendous dogs ever, which were admired by the other women! Lamma is the third largest island in the area and after lunch we walked amongst banana trees and trees with metre–wide leaves and 'vulgar' flowers. I saw huge scary spiders which upset Tracey!

The roads around the islands are too small for cars. The beaches were sandy and inviting, but netted for sharks. It had almost a Mediterranean feel to it really. I walked the long way back to the ferry with the only other three women in the party who were fit enough to walk after the trek before lunch. Tracey entertained us with a story of a loo in Tonga where you could see the pigs waiting in a trench for their dinner to drop down from under the loo seat......

We passed the Bookworm Café which we glanced into on the way to the ferry. It sold new and secondhand books and vegetarian meals. I must go back soon!

9th July 2000
Mandy's Birthday

All Mandy's friends contributed dishes to take on the trip, and, since there are very few private cars, the food and drink had to be transported by public transport It was quite a feat to get the mountains of goodies and drinks to the junk. As it was Sunday **lunch-***time the Filipinos had taken up all the buses and were massed in the streets, but we staggered through them and met on the quay. Bridget and Cathy - Australians living and working in HK - adopted me, but everyone mixed and talked happily all day. The picnic lunch was consumed on board and we swam and water-skied off the junk - o.k. I swam!*

The views of HK as we sailed along were wonderful in the sunshine and the grand finale was supper at a seafood restaurant crammed with hundreds of very noisy Chinese. I couldn't help wondering what Chinese people think of the mostly funereal atmosphere in restaurants when they come to England. We ate octopus. langoustine, lobster, prawns, fried lettuce, fish soup with tofu and spinach, crab, and pak choi and drank gallons of green tea and alcoholic beverages! I had a teetotaler on one side of me, declining champagne and wine, and a woman from Manchester (over to check on a clothing outlet) on the other, who couldn't bear Chinese food and didn't eat a thing. I didn't let these neighbours inhibit me though...

From new Chinese friends I gained: a recipe for cooking chicken in boiling water and all about shahtoosh, a shy alpine goat in Tibet. The coat of this endangered goat makes wonderful cashmere type garments which sell for hundreds of pounds. I was also told the best way to adopt children from another country and details of how to adapt to life in Hong Kong.

I got a bit fed up with how incredible they all thought I was – *for my age!* I was used to this comment from the Indians when I lived in Tamil Nadu for a year but I could see the difference in my contemporaries *there*. My lovely easy life in Britain had made me fairly wrinkle free but those poor, overworked, poorly fed women looked years older than me. Perhaps these young people were talking fitness or energy, and not appearance at all. I am certainly blessed in this department and the heat doesn't affect me either. On this lovely trip I was totally warmed by everybody's kindness and affection for each other and for me, and I loved their company.

Another lovely girl called Debbie, who couldn't come to the party, had 'emptied' Molto for me during the day, and he didn't appear to hold a grudge when I got home. I would have done anything not to have had to walk him again though, at 10.30 p.m., because I was on my knees and possibly feeling my age?

10th July 2000

I bought a single special orchid and delivered it to Debbie to thank her for walking Molto yesterday. Then I took a thank-you bunch of flowers and a card, which portrayed a garlanded 1920s nude, to Mandy's block. This message of thanks included the suggestion that it was me in the picture, at work. Jim and Mandy had been tickled to learn of my earning extra pin money as a model for a local art group in Ipswich. Anyway, I gave the items to the security guard in Mandy's block and he seemed happy to deliver them to Flat 2, 7th floor, as clearly marked on the envelope. However, next day it became clear he thought the items were for *him* and he thanked me most sincerely and said how lovely they were, and how kind I was. Mandy is in fits and apparently mustn't enquire further because he would lose face!

I am intrigued with the bamboo scaffolding everywhere and an engineer on the boat trip told me that it is stronger than steel as long as it doesn't split. It looks like something from a cartoon. I was admiring this, looking upwards, when I was walking Molto and didn't see a man with three dogs, NOT on leads, heading towards us. I thought one of his dogs attacked Molto, but our lead gave me friction burns and therefore I have to admit Molto may have attacked *him*. Anyway the man and I shouted and hauled our animals away and there was no harm done.

We then watched the Finals of Wimbledon with Molto in a licking-feet mood, but as I had walked my feet off with him that day, it was immensely pleasurable.

Western Market

11th July 2000

Today I went to Sheung Wan on the tram. I found the Western Market selling fabric, and the tailors' block, known as Shun Tak. I traveled there on the open-topped tram again which was fun but very hot. Although I found both buildings, I couldn't find fabric or tailors. However, I did find a shampoo dispenser which I had craved – you fix it in the shower and fill one side with shampoo and the other with liquid soap – or conditioner - and just press a button each time. I nearly bought two pairs of shoes but realised in time that they cost one hundred HK Dollars and not ten HK Dollars!

At home I dined on left-over boat party crabs, langoustines, chicken and rice which were just as delicious cold, then watched David Copperfield on video. To crown the evening I had a lovely telephone chat with my daughter Jane who told me that her new dancing school, Shiny Shoes, in Tring, is doing really well.

12th July, 2000

Another trip to the Western market – this time with Scottish Mary McGinty. She is a Social Worker and has lived in Hong Kong for sometime. We lunched with her husband Terry who left his office to join us. He had been in the R.A.F and Radio but evidently was very happy in Hong Kong.

Mary bought material from the wonderful selection *upstairs* – which is where the market was and I hadn't looked *upwards* yesterday to find it on the first floor balcony overlooking the ground floor! I bought enough pretty green stuff to cover my button-back chair at home, but don't think it was particularly cheap and there is no way I shall afford to have it made up here. Prices are decidedly high in Hong Kong, compared to England, let alone Nanjing. My dream of a new wardrobe is unrealistic!

Plants

14th July 2000

Hong Kong is not as *Chinese* as I found Nanjing, but was more exciting in architectural, botanical, geographical and climatic terms. Exploring it has been for three hours at the most, partly due to my lack of stamina in the heat or torrential rain and partly due to Molto's needs.

Today I rose at six to take Molto walkies so that I could join Mandy early for swimming and coffee at the Cricket Club. It was absolutely scorching by the pool and I am now tanned. I talked by the pool-side to Andrea, a qualified architect who is also studying herbal medicine. She told me that spider plants definitely improve the atmosphere in a room and suggested planting things in window boxes that combine well when cooked together. Her own favourite was tomatoes and basil. She described various orchids and mosses and a sort of strawberry called guava apple which grows all over the place in China.

I keep finding small plants such as Busy Lizzies and baby bamboos in the streets, which have been dug up in their entirety, perhaps by some sort of animal? Anyway I bring them home and plant them because they are so nice. The windowsill in the flat is amazingly full now but I think it may be getting a bit 'jungly' for Jane's rather minimalist taste. There are many more butterflies here than at home, black or broadly striped, and I have noticed very large caterpillars on the numerous camellias that line the streets. Oh and the snails are enormous too. I found two huge purple-flowering plants on a rubbish pile up Hatton Road when I was walking Molto. I lugged them home in their terra cotta pots with Molto pulling me - but it was well worth the trouble when I resettled them in the soil from a sack on Jane's balcony.

Cemeteries
15th July 2000

The Chinese don't feel sad like us about cemeteries. They meet and picnic on the graves on special days or anniversaries, bringing fruit and flowers and candles and incense. There is even a Hungry Ghost festival, when the unhappy ghosts of people who have not been happily dispatched, roam about seeking revenge.

Today I visited the main cemetery in Hong Kong that I had spotted from the tram during my first days here. I found separate grounds for Buddhists, Taoists, Muslims, Catholics and Protestants. I noticed that the Muslim cemetery had many young people, mostly between the ages of 4 and 27. I only saw one 75 year-old's grave and I wondered why.

In the Catholic section I saw the grave of Thomas Campbell, a Hong Kong policeman from Drogheda, Ireland. His epitaph was 'God has you in his keeping – We have you in our hearts'. Dr Lim Shui Wah was 27 when he died in 1934. Anna Mackenzie died in 1980 aged 95. She was preceded by her daughters, Chan and Jane, who died in 1919 aged 30 and 25. There were many Irish and Scottish graves and so many interesting descriptions that I completely forgot I had no hat and it must have been 35C in the non-existent shade. I saw the grave of Frank Summers, 24, born in Hong Kong and killed in active service in Ypres, Belgium, and also that of William Graves, a seaman on board an American ship, U.S. Vandalia. He was killed in an attack on pirates near Lantau Island in May 1855. There is a Cenotaph here for seamen who died of smallpox, fever or dysentery. I was moved to find the grave of an Olive Batley who was an air-hostess in a Cathay Pacific Airways crash on Mount Butler in 1948. Her epitaph read 'As a star that is lost when the daylight is given, she has faded away to shine brightly in Heaven'.

Hair
16th July 2000

I ventured into a hairdressing salon today and Michael in "Joyce's" on the Hollywood Road offered me a shampoo and cut for sixty Hong Kong dollars. I had a wonderful head massage whilst being shampooed and then had another rinse and mini-massage after the actual cut. Michael only spoke once to point out, morosely, that the colour had gone from my hair – "it is white" he said. He snipped away with various scissors, then 'moussed' it and blew it up in the air. He seemed very pleased with what he had achieved. He had copied his own style onto me! After only one shampoo at home I realised the damage one man can do with thinning shears – I was absolutely shorn and looked like an animated carrot in a children's' book.

Henry Litton

A pleasant man on the bus today told me the tale of a bad landslide. They are a recurring hazard in Hong Kong. He said that in June 1972, during torrential rain, part of the Po Shan Road – one up from me – and a thirteen-storey apartment block, Kotewell Court, slid downhill and 67 people died in the rubble. Amongst those trapped was a barrister, Henry Litton Q.C. He was pulled from the rubble 23 hours later, after firemen heard him singing 'When I'm 64'. Now he is a judge and happily he made it to 64 and is now 66!

Mudslides like this are apparently a continuing threat here and in 1992 a record rainfall (180mm in two hours) sent mud pouring into another estate and two people died including a 7-year old, Brendan Murphy. Shotcrete is a system of retaining banks which prevent the soil sliding and it seems that landowners are responsible for the maintenance and safety of these hills.

Ian Wright
17th July 2000
Ian Wright (traveller not footballer), was in my daughter Jane's class in school in Ipswich. He was today featured in an article in the Sunday Morning China Post. He also featured in a wonderful TV programme called Lonely Planet, as a travel reporter. My most vivid memory of him is at my daughter Jane's fancy dress birthday party. He stood on the front doorstep, practically nude, asking me to pin his nappy on as he wanted to be a baby and didn't know how to do the essential pinning part! He is *such* good fun and all the girls here love him.

I loved the episode on TV when he was on a ten hour bus journey in Ethiopia. He became desperate to visit the loo. However, when he finally found one he said he would rather wait the next ten hours than use it! The cameras then followed him on another bus, then a train and even a cycle but the programme finished with him bolting *very* urgently into some bushes!

I subsequently enjoyed many of his programmes while I was in Hong Kong because it seemed that I followed him as I travelled around the world, and his great sense of humour and laid-back approach to the challenges thrown up in foreign parts, appealed to me greatly.

Today Molto again chose his moment for maximum embarrassment for me. He performed exactly at the bus stop when a bus, loaded with onlookers of course, stopped. Everyone watched me avidly, with my plastic bag and very red face.

Dalmatians are rare in Hong Kong - well, there aren't really many dogs. This means most people are scared of them, and excited or frightened children flatten themselves against walls when we pass. Many dogs are kept by the Chinese as a status symbol. Molto's friends are: Dolce, a short-legged golden retriever, Patches, a brown spotted Dalmatian, and Bo, a little black dog. Apart from these friends, I tow him across the road to avoid meeting any other dogs because they fight. They all live in flats and I could never keep a dog here. They can't be exercised properly because of the heat. It occurs to me that dogs in Mexico weren't walked much, either. Perhaps it is an English habit?

I am wondering about getting some chlorophyll tablets for Molto. He keeps trying to eat grass and vomited what seemed like a whole rattan chair one day. I note that he likes the occasional apple and yesterday he ate a raw egg, which I had dropped, and it went down a treat.

Jo
19th July 2000
Jo Lusby became my very good friend in Beijing, where we taught English in schools and colleges for six months in exchange for basic accommodation. We met in the plane going over and she had us all in fits about being a reluctant bridesmaid at her sister's wedding.

Jo stayed on alone in Beijing, working as editor of a newspaper. She kept in touch with me following our stint together and I had several e-mails from her whilst I was in Hong Kong, including one today. It was to tell of an accident she had in the shower, which resulted in her having eight stitches in a rather unsavoury hospital. She had to give them money before they would do anything at all, but, as she had no health insurance of her own, she found herself in a financially tricky position. Eventually, however, her employers agreed to pay for her to be seen properly and she got appropriate treatment and drugs. She hadn't told her mother about it. I told her about my daughter Jane not informing me of 'nasties' that had happened to her whilst she worked abroad. Jo then hinted at other problems that she was encountering. She promised to keep contact with me until she came to stay with me here for a holiday.

Teaching
19th July 2000
John Wong has a teaching agency and has offered me work. I will be teaching for nine days in August. He arranged an 'integration day' (unpaid) with the other novice teachers at the International English Centre, easily reached by train from Admiralty. Of course on Integration Day I got lost trying to find it because at Jordan I came out of a different station exit and it definitely *wasn't* easy to find the school. I puffed into the Centre feeling sweaty, fat and old – and entirely put the other teachers at their ease because of this. They forgave me for being twenty minutes late and relaxed and chatted happily. There were four of us, including an American Andrea and two boys, Gordon and Tim. Tara from the office explained the drill for Monday next. We have to meet together at Prince Edward Station and walk about two miles to the school. We work for four hours with only quarter of an hour break and my enquiry about availability of coffee met with a blank stare. Finally we were given a ton of textbooks for the students, to take home and bring back with us on Monday!

Jo again
No news from Jo and I am wondering is she is alright in view of her recent accident. I am really anxious about her as she doesn't reply to my e-mails.

25th July 2000
Happily Jo has sent a long e-mail and I now know where she is. However the e-mail described graphically the serious sexual harassment she had endured. It was so bad she had 'flipped' and had taken off to stay with friends on a beach in Indonesia where she could scuba dive and recuperate. I quite understood her lack of contact when I knew the details.

Repuls(iv)e Bay
31 July 2000
A Yum Cha, or Tea Party, was arranged by the YWCA, in the Veranda Restaurant, and I went early and had a good look at the dirty, crowded beach (yuk), and the Tin Hau Temple. This bizarre collection of statues and other deities included a four-faced Buddha and other garish but fascinating objects. A bridge in front of it all is called Longevity Bridge and crossing it is supposed to add three days to your life. There's a huge collection of apartment blocks and *one has a 'hole' purposely designed and inserted at the behest of a Feng Shui master, as the 'eye of the dragon', which brings good fortune.*

I admired lovely sepia photographs in the Repulse Bay Hotel, of 1920–1930, when the Stubbs Road was cut through to Repulse Bay and the motor car arrived in Hong Kong, making the beach and hotel a popular place to visit. A hundred-year-old bell from Guangzhou is preserved in the hotel.

I sat next to Americans Donna and Denise, who were friends of Jane, and were interested in me and my travels and particularly in publishing my book about India. I was encouraged to return to Hong Kong to experience it without Molto. Tea was English-styled and delicious - chocolate cake to die for and little tarts of fresh fruit in a banana custard base.

I met an English girl on the way to the bus stop, who had a baby dangling in front of her and wanted to know where I got my Mexican sandals. We talked for a while but I sort of left her before we both wanted to,(I later admitted to myself) from some sort of misplaced guilt on my part, about taking up her time…….

Today it was 29C and only reduced to 28C when it rained a little – there was an electric sign on the beach telling the time and the temperature. I bought a tin of Blue Ribbon Beer imported from the U.S. and a packet of grilled corn, covered in spicy powder and ate them on the beach. I also bought two dainty Kleenex box covers, which was against my economic instincts, but they were so pretty.

2nd August, 2000
Dolphin Watch
Another 'Y' inspired trip today, and it was absolutely tipping down when we all met in the Mandarin Hotel's beautiful, vast and opulent foyer. There were the usual mix of American, Australian and about three English/Welsh people

and I kept company most of the day with Beth-Anne from near Aberystwyth. She was a housewifely, very pretty 65 year old with boys in their late twenties whom I enjoyed hearing all about.

Shirley, the tour guide, was from Yorkshire. She had been to Tokyo with her American husband and thought she might as well take free Japanese lessons offered to servicemen and women, whilst she was there. She found she was good at it so took some more, paid, lessons. Then her husband suddenly got posted to Hong Kong by his firm so she thought that the lessons had been a waste of time. To her joy she landed this tour guide job, showing people the dolphins. Her Japanese was really useful because of the hundreds of Japanese tourists. She had always been eco-friendly (Green Party and all that) so this job was made for her. Her parents are coming next week and she says they are going to be SO proud of her…..

The boat wasn't 'fumey'. I had given my Kwells to Beth-Anne hoping that it would be O.K. for me – and it was, I felt fine. However, I felt sick as a parrot on the way home on the bus….

After a half an hour of 'full steam ahead', the rain stopped and we could scan the sea for dolphins and, after about twenty minutes, there they were! It was such a beautiful sight – and I was unexpectedly affected by them. I'd been thinking "Well they are PINK so I had better go and have a look" – but they were really wonderful. The babies are grey and the teenagers spotty (!) and the adults decidedly PINK and their movement or their proximity or *something* - makes it a most emotional experience.

There were a lot of Japanese on the boat and one lady my age slept throughout the trip! The whole of the boat was oooohing and aaaaaahing and cheering when we caught sight of the dolphins, but she was snoring!

When I returned from the Dolphin Watch, Molto seemed extra pleased to see me and I gave him a great brushing session. Everything has to be covered up in the flat because of his hair loss and it is so spiky and profuse. A couple living downstairs complained when the covers were shaken on our balcony and blew in their windows! He has a monthly flea treatment and a monthly bath unless he gets smelly. His skin problem - a sort of pinkness that comes periodically - isn't too bad at the moment. I have to keep his ears and eyes as dry as possible when bathing because they are sensitive. I didn't know about Dalmatians often being deaf - due to a genetic fault. This makes them more difficult to train so they are sold cheaply from Homes and Refuges where the costs are offset by selling fit puppies.

4th August 2000
Ikea
I went looking for Ikea in the Victoria Park area of Hong Kong and found by accident the gun which has been fired at noon by the British since 1901. Noel Coward made it famous in 1924 in his satirical song "Mad Dogs and Englishmen" which goes "In Hong Kong they strike a gong and fire a noon

day gun, to reprimand each inmate, who's in late". I had been walking through the Victoria region, humming this song, enjoying a notice to joggers: DO NOT CRASH, - and there it was, situated on the harbour wall in a little garden. Lengthy engraved notes explained how it had been fired in error as a salute and the tradition started for daily firing at twelve noon. Covered with a waterproof sheet, it sat between pretend cannons and beside a brass bell, which I presumed to be the gong.

I found Ikea and bought a yellow washing up rack, matching beakers, a shower curtain and a toiletries bag. How sad is that?! I expect they are the same price as at home and I know I will have difficulty lugging them on the plane, but I *love* Ikea and couldn't resist buying these things. I was quite proud of *not* buying lovely black towels, fine sheets and quilt covers and an arm/shelf for a TV, all of which were very cheap.

8th August 2000.
Teaching
I met the some of the teachers at the meeting place in Prince Edward Metro. Gordon Arthur (from New Zealand but born in Scotland) was a bit like Ian Wright but thin and then Tim (US) – rather bored by life generally. Andrea is an American living with the parents of her half Chinese lover and finding it a bit heavy I think. She looks like Miss World in a very unselfconscious way.

Fanny Cheung, the project organiser, is calm and nice and laughs at my jokes even though she has a somewhat incredulous look about whatever I say. We walked for about ten minutes to the St Helena school and got the usual *unwelcome* from the staff and found our two sterile classrooms. However the 20 boys in each of my two classes were absolutely gorgeous. They are called names like Tam Yik Yu Ivan and Pang Yin Pong Dennis and Man Long Tin Charles. The area of the school is called Sham Poo or something similar.

I started them off with a sort of relay race to the blackboard when they whisper words I have told them from the back to the front of the row. They all wrote Cheers on the board instead of Cherries – it must be the US T.V. programme that they see – and when I whispered the singular of a word to the front person they were supposed to whisper it back and run forward to put the plural on the blackboard and they all wrote the word plural.

We then played saying numbers round the room and then inserted 'Buzz' when the number was dividable by two or by five. This was fairly successful, but I later realised that they were saying 'Pus'…..

The children bowed and said 'Thank you Mrs. Jenny' when collecting their marked books, but I can't believe it will last.

Today's list of proper nouns in the curriculum leaflet given to each teacher was: Hong Kong, Jamaica, England and Harrods. The children had to write sentences including these names. They are to learn about superlative adjectives, conditional somethings and adverbs, tomorrow, so there will be some frantic swatting up by teacher tonight!

Tim told me he had photocopied a whole lot of stuff and distributed it but they designed aircraft with the papers and threw them about the class!

I met Fanny at her office and talked doggies for ages and she gave me loads of dollars and she said that she would try to get me cash for my final pay–off. She didn't advise trying for a work permit when I come back in November as it is complicated and you need to offer more than six months' work and full time commitment. She thought we could continue as at present but advised me to get a bank account next time.

I bought candies for the boys at the end of their sessions with me. I opted for M&S small chocolate bars in spite of advice that Chinese people prefer Chinese goodies. Grace the Security lady in our block says she loves M&S though. She was wearing a huge peaked cap today when I returned, because the big boss was coming!

Flesh eating Fly
Meanwhile, throughout all this education stuff, I was worrying about a ghastly flesh-eating fly that Jane and Adrian had e-mailed me about. They had heard about this lovely critter in Australia, and warned me not to let Molto dig in sand. Apparently these flies invade open wounds on dogs and eat them away from the inside. Charming isn't it? Fortunately Molto isn't a digging sort of dog and I only have to worry if there are builders with sand in the road. Another delight to avoid is poisoned food left by a crank who is well known in HK and has polished off several pets. Even Chris Patten's dog fell ill because of this lunatic. I e-mailed them back to say I would be very vigilant and told them that I had just read how Freddie Mercury used to telephone his cat when he was away – did they want a word? Of course within days I only just stopped Molto from nibbling a Chinese takeaway which he found at the side of the road. I yanked him away just in time, happily, since its owner was doing his tai-chi-ing behind a nearby bush.

The water supply had been cut off in our apartment block for three days and came back today just as the rains came. It was rather a wonderful rain: soft, very heavy and warm, and I welcomed the cleansing bit on the streets because Molto alone has done – to my calculations – nearly fifty wees and nineteen poos during this drought. I feel reluctant to bother with an umbrella because you get soaked anyway as the heavy rain splashes up after falling down!

9th August
Irish Lorraine.
I took the Wan Chai ferry, which takes 317 people across from H.K to the island of Wan Chai in a few minutes. I wanted to see the Kings College Choir for their Christmas concert but there were no tickets left. Another disappointed woman introduced herself as Lorraine from Ireland and invited

me to have a beer with her. She treated me to an enormous Carlsberg lager in a café which I had admired but not visited, near the Escalator. She told me that she reckoned one needs three or four thousand dollars per month to live here and one can make a lot of money teaching, as she does.

From the café, we watched some dust-*women* with their sunhats, wellies, aprons and handcarts, and were intrigued by a ginger-haired man with spectacles and a goofy expression, who talked non-stop to an adoring Chinese girl in twinset and pearls.

Lorraine was good company and made me laugh. At one point I mentioned buying presents for people back home and she protested. "Oh Jenny, FOK presents! No real traveller buys presents!" She invited me to meet her for tea next week at the Helena May Home for Women of Limited Means and I happily agreed.

10th August
Stanley market
A double-decker bus took me on a wonderful scenic route to Stanley market. I had the front seat and the woman asleep nearby reminded me of my old friend, Maureen, sleeping through a Frank Sinatra Concert. I wanted to wake her up and say "LOOK!" A Chinese woman next to me said that the swimming pools and sea were empty of bathers because the Chinese don't like to get brown, they prefer to stay white. She also told me that her generation, living in Hong Kong, is still not saying they are Chinese – they are saying they are Hong Kongers. She knows that the next generation will adjust to the new arrangement and call themselves Chinese but in the meantime they should be writing "SAR" which means Special Administrative Region or even "China" at the end of addresses instead of Hong Kong but they forget.

I loved the stalls and shops in Stanley Market, and saw so much that I would've liked to buy but had no money. There were kites, night-shirts, sequinned tops and dresses, silk ties, tiny blue and white tea-sets, a Buddha made from a walnut, Chinese dolls and good quality men's shirts for next to nothing.

11th August
Fringe Theatre
This little theatre has a café/bar on a street in Central where Happy Hour beer was only $12.50. Hessian pictures in the foyer were stuck with steel pins and it was decidedly atmospheric and 'fringe'. I loved it here, and for only 150HKD admission I got to see many good plays.

A group called The Playbox Theatre from Melbourne, Australia and the Ilbjern Aboriginal Theatre Co-operative, presented Jane Harrison's uncompromising drama, telling the true story of a whole generation of Aboriginal children stolen from their families and adopted by white people. I cried for two hours solidly.

There was a great discussion session with cast and audience after the curtain went down, and several people spoke up who obviously had suffered from inappropriate adoptions.

12th August
The Helena May.
The Helena May club was opened in 1916 by an Englishwoman married to the Governor of Hong Kong. to care for wives and daughters coming to Hong Kong to join their men-folk or look for work and/or husbands.

The current cost of living in a flat there is the equivalent of £121 per week. The rooms are small and the bathroom shared but it is all very 'refined' and there is a waiting list for the flats and the rooms.
The menu in the lounge was superb – Western and cheap. Lunch was $35 to $45 and a High Tea, which would be enough to feed you all day, was $25. Drinks were cheap too. Most of all I loved the library and the elegant Twenties-style lounge, with comfortable sofas and cushions, sepia photos of the old days, and pleasant people just chatting, eating and drinking.

Lorraine showed me all this and we ordered up an excellent tea. Unfortunately the waitress told the Manager about us and because we weren't members we could have been refused! I was so embarrassed but when I told the manager and the waitress that I was interested in living there – I could afford it if I had a full-time teaching job – she let us stay.

The next embarrassment, well it was more of a shock, was that my budding friendship with Lorraine suddenly ended, as, in the course of eating our tea, she decided I wasn't a Lesbian, so she upped and left me!

14th August
The Findhorn Community
Tracey and four YWCA girls and I came back to the Bookworm café on Lamma Island to hear Peter Lloyd give a talk on the Findhorn Community Centre in Moray Firth, Scotland. Children are raised and educated there using Steiner's principles, - a holistic and practical approach to living. The dream of these people is to get the United Nations to make their prime goal the rescue of the Environment. Peter quoted G.B.Shaw "Those who cannot change their mind cannot change anything".

I was more interested in Peter! He had been born in Hong Kong but spent most of his life in Britain. He lives on Lamma now, working as a publisher, and he showed us his published works. He said he would consider my book so I am pretty excited about that.

15th August
American Women's Association.
On the tram to the very posh hotel where these American women meet, I learned from a Chinese man that the fine for smoking in public places is

50,000HKD and that the punishment for dog-fouling of pavements is fines and even prison!

There were about thirty women at the meeting who were mostly from America, sitting round in a circle. We introduced ourselves, telling our reasons for being here and how we were finding it. I was most impressed with their confidence – I know that a similar group of English women would've been very nervous standing up like that. My own heart was bumping when it was my turn. Their speeches were funny, or had practical advice, or were simply confessions - if they weren't settled or hadn't wanted to come to Hong Kong in the first place. They were all friendly and interested in *my* story - in the genuine, if overwhelming way Americans have.

On the way home an Indian man told my fortune but didn't mind that I couldn't pay him any money, and believed me when I said I hadn't any. He says September will be good for love, money and job. He ended up saying I thought about things too much, but I don't know what I can do about that! I'll have to *think some more*, won't I?

16th August
I spent a lovely couple of days on the roof of the flats next door with Scottish Mandy, who is the most appropriate person to talk to after three days of not speaking to anyone! She is going home on Wednesday to her mum, who has just lost her husband. She is living through what must be the horrible bit after the funeral – what to do, whether to move house, who to live near, what size of house to live in, why hasn't so and so telephoned etc.

Mandy invited me to a reflexology demonstration on Tuesday evening and wants to treat me. It is only $120 though, so I can afford that this week. She says she will download my manuscript if necessary, for publishing, though she says an 'attachment' is the answer and she doesn't know why Peter didn't suggest that. She's so kind and helpful about everything.

18th August
Cheung Chau
Once famous as a refuge for pirates and later a place for the British to retreat to for a break from Hong Kong, it is now the most crowded of the outlying islands, with a population of twenty-two thousand. Hardly any foreigners live there now and many of the inhabitants live on junks and sampans, which are anchored in the bay. There is no motorised transport, and it is rather scruffier than Lamma but perhaps it looked less than lovely because of the damp, terrible weather when we visited today.

I was with a group from the YWCA and we tramped miles. The views were beautiful and the path well made. In a village we came across a garish temple, Pak Tai, built in 1783 to honour a Taoist deity and his allies, a tortoise and a serpent, who overcame a demon king. This temple was attached to an old peoples' home with a sort of Catholic mission feel about it.

We had a good seafood lunch but American Lana did her American bit and complained at the non-appearance of her steamed prawns in garlic water. I don't suppose she would have ever seen them if she hadn't though. She was quite taken aback when I said I felt sorry for the waitress and wouldn't have spoken to her like that and Lana then felt sorry for her and left her a huge tip!

We didn't see the famous cave, Cheun Po Tsai, which is said to have been the hiding place for a ruthless, bloodthirsty pirate in the 19th century. Must've missed it because we were all talking so much.... Hundreds of jokes and anecdotes in the course of the trek and Oh, I thought this was funny:

WHAT TO DO AS THE ULTIMATE REVENGE ON A HUSBAND WHO IS STOLEN BY ANOTHER WOMAN – LET HER KEEP HIM.....

We fell into McDonalds with glee for coffee and/or ice-creams and got the ferry back but before we left I bought Vaseline in a chemist for my cracked feet. You could buy something for everything that ails you and stuff for enhancing breasts, reducing fat, stopping snoring etc. At first I couldn't find Vaseline but when I asked the girl behind the counter, she pointed behind me and there was a floor to ceiling rack with every size and shape of Vaseline you could imagine!

16th August
Reflexology
I had been invited by Mandy and her darling Jim to go for a session of reflexology because they are so thrilled with it. The salon was a train journey away and before I met them I was 'adopted' on the station by a pleasant woman who guided me on to a train and advised me to change half way. She then sadly bid me goodbye. Mandy said I had been on the right train originally and could've kept on it, but never mind!

Jim's brother John, newly arrived from Manchester but already flying high in Hong Kong yuppiedom, came too. He had a rather low pain threshold and had to keep biting his towel and crying out while his feet were 'being done'. The salon was immaculate and rows of pink armchairs and pouffes were filled with pink-towelled men and women who had their feet submerged in electric footbaths full of what looked like tea.

We joined them and while our feet soaked, our shoulders, neck and arms were savagely massaged. Very invigorating! Then to the feet! My masseur told me, through Chinese Lucy, Mandy's colleague at work, that I was retaining fluid in my knees and that – even if I said I wasn't – she insisted I was the most *tired* person she had ever had. I suggested that it might be because she didn't have such *old* people as me usually but she insisted she had a lot of old Chinese – older than me – but they were in better nick because of Tai Chi (the exercise they do in the mornings).... Ah, well! Meanwhile John was still crying out – his masseur was a burly man who kept stopping to have a ciggie, so that might have been something to do with it! The charge was about twelve pounds ($158 HKD) but Mandy and Jim paid for my treatment with some vouchers they had been given at the beginning of their ten week session, so that was lovely.

We all repaired to a Chinese restaurant - there are several here I notice - and though I had eaten at home, I sampled the lovely broccoli in Thai sauce, beef in something or other, and Tiger beer made in Singapore.

19th August
Godown Club
Located on the ground floor of Citibank office block, the Godown Club was posh and marble and lovely and the *food!!* I had been invited by the girls at the Y and, coming after several days of eating noodles and iceberg lettuce, it was a welcome indulgence. There were Japanese and Chinese delicacies of vegetables and fish, frittered everything and stuffed chicken legs and I thought 'Wot the hell', and paid a fiver for a Carlsberg, which was worth every cent.

20th August
Roberta's Adopted Baby
Roberta is from New York and sounds it. Her adopted baby, Sara, is three months old and *absolutely adorable*. I can feel energy or something coming from that baby – it just feels so good to hold her. She is very pink and round and cuddly and smiley. She was surrounded by the most wonderful contraptions to play with, and her wardrobe was fuller than some baby shops I have seen.

Apparently they got her by first of all hiring an 'attorney' in the States. He holds all their details and waits while they advertise for a pregnant girl who is willing to give her baby away immediately it is born. There is a free number that pregnant girls can ring from anywhere in the world and discuss their situation. If it sounds promising, the prospective adoptees pay her living costs throughout the pregnancy and sometimes for a couple of months after. She has to send her personal details and medical reports to the attorney to be approved, and meetings of both parties are arranged by him.

Roberta had had several perverts calling, as well as several desperate girls and two that were using the system as a way of life – not pregnant at all but pretending! Sara's birth mum, a beautiful 19 year old, is in college studying to be a doctor, and not wanting to abort or give a less than lovely life to her baby. She would like – at the moment – to meet up with Sara once a year. I have never seen such contented parents and baby as this family and you can't feel anything but optimism for their future.

Since my travels - and through my interest in adoption agencies in England - I now feel more optimistic than pessimistic about the chances of successful adoptions between countries. I especially found Romanian babies in such depressing circumstances that there is no doubt in my mind that a loving home *anywhere* that had been carefully inspected and monitored, must be a good idea. The other aspect which I feel hopeful about is that mixed race families are a way forward in the battle against racism — am I being unrealistic?

Tongue Analysis

I love to wander round the chemist shop in Central Hong Kong. You can buy so many interesting aids and potions here. I have spotted Night Trim and New Figure Gel which are fat burners; a colon cleanser (to be taken with *eight* glasses of water); Cardiwine Dietary supplements made from red wine extracts in France, for reducing the risk of heart attacks; Oyster Extract, sold to men with sexual potency problems; Vitacalm sleeping pills were stacked up against a girl assistant yawning her head off, and intelligence pills called Neuro Plus had pictures of children on the front!

A Chinese friend told me that *everything* could be analysed about your health by looking at your *tongue*. Anyway here is the list to help us know what your trouble is:

Red — you are dehydrated
Red tip — you have an emotional problem
Red sides — you are angered or stressed
Pale — you lack energy and could be anaemic
Purple — you have poor circulation and should exercise more
Crack in middle — you have digestive problems or heart disease!
Cracks at side indicates poor food/fluid metabolism — don't rush meals and exercise more
Yellow — imminent cold
Grey - cold or 'flu virus likely
Peeling patches — another sign of dehydration

Soft Ware

At a Tupperware-style party, a lovely big lady demonstrated her 'Micro-fibre' clothes, which breathe and are non-static. They came in mix-and-match styles and she was as big as me, but put them on and looked wonderful. I ordered three hundred pounds worth on the strength of my teachers' pay - they were that good. Delivery was promised within a week and I feel confident that these things will be totally appropriate for my life in this climate *and* at home.

Mary McGinty's "Special" Youth

Mary had been a social worker in England and she volunteered for an Integration Programme to help handicapped Hong Kong youngsters when they start work. She agreed to go swimming to get to know them, on the first day, and told me what happened: One of her colleagues was an Armenian, pony-tailed social worker and he assured Mary that one girl, Minnie, never had fits, despite having been diagnosed as epileptic. Another girl, Nancy, was a precocious teenager who refused to use the changing rooms at the pool and proceeded to undress in public. Mary held up towels around her and scrabbled her into a swimsuit. Nancy then put a huge shower cap over her masses of hair and jumped in the water completely saturating Mary. In the meantime, Minnie *did* have an epileptic fit and Mary had to call the ambulance. She looked desperately for other social workers to help but they were all in the male changing rooms. She dealt with Minnie and the ambulance and eventually staggered back to Nancy, to find her proudly wearing a t-shirt proclaiming Do Not Touch What you Cannot Afford. ....

21st August
Lantau Island
It is Sunday, 8.10 a.m., and the Filipino girls waiting for the courtesy bus outside the flats were in holiday mood. I joined them, on my way to catch the Ferry to Lantau Island. The bus driver looked like the pilot in war films on Saturday morning pictures in the 'Forties – glasses like goggles and a sort of sneer as he looks round to check you are authorised to use his bus.

The Ferry was rocking madly when we left the quay and a large notice saying Vomit Bag is Placed at Seat Back wasn't very encouraging.

After landing, I went first to Mui Po and fell into a café which looked a bit French, with its blue and white checked tablecloths and very good coffee. I enjoyed the 45 minute wait for the bus to see yet another Buddha- an incredibly tall, golden statue situated in a hillside monastery looking out across the South China Sea

Whilst waiting, I saw a notice for a Playgroup called Mini Genius and it advised that you "Don't let your children stay at home and pick up bad and slothful habits." I walked round a rather unremarkable village and noted The Friendly Bike Shop which offered the bikes for 550 $ – for hire or deposit or price I wondered? Bit hilly here for me I thought.

The Bus came eventually – No. 2 – and the scenery on the 25$ drive to the Buddha was absolutely wonderful. I noticed 'mottoes' written up in the picnic spots on the way and my favourite was

> Fake becomes True
> It Depends on You

I sat next to Joseph Dunn on the front seat. He was a wonderful Chinese man, who told me he was 70 and had learned English for six years in his middle school and had retained most of it. We exchanged names, ages, and children details, and he was most impressed when I spotted the Buddha before the other people on the bus. He was less impressed when I couldn't tell him the population of London – what a drip I am. He said he had loved practising his English and shook hands and bowed when we separated at the end of the journey.

The bronze Buddha was atop a 520 m high plateau, and has been there since 1928. Po Lin (Precious Lotus) is the largest monastery in Hong Kong but I didn't see a single monk or trainee monk all day. The climb to see the Buddha wasn't gruelling and the atmosphere amongst the climbers was very relaxed and happy. The monastery itself was decorated with brightly coloured tiles and memorable for some cartoons with mottoes on shelves and on the walls:

- Gossip frequently and your mouth will be irregular in shape
- Beat one's parents and you will grow a bent hand this present life.
- Laugh and scold at beggars and you will starve to death at the roadside
- Be Jealous of others and bad smelling will grow on your body
- Point out to other people the solution to any problem and you will be loved by everybody....

I found The Tea Garden after walking for five minutes along a tree-lined road away from the main monastery. Although the garden was a bit disappointing, they produced a lovely pot of tea and plate of spring rolls. I don't know why there was such an element of surprise in his face when I asked the waiter for tea — "Tea?" he said. "China tea?" However, a girl bought a white teapot with the lid wired loosely on, filled with what looked like clear boiling water. The man then hurtled off to a nearby shed — I thought he'd gone for the tea leaves but I never saw him again. However, when I poured the contents of the pot, it tasted delicious - jasmine-flavored. The spring rolls were lovely too and I was entertained while I ate them by three huge geese with funny floppy bits under their beaks. I then read the Sunday paper, bought a sun-hat with a pointy middle that the labourers wear in the fields, and got the bus and ferry 'home'.

22ndAugust
Stanley Market
Armed with a huge 'wodge' of wages from the teaching, I caught the Stanley bus without too much trouble and it all looked nicely familiar from the time when I had been when I had visited my friend Mo from Felixstowe.

 I went straight into the market street and within a very short time bought two mandarin-styled linen blouses, a navy linen over-blouse and a nightie for me, pyjamas for Jane, boxer shorts for all 'my' men at home, army style t-shirt and cap and t-shirt with his name in Chinese and English for William, Mandarin-styled pyjamas for Holly, table lineny things for me, slippers for everyone, and loads of tattoo transfers for the small boys I look after in the holidays.

Further up the road, I ate at a restaurant chosen for its intriguing name "Tables 88" and the weird décor. There were strips of metal like giant tagliatelli made into trees, and chairs made of twigs. A fan, an air-conditioner and extractor fan were just above my head in a row together, and sheets of steel made into cones for umbrellas at each table. There were coiled springs with round blobs of velvet cushion on the tops as bar stools and steel girders to put your feet on as you sat at the bar. The floor was made of tree trunks, herringbone-patterned and painted black, and with small lumps of steel, bronze, brass etc. randomly scattered in it!

By chance I noticed the difference eating with and without my glasses for the first time today. Finished my curried veg. with green tea and the bill was 103$. I noticed a couple tucking into simple chunks of sweet corn on the cob and watched a man opposite poke his lamb slices into pitta bread. An electrician on the corner table sat surrounded by amp testers and coloured rolls of wire and did things to a speaker without eating at all. Lots of very young couples ate here and I could understand why - it was fascinating in all respects.

The weather report given on a T.V. on the counter, told us that the temperature in Hong Kong cemetery today would be 33 degrees. Oh, and that by 2002/3 there would be seven million people in Hong Kong!

23rd August
ChiLun Nunnery
I took the MTR to Diamond Hill, changed line several times, and came out of the wrong exit, as usual. I ended up hopping about crossing motorways and climbing overpasses. I desperately asked an elderly couple at the entrance to Hollywood Plaza, if they knew where the Nunnery was, and they assured me they did, and ushered me into a lift which took me to a huge branch of KFC! I thus had the nicest 'elevenses' so far - a hot puff pastry egg tart and half a pint of divine fresh orange juice!

Feeling totally refreshed, I descended in the lift and trekked about as instructed by several children. They were all with their mothers (who didn't speak English) and their instsructions took me to a Monastery which looked promising, so I went in. I asked at the door where the Nunnery was but they didn't know and didn't want to help me. I enjoyed looking round the Monastery and then found it *was* the Nunnery!

In the courtyard there was a two thousand-year-old bonsai yew and loads of hundred year-old trees which are normal, according to a grey-robed, middle-aged, American-accented Chinese nun in the 'gifte shoppe' section. She told me of the 'integration' of male with female inmates – they are celibate but their aims and lives are identical. They care for 400 old people in an adjoining building with outside help because apparently they don't die off like they used to. If they didn't have help they wouldn't have time to do anything *but* care for the oldies. There are fifty nuns living there. She was the only one I saw though. In fact I only saw two other inmates - youths in maroon robes with shaved heads and baseball caps! I bought four elasticated bracelets for serviette 'rings' or presents, which are painted seeds of the Bodi tree. This is the tree under which it is alleged Buddha found enlightenment.

27th August
Molto and the Firemen
The morning after the adventure, I was awoken at 5 am by the fire bell! In retrospect I think I was very calm and organised. I collected up my passport and some money, donned a housecoat and put Molto on his lead and went urgently down hundreds of stairs, heeding the warning written in all lifts to only use stairs when the fire bell rings. Molto and I got up speed by the time we reached the ground floor and burst into the foyer to be greeted by a 'guard of honour' of more than a dozen small Chinese firemen. Even *their* eyes were round at the spectacle of a tubby woman with a huge spotty dog on a lead, hurtling out of the stairwell. They explained to me that the alarm was because of a flood or burst main. There wasn't another resident in sight. How could fourteen floors worth of people ignore the fire bell? I thought we might as well go walkies then, even though it was thundering and lightening but it was raining so hard that Molto put his four feet solidly into the floor and wouldn't leave the building..........

28th August.
Nabia
A woman I met at the YWCA invited me for dinner at the Kathmandu restaurant because we both had happy memories of Nepal. It was lovely to meet her at the bottom of the escalator on a very rainy night and sit in the colourful and welcoming restaurant. The staff wore their National dress, including the head-dresses with coins jingling. It was fun, too, to taste Dhal Baht again. This is a very bland sauce on rice but the Sherpas on our trek insisted it was the only food for them. They could never be coaxed to try our food.

Nabia is a Malaysian Muslim and as I had never talked with a Muslim before, she was happy to tell me a lot about it. I didn't know, for example, that they mustn't eat pork, and was surprised to know that they are not allowed to touch dogs because there could be noxious bacteria on them.

She has two Internet friends, one of whom is a blind Californian called Norman. She has visited him twice, driving his family's car and staying in a log cabin and walking (scared to death) in the woods with him. Malaysians are well into ghosts and spirits of the past etc. Norman had a guide dog and Nabia was impressed with how he could 'scoop the poop' etc. without help. She, of course, couldn't touch his dog but managed the visit without making an issue of it.

She loved America when she studied there for four years and she kept 'forgetting' to go home to Kualalumpa!

She talked about her rather solitary life of a seconded Bank Manager in Hong Kong and how difficult it is for her to make friends. She says she would like to marry again, having had an amicable divorce. She had been wife number two when, after ten years of living separately from him and wife number one, she divorced, hoping there could be a better life than this. He had not told wife number one about her! He and she still meet occasionally. She was advised by an older friend, when she married, to celebrate his visits and not complain about how little he visited, and the fact that he couldn't stay the night! The evening's conversation with this highly intelligent woman highlighted for me the differing states of singledom in the world today.

Going Home!
Even after all these weeks as constant companion to Molto, I couldn't decide if he was very intelligent or very stupid. All I know is, he is very emotional! I pulled my suitcase out from under my bed, where it had been for months, and he started to whine and whimper as if he knew I was leaving. He was delighted to see Jane and Adrian, though, and I don't think he'll miss me. I felt I knew him as well as I had known my dog in England, and it had been fun and a privilege to care for him because he was such an emotional mixture.

Molto had shaped my experience in Hong Kong and certainly whetted my appetite to return for a stay which would not be restricted to dashes between wees. I loved the many friends I had made and so many had invited me to return, that I feel it is a possibility.

I booked my luggage in at the station and didn't need to worry about it until Heathrow. Marvellous! I did a little walkabout in Central and boarded with sadness mixed with huge excitement about seeing my family.

There was a Julie Andrews type on the communal T.V. at the start of the flight and she told us to stay in our seats for landing, but Bangkok was lit up and lovely from the air and everyone stood up excitedly and got their stuff out of lockers while she spoke. We had eaten fish and white wine and I had again enjoyed my big cup of tea.

My companion on the flight was Shamayan Showmit - a 22 year old Indian boy who is studying B.Admin. in Windsor. In reply to my enquiries about any racism he might have met, he said he really doesn't know how the English would treat him because he is in such a tight social circle – sharing only with Asian boys at home and school.

There were several German passengers with Phuket written on their souvenir tee shirts. I say this scornfully but there was I, writing with my Hong Kong biro with a little mandarin dolly on the end, and my Mandarin hat was safely in the locker with a Mooncake given me by Grace, the security lady in Mandy's block, as a going away present.

I transferred my English money to my purse, found the door-key to my own home and the bus ticket to Ipswich, and was *so* excited. As always, when landing in England I said: -

I AM SO GLAD TO BE HOME, I'M GLAD I WENT!

HONG KONG - 2001

It was so good I did it twice! I wanted to experience Hong Kong *without* caring for Molto the Dalmatian, which had been my reason for a six months stay last year. Since I had made many good friends who had invited me back, I set off with great excitement.

At Heathrow I successfully called my daughter, Jane, in Tring, using a complicated numbering system which didn't demand money and billed me at home in England. It freed me up to call without worrying about coins. This call was a lovely treat while I waited for my flight and isn't it surprising how much a mother and daughter can find to talk about - even after one day?

I then had a lovely chat in the airport with an English mother and father who were going to live with their son and daughter in law in America - the young people are teachers and want their parents to join them - and they were so happy to tell about their proposed new lifestyle.

From Heathrow to Schipol we were only given Twix bars and tea as it was too early for breakfast. I proffered my large enamel mug bought specially for flights, and it was filled generously with tea without complaint. The Boeing 747 took us on to Hong Kong in ten hours, stopping for a time at Houston for some unknown reason. Here I talked to a Canadian who told me about all about his Rottweiler while I had a cheese pastry and a mug of hot milk with a teabag dropped in it.

We went over Poland (drinking G and T) and over Minsk towards Moscow it was -59C with a tailwind. Over the Gobi desert it was 18 C and the sunrise was spectacular. I didn't enjoy a rather horrid breakfast but after loads of lovely tea in my mug I couldn't believe it was already time to land. We touched down at 10.30 am and had covered 9,800 km mostly at minus 23 C and an altitude of 12000 feet, and I hadn't read everything I'd bought with me, or even shown anyone my granny pictures......

I easily found my way from the airport to my friends Mandy and Jim's luxury flat. Grace, the Chinese security lady at the flats, was cross to see me back because she had a Christmas card written out to post to me in England!

Mandy and Jim were at work and so, after a welcome shower, I fell gratefully into a purple fluffy bed, and slept for a few hours. I then went next door (next apartment block) to visit Hong Kong Jane - a *very* English Jane really, but so called by me because of the other Janes in my life. She told me of Geraldine, a tiny Filipina, who is Molto's new 'slave'. I had looked after him for several months while Jane and Adrian went to Australia and I was surprised to see him now weighing 37kg. He seemed pleased to see me! Jane had settled back happily into her Hong Kong routine after my stay in her flat, and invited me to supper next week.

After my visit there I prepared a smoked salmon salad for Mandy and Jim's tea but they didn't come home so I converted it into a sandwich for myself - in the dark because I had fused the lights! Jim fixed them without any trouble and they made me *so* welcome. It was lovely to see them. I had my own en-suite bathroom and a front door key and they insisted I could stay forever if I wanted!

I was anxious to work at something because I only had the money from letting my house in the UK to live on, so I went off to the Explorer Teaching Agency which I had used before. To my dismay, my friend Penny Cheung, Chief Administrator, had gone away! However, they interviewed me again and promised to call me when something came up. I didn't need to know Mandarin because I simply 'teach' conversation wherever I am. When I let pupils get a word or two in, they improve rapidly with my tuition and I have taught in Mexico and China as well as Hong Kong and love it. I suppose it is a bit like theatre - one has to mime and enthuse and encourage your audience to participate in your ideas. I have been a social worker for ages and most of those skills were useful in that role.

I called and saw friends working at the Hong Kong YWCA which is very well run by a friend from last time, Tracey. As you get off the nearest bus stop, you see the Aviary and Zoo and it is impossible to bypass it. A little sortie today revealed a new (to me) chestnut-backed scimitar babbler, a white- romped Sharma and scaly breasted bulbuls. They were perched in ramflory trees which have their fruit or flowers growing straight out of the branches, and incredible flat-trunked trees which someone said are called plank buttresses. All that before 10 o'clock am!

I volunteered to do 'cold calling' from the "Y" office, for a few hours a week. This would be to confirm members' wishes to register for further courses and events. There is a lovely library of used paperbacks there which I enjoyed 'filing' for them, as well as borrowing. Newcomers and residents call in this office from all walks of life and different countries, and they are helped to settle here and to make a success of their stay in Hong Kong.

During my first month I was absolutely spoiled by everyone. I was breakfasted, lunched, and suppered by all my old friends. I was loaded with presents and given tickets to fantastic events in the future and all I did was water a few plants for people and lend a motherly ear from time to time. Every day something funny or interesting happens here and I got into the swing of life in Hong Kong really quickly.

17.12.00
The Peak
I walked there and back one Sunday morning - without the anxiety of Molto - and enjoyed it very much, particularly a long discussion of grandchildren with a visiting Australian grandmother. She is totally disillusioned with her grandchildren and thinks they have been spoiled in Hong Kong. Her own daughter was rather unhappy in Hong Kong, particularly because one loses

friends all the time because of the transient nature of jobs in Hong Kong. She explained that a lot of energy is necessary to keep replacing them, and the novelty is wearing off for her.

One of my first jobs was modelling outsize jeans for Mandy's Chinese boss, Mr. Yick. Their firm - Arcadia - makes clothes for Marks and for Mothercare etc. but they hadn't got a big Western model for clothes destined for Evans (Outsize) shops, and all the Chinese girls are built like children. I was happy to oblige and they gave me two lovely pairs of stretch jeans as wages! Mr. Yick was very sociable and in the course of our conversation about the size of Westerners suggested that we probably eat a lot because of the poor weather!

I lurched from this modelling assignment to a lunch of crab salad and noodles, then to a performance of The Nutcracker Suite in a fabulous concert hall. I ended the day having Supper with American friends, 41 floors up, overlooking Hong Kong Harbour. What a day!

Next day I went walking with Mary Mac - an ex-social worker friend that I had met at the YWCA - and we had a wonderful day hiking on an island just off the mainland, and admiring practically everything we saw. There was a tiny temple where we lit incense outside with a gas lighter provided, we viewed rocks, had a swim, and ate seafood rolls and other delicacies in a seaside restaurant. Mary rather disillusioned me over the seafood which - in spite of being eaten in one of many cafes strung with fish nets and other seaside paraphernalia - comes from Australia. The journey home from the island was memorable for the colourful Christmas lights all along the shore to our right, competing with the sunset on our left.We obeyed the strict notice by the ferryboat gangplank, asking us not to disembark until they instructed us to: - "Please Wait for a Moment!" it said, in big red letters!

LETTER HOME on 19th December, 2000

Hello World: just a few lines from Sunny Hong Kong wishing you all a lovely pre-Chrissy week and thinking of you all so much at this time. Life here is still humming – every day different and it seems like it will become even more different! Tomorrow I move from this luxury apartment to house-sit while some friends go to Sri Lanka for a holiday. While I am living there I have two rather intriguing interviews: one for teaching work in a place called Causeway Bay – not as well paid as last time I was here but work anyway which will be nice.

The other is to become a Caretaker Nun! I will be looking after a sort of glamorous shed on the island called Lamma which I have always loved. The Buddhist teacher/important person, is leaving for Brazil and she wants to check me over before she goes to see if I would be an appropriate resident in the Buddhist Retreat that has been her home for nine years. She is going on to open another similar place in Brazil.

There is electricity and water but the Buddhists –to whom it belongs – are worried that I will not like the many insects and animals that will be sharing with me. It is a half mile walk from the ferry, up a small mountain. The Buddhists will want to come for a weekly session on a Sunday, but of course I will love that. Doesn't it sound intriguing? They also say it is difficult to stop your things going mouldy because of the damp conditions and you have to hack back the vegetation or become overrun. Now hands up who wants to come for a holiday with me?

I am still helping out with the modelling job for Mandy - still Evans clothes mainly! Good job that work came up <u>before</u> I shave my head to be the stand-in Nun isn't it!

Before leaving for Lamma, I have had dinner with a chap called Toby who was in charge of making the Jubilee line, tea with a glamorous M & S undies model, a day in the Chinese mainland shops, buying material and hopefully getting them made into clothes, visits to an Aviary, a Conservatory, a Tea-ware Exhibition in the oldest building in Hong Kong (1846), and at every possible opportunity I call in to commune with two beautiful jaguars, in the Hong Kong Zoo, one black and one spotted. Not boring, is it?

Well I will stop rambling on and send you all the Very Best Wishes for Christmas and 2001 and loads of love from Jenny.XXXX

After school English class

25.12.00
Christmas Day! I fulfilled an ambition to spend it completely alone and I didn't want the day to end – I mostly read and watched t.v., and ate and drank lovely things, while I 'house-sat' Tracey and Steven's beautiful flat. They were in Sri Lanka and e-mailed me that they were having a great time.

I loved every minute of my stay, and it was no hardship to be alone.

Tomorrow I meet a newspaper editor who is apparently famous in Hong Kong - for lunch! Some of the girls at the "Y" got me this treat, to discuss publishing matters daaaarling! I have finished a book about my year in an Indian orphanage and don't know how to get it published. The girls at the "Y" belong to a Writers Group and have given me some other contacts, and have invited me to their regular meeting.

My friend Jo, in Beijing who edits a paper there, asked me for some travel articles so I must get a laptop organised soon! I hope my earnings from teaching will buy one as they are cheaper here.

I couldn't find the Writers Group people, when I tried to go their seminar the other night. I looked everywhere in the Fringe café and the Verandah of the FFCC which seemed like a posh men's' club - full of film star-looking men and no sign of the nicotine-lipped authors I expected, so I will get back to Mandy's friend and try to meet them another time. The film star types were unimpressed with my sweating, ageing hippy entrance I'm afraid, and I went over the road and had a conciliatory bowl of spicy chicken broth at the Noodle Box and a Happy Hour beer at the Fringe Club. I noted that there were also seafood noodles available in a coconut broth - all served with green tea for the remarkable price of 25$, so I will return!

The lunch with the Important Person from the main newspaper was a unique and - to me - wonderful experience. He was a gentle Indian who was so interested in my adventures I was completely won over by him. He gave me a lot of advice about book publishing and printed an article about me - British Granny Abroad type article - and the girls at the Writers Group were so impressed at my good fortune in meeting him.

When I visited the Bookworm Café on Lamma, the first time I was in Hong Kong, I met an interesting and intriguing chap called Peter Lloyd, who was to become a very helpful friend, particularly with regard to book publishing. It was on this second visit that he introduced me to the Buddhists who might allow me to use their retreat, called The Heart Wisdom Centre. I tracked him down at his house in the middle of dense vegetation to talk about the Centre, and he emerged from his house, wearing sort of pink pyjamas and a sandy pigtail and looking like Jesus and sounding like Jeremy Irons.

Peter had his little boy staying with him on holiday when I called today. He told me he had lived in India and would like to live there again, and was therefore interested in my book. He has published collections of pilgrims' experiences - similar to mine but more spiritual I'm sure.

Peter made me Earl Grey tea and offered to read and consider publishing my book, but he thinks I should self-publish if I just want to raise money for the orphanage, and feel that I could sell a lot. We sat under his banana tree and talked books while gazing at his orderly vegetable patch and the sea - lovely!

I later went to a "Fun Day" on Lamma in aid of Nepalese children, and met Peter again. He had more information about the Heart Wisdom Centre, and it looks as if it *will* be my new home. I had a swim on an empty beach at the end of Fun Day. There had been crowds there all day, in brilliant sunshine, but as I came out of the water in the cooling air, the beach was empty, save for a woman with three of the fattest hens I have ever seen – was she taking them for a walk I wondered!

CHINESE NEW YEAR
24TH January 2001
Jo came from Beijing to visit me and timed it perfectly for the famous Parade on 24th January. We positioned ourselves with not a huge crowd by the roadside and a Dalai Llama type person came along, blessing the road by sprinkling liquid from a bowl while sitting in an open car. All the people lining the street were dressed in new clothes with the children looking particularly good, many in little Mandarin suits.

He was followed by red and green coloured Dragons, formed by six boys standing on shoulders or on stilts with masks over their faces. Air hostesses marched in the parade next, looking rather self-conscious but very smart. Then there were Koreans, Scots and Chinese playing bagpipes and dozens of people dressed as fish or tomatoes! I loved the Tai Chee women – particularly one with what looked like bound feet who couldn't keep up. She had a huge smile though and scuttled along at the rear.

There were dozens of Disney characters with majorettes alongside them, and Minnie and Mickey waved from a red open-topped car and they were the most popular float because of the imminent Disneyland venture, I suspect.

The girls and boys from The Budding Violet Dance School and five other similar schools, were a mix of Chinese and Western children, and looked just like those in England in my Jane's Dance school.

The many Bands were tear-jerkingly wonderful - why do they always make you feel so emotional? The Customs and Excise men marched with bayonets and the Japanese Airline people were a blaze of red flowers and birds – spectacularly vibrant. There was a Norwegian marching band and men and women from the Phillipines in masks and tribal gear. The Hong Kong Beetle Club Classic cars bought up the rear in style – very Twenties and Thirties-looking and gleaming in the sunlight. It was lovely seeing all this with Jo who entertained me with her cynical humour about it all, but despite her sardonic, amused comments, she declared it well worth the visit.

30th January
I'm still unwaged but not unhappy about it - managing well on very little even though the cost of living is high. Yesterday I went to an awesomely lovely, free, recital in the Cathedral – Mozart, Schubert and Purcell, and then, blow me, the soloist did a terrible rendition of "Eternally" (Charlie Chaplin's theme) with a microphone and it was like the worst karaoke. I would've got

71

the giggles if I'd been with anyone, and I wasn't the only one to make for the door in a hurry.

I was happy to find that the Poste Restante section of the enormous post office in Central *works!* The receptionist is as thrilled as me when I find letters and laughs when I say "Nobody loves me" when there is nothing for me. It is unusual for Chinese to appreciate that brand of humour so it makes my day when I get a laugh – how pathetic is that?

2nd February
Today I saw a woman taking her supper fish home, still alive and flipping about on a string. I found a lovely clean beach near my new home on Lamma, and had a swim and read most of a Nick Hornby book bought at the Bookworm Café. I had a goat's cheese baguette and watched the sun set before taking the ferry home to Mandy's. A woman was sitting on the ferry stripping dill leaves off stalks and she told me she would put them in ice-cubes when she got home – good idea, isn't it?

Hong Kong is wonderful for the unexpected – I planned to have a noodle lunch in a new café and then visit a pottery exhibition but Mary - the Scottish ex social worker - suddenly invited me and several women from the "Y" on a day long hike and swim with seafood lunch on a neighbouring island! It was a sparkly, sunny day and with the blue sea and dense trees and bushes on the island, the ingredients made a perfect day.

There was a poster advertising a Royal Geographic talk entitled "A Horse ride Through Mongolia" which appealed to me. I telephoned for details and they faxed a map to me so I found the hall but I was far too early and of course didn't know a soul in the adjoining café. I waited there and had two very lonely cups of coffee and reminded myself not to leave home without something to read for times like this.

The Speaker was a handsome young man, wearing a very colourful Mongolian coat. A woman called Carolyn (from the Manulife office) came and sat with me, so we enjoyed his photographs and 'lecture' together and she walked with me to show me an easier way home. He had certainly had the adventure of a life-time and I was intrigued to hear his feelings as a *sole* traveller with little of the local language, even when he had the Mongolians for company

Today was the appointed day to meet the departing Buddhist Nun and be vetted for taking over residency. I went to the ferry and saw an old lady; Lee Kwai Wu was her name, hobbling on to the ferry to Lamma. I helped her on to the ferry, on her crutches, and she told me all about how she had recently fallen on the gangplank and had to have stitches and operations. She also told me about her son who was a policeman and we compared granny notes and she filled my bag with coca-cola sweets. By the time she had shown me her letters from the hospital and from her psychiatrist, she said it was time to get off the ferry. I helped her hobble off and, too late, saw that we were on the island Cheung Chow, not Lamma......

While I was looking for a telephone kiosk to tell the Nun of my mistake, I noticed fishermen going out to sea and pensioners sitting doing pedicures on themselves along the sea front. I telephoned the Nun and told her what I had done and I think she thought *I* needed a psychiatrist. I never did meet her but she agreed I could live there on a very small rent, if I cleaned it up and I was more than happy about this arrangement, but very sorry not to have met her. It would have been good to picture her while I was working about the house and garden.

Buddhist Retreat – Lamma

MANDY & JIM
Jim came home one night and Mandy was expecting him to pack for his trip to the Phillipines the next day. He has to do a lot of travelling for work - I think he works for a firm to do with Walt Disney - and tonight he was packing for the trip, but had to go to a business dinner first. To my amazement he asked Mandy for a spaceman suit in which to deliver his speech, and a seventies outfit which he needed for the party afterwards - *that night!* Mandy made them in about half an hour *and* shortened his new jeans for his business trip! What a couple they are!

Jim returned in the middle of the night, while we were watching tele and was wonderfully tiddly – and his outfits had been really successful. He went off to the Philipines before Mandy and I were awake next day!

HEART WISDOM CENTRE
The Nun who was leaving for Brazil had lived in the Centre for nine years on and off. She expected the centre in Brazil to take two years to set up. When I telephoned again, she was full of tips about living in the Centre on Lamma -

things like pruning the hibiscus after slugs in March, shutting down the house daily when the mosquitoes were worse - close to sunrise and sunset, and the need for a cooker of some sort. She sounded very poorly to me and I was not surprised to find the Centre in a bit of a muddle, as she told me she had been on strong drugs because of operations and has steel pins inside her. She told me that she needs further operations but is delaying because she wants to open the new Centre first.

I learned that Meetings in 'my' house will be on Sundays from 10.15 a.m. and the number of people varies widely. Water and electric and telephone are laid on so that will be great!

I went to a very elegant and action-packed New Year's Eve party with Jim and Mandy and we came home very late, but I woke very early with excitement at the prospect of moving into my new home. I crept about at the crack of dawn, without waking my friends, and collected all my stuff and departed on the ferry for Lamma and my New Life. It was a bit of a struggle up the hill with my belongings, but turning the key and entering was lovely - I quickly made a cup of tea and sat outside and revelled in the beauty of everything.

It was indeed very run down and neglected but I love clearing up as there is nothing as satisfying as a good Before and After project on houses, in my opinion. It is built rather like an Austrian chalet and is absolutely covered in bougainvillea, gardenia, frangipani, hibiscus and mulberry trees as well as the thick bamboos and hundreds of the plants which we have as indoor decoration.

It comprises one large room for the assemblies, one bedroom, one library and a kitchen with a wall that doesn't go all the way to the ceiling, and divides it from the shower/loo. It is somewhat dark everywhere and there is a permanently running shower head leak, so you need Wellingtons to use the loo, but those things don't detract from the pleasant layout and exotic feeling of living in a jungle.

A young Chinese couple are the nearest neighbours. They have two dogs which they have gone away and left in the care of an American, called Jo, who bikes from the other side of the island to look after them but they have water and food somehow 'piped' to them in their garden so he doesn't need to come often.

One of my first visitors was a Buddhist called Kirsten, who called for a cuppa. She teaches in New Territories and stays over on Lamma sometimes to clean it up and put flowers on the altar etc. She isn't a strict Buddhist but says her boyfriend is – he is "prostrating" in Nepal at the moment. She told me that the Chinese who are Buddhists are usually *strict* Buddhists, but not many come to the Heart Wisdom Centre to worship.

Kirsten and the other people don't seem to know exactly what rent I should pay so I'm going to list the new things I have had to buy, note the days work I did and then ask them to let me know how much I owe before I go.

One day when I came home, there was water absolutely gushing out next door from the pipe system that served the dogs. I rang seven people but no-one could advise me and I really didn't know what to do but was ever so anxious about the loss of water. The dogs just watched patiently when I eventually joined two ladders together and got over the wall and turned it off at the main. Whew!

I met Jo, the American, in the village and he was buying pipes and bits to fix things, in response to my desperate answer-phone message. He was amused and impressed at my 'agility' in temporarily solving the problem.

Another couple who live nearby are Born Again Christians and they didn't want to walk under the Buddhist flags fluttering over the path to both their house and mine. They removed them and handed them to me, so I folded them up and worried about what the Buddhists would say. I needn't have fretted because they all have a very 'live and let live' attitude and just accepted the neighbours' complaint. It wasn't at all a Northern Ireland situation as I had feared!

They told me the next Sunday session would be billed as Loving Kindness Meditation to Welcome the Year of the Snake.

In the meantime, a dear little red mini-oven and a huge duvet contributed by Jim and Mandy have made my life much more comfortable in the Centre. The bed is home-made by the Nun from tree trunks, and Kirsten donated a very attractive mosquito net that had been a present from her brother so I was very grateful and it all looks very 'Out of Africa' in the bedroom. I threw several bin bags of rubbish away but was uncertain if some of the Nun's old but personal stuff, should be ejected - like *nine* used toothbrushes - and there was a long, green, plastic *leg* which confused me….

Within a couple of weeks I had a really clean and attractive home and by March I was eagerly looking forward to a visitor from England - my friend Patti, who had been co-driver with me when I went to Romania. We went together that year when everyone was taking medical supplies and toys to the Orphanages and she is such an enthusiastic and curious traveller that I was looking forward to showing her Hong Kong and mainland China.

I spent all the day before Patti arrived, watching an amaryllis opening and reading books on Buddhism. What luxury!

Patti's Visit
6.3.01
It was great to meet her from the airport train and, within minutes we were on a tram so I could show her Hong Kong. I was clasping a duvet I had

borrowed for her from the "Y" and she had her luggage but we gained an upstairs seat and loved rattling along, sweating away, seeing the sights and loving the prospect of another adventure together.

One day we travelled to Ngong Ping by ferry with rowdy sailors, possibly Turkish we thought, and Patti happened to be looking when I slipped and nearly fell down an open hatch. She lost no time in drawing a charcoal picture of me with eyes like halves of hardboiled eggs!

We ate bean curd mapoy (hot sauce) and rice, with orange plastic chopsticks and had jasmine tea in the Tea Garden - from the tiniest teapot - and saw that 'vegetarian' honey was available. Patti is a painter and a potter so I quickly slipped into viewing everything with her heightened appreciation of colours and textures in China. We went on searches for painted tiles and that led us to really 'Chinese' areas of Hong Kong, very different to the glass and concrete centre.

My favourite pink Hong Kong Tram

Another treat for us was Afternoon Tea at the Peninsular Hotel in Hong Kong. Looking our usual 'rather less than smart' selves, we loved every minute of this luxurious afternoon. Patti came back from the 'bathroom' there, grinning from ear to ear - she had had the tap turned on for her to wash her hands and there were *ironed* towels to dry them. The clientele were mostly Westerners and there was a quartet with pianist at a grand piano, playing classical and romantic modern music up on a gallery. We ate crumpets and sandwiches – cucumber, smoked salmon and ham, and tiny delicious pastries. We were surrounded by palms and gold paint and elegance and it cost 268$ for two....... We don't quite know how we came to be *there*, since Patti had claimed an ordinary buffet style café which we initially entered, was too posh........

I was a bit weary of arranging my teaching hours, routes, and syllabuses and getting up early and coming home late, so I handed all the arrangements for her proposed visit to the mainland to Patti. She took it on and effected an absolutely great itinerary and did the tickets, passports and visas and everything so it was great to set out with excitement and pleasure, without having had the hassle of the organisation.

China Trip on 11th March
After a McDonald's breakfast in the China Ferry departure lounge – which I have to admit was delicious - we survived the rest of the day on buns bought in a lovely patisserie in Arome. Oh, we were given a free sachet of shampoo with our breakfast too!

At Shenzen airport I successfully telephoned to cancel my English lesson with Alena and Richy, a mother and son who came up 'my' mountain once a week hoping to improve their English. I'm always a bit surprised when I make a connection on the phones here.

Our airfare from Shenzen to Guilin, single, was only seventeen pounds. We filled in terribly complicated immigration forms and got the giggles because two men had a huge argument, filling theirs in, and we and the rest of the passengers stared mercilessly at their Immigration Rage.

We arrived in Guilin and chose our lunch carefully, having seen extract of sheep's' placenta on the menu.

In the streets there were bikes galore and we saw one girl with dumplings hanging from her handle-bars. There was a definite change of ambience here - a really Chinese feel.

At a lovely riverside hotel called Blue Skies Sun we slept soundly in spite of a big hole being dug opposite this hotel during the night. We saw pansies and nasturtiums growing outside the hotel in pots, and people carrying scales and handcarts and dragging loads of different materials. A woman had handfuls of spring onions for sale, and a Downs syndrome boy showed passers-by his bag of buns. Everyone seemed pleasant and patient with him, and there was a very relaxed atmosphere in spite of the crowds of people.

The temperature averaged 19 degrees, and they told us the rainy season is from April to July. We saw the cormorants that work at night, fishing, and bamboo rafts everywhere. There were sedan chairs for hire as taxis.

We took a boat tour and John, the courier, told us that his family live in the country two hours away. They grow rice and fish to sell locally because

Guilin is too far away to transport it – it would go bad. John works 6.30 a.m. to 7.30 p.m. and only goes home once every three months. He wants to buy a house and live in Guilin and thinks farming is too much hard work.

We enjoyed the leisurely rate of progress in the boat and were intrigued with the mountain formations everywhere. John insisted that the Chinese think they look like all sorts of weird and unlikely things. We kept giggling at their names and what they were supposed to represent but we thought the best of all was the Hunch Backed Man Sitting on a Hen......

We met a friendly couple called Manfred and Margaret from Spain with their two unexpectedly blonde sons and shared our lunch with them. Lunch proved to be eight dishes and three bottles of beer per person. "Snake" on the menu turned out to be bean curd thankfully.

We landed on an island and were treated to a dancing exhibition and on passing a temple a pink ball thrown from balcony meant the woman catching it would soon have a husband. I caught the ball but hoped desperately that this wouldn't come true for me! Wine in tiny cups was then poured into us by ranks of beautiful women.

Our tour continued in weird and beautiful caves which we explored by boat. The trip round the islands included native dancers in the bushes which worried Patti. However, they looked jolly happy to me and she agreed they were probably better off there than working in the awful industrial area we passed through on our way home, and she needn't worry.

Returning to Guilin that day, I drew a cow to describe the milk needed for our tea in a café and I heard Patti asking for No. 14 on the menu. The waiter assured her it was delicious but when she passed the menu to me to see if I would like it, too, it said Spicy Fried Pigs Penis! She thought she would have it with two dumplings....

Also on offer were bee chrysalis, roasted in pepper-salt, quick-fried fatty intestine with Chinese chive, fried frog in a casserole, quick fried fragrant ducks' tongues, braised carp with fresh beer in a little pot. We contented ourselves with a whole fish in ginger and soy sauce provided by a very grumpy café owner, but proving to be delicious.

Patti bought a lamp and had fun getting a wick for it, plus a padlock for her friend at home. I was tempted by a shower handset to replace my leaky one at the Heart Wisdom Centre, but didn't know if the plumbing bit would fit. We were guided about Guilin by a boy called Robert who attached himself to us and told us his sister lives in Wimbledon and he has two teaching parents living there, too.

We had a most successful trip to hairdresser. It *was* dingy but there were two smiley girls who knew no English and wanted so badly to help us that we thought we'd risk it. Patti's face was a picture when she was offered perm rollers since she has never used a roller in her life, and definitely didn't want to start now! We looked at pictures on the wall and mimed what we wanted but the girls just confirmed that the price would be the same for both of us and started work! Patti was head-massaged energetically, while I was attacked vigorously with the scissors, and given a very professional all over cut which was lovely. You stood up to be shampooed first and the whole treatment cost us the equivalent of a fiver each. Patti's 'bob' made her look so pretty. She was pleased with it and said her new look gave her confidence.

Next day I got confused and asked for change for an l00$ note in a café but I hadn't given that note to them in the first place! I also kept telling Patti anecdotes twice so she thought perhaps I must have just started to be elderly and confused - at age 59! Worrying!

We went for a walk in the evening and a man was so urgently re-lighting his lamp to show us his wares at the Night Market, that he set fire to his stall and it seemed the whole stall would go up! It didn't, but I felt compelled to buy something and ended up with navy, sun-and-moon-patterned pyjamas for 40$ which still smell a bit scorched.

On our return to Lamma, the Buddhists came for a session one Sunday and we all discussed families and the good and bad aspects of them. Everyone seemed happy about my place in their Centre, and the work I had done.

However, when the men left, Kirsten and Maria suggested that I had been discourteous in having a visitor to stay there, before discussing it with them. Since I *had* mentioned it previously - to Eric and Rodney - and they hadn't complained, I didn't worry too much. I recalled Kirsten being disturbed that I had put mail which had been delivered to them, on what looked like a mantelpiece, but was apparently another altar, so I could sympathise with her worries that I might make the Centre into a bed and breakfast venue.

In my bedroom I laughed out loud one day because a little frog was sitting so neatly admiring a photograph of my grandson, William! Another unusual sight was ants hatching in the fax machine - there was no shortage of 'company' at home, and Patti was ever ready with her paintbrush or charcoal to record them.

KOWLOON
5.3.01
Here, courtesy of the Lonely Planet guide, we found the best fish market ever. There were hundreds of live fish in bags and in tanks for eating or admiring at home, and coral and shells everywhere. There were puppies and flowers and fronds and orchids and lotus flowers in huge purple bunches. There were birds in cages in three or four streets and it seems old men and young girls like watching birds in cages in China, and we had often seen them being taken for a walk! The cages were so attractive to me but Patti was worried about them being 'trapped birds.'

We ate hot custard tarts in flaky pastry and coconut drink from the coconut with the brown husk removed so they looked like giant dumplings.

An art gallery impressed Patti with the high standard of paintings, but I had a bit of trouble 'getting rid of' a man who had given us directions to the gallery and then came with us!

Teaching

I missed Patti when she left but she had thoroughly enjoyed Hong Kong and went home loaded with samples of painted tiles which she would use in an Exhibition in the Midlands. We had had a lot of adventures finding them - including climbing on a roof after getting permission - to claim one tile from a derelict building! I soon got into the swing of my new working life though, with new schools and individual students calling me daily to enroll. I had placed an advertisement on the wall near the Lamma ferry saying:

Do You Wan t To Improve Your English Conversational Skills?
If so, please telephone Jenny on 329857 any time.

Several lovely people replied and I particularly enjoyed working with a mum and her seven year old son who came twice weekly for sessions with me. Her husband was Italian and she was very keen on her little boy -"Rizzy"- becoming fluent but he was rather spoilt. He had behaved so badly at lessons in their house that I suggested they come to me, and indeed he improved there and his mum didn't seem to mind the walk up the hill with the pushchair. She sat under the mulberry tree with her adorable baby and we had cups of tea and talked. She said she was mystified why I was always happy and other people were always serious and she said being with me made *her* feel happier - wasn't that nice?

Another couple, called Annie and YK, who had been visiting Lamma and saw my ad., invited me to join them in Delifrance (a lovely café in Central) to talk to them for an hour every Saturday. They plied me with hot cheese croissants and coffee and paid me £30 to talk to them and correct their accent. I helped YK (the husband) with business phrases and some American expressions (!) because he needed them at work, where he had been told his accent was deplorable. He and his wife Annie loved telling me all the things I wanted to know about China and Hong Kong - their one child policy, the extended family system and the take-over of Hong Kong, and they loved hearing about our customs and habits.

Annie subsequently told me - YK was too modest to say - that he had delivered a 'paper' in English, to his colleagues, and had been complimented on the improvement since his 'lessons' with me. One day Annie and YK told me they thought I looked like Chris Patten – big eyes and big nose - and perhaps I came from the same part of Britain?

At the School run by the Oblate Fathers – persons dedicated to monastic life - at Tok Wa Wan, I had a 9.30 a.m. start and it took an hour to get there.

The children wore purple collar-less blazers, black dickey bows for the boys, shiny shoes or bright white trainers and most had John Lennon specs. They all paid $120 per month to the school for English lessons, which worked out at about three pounds a lesson each.

On the first morning I did introductions, talked them through the Union Jack, played Hangman, Head and Shoulders, and saying a word for each letter of the alphabet round the room. When we asked each other "What is your father's name?", one said "Deddy?"

We finished with acting the three bears as a play and they enjoyed this so much we repeated it for Alex the Agent who had come to check on me.

Mrs. Joanne Wong was a Teachers' Agent and she took over my teaching life for a time. I worked three days a week for her in an apartment block in Happy Valley and it was 'teaching' 3 to 5 year olds from 6.30 p.m. to 8 p.m. and 4 to 8 year olds from 8 p.m. until 9 p.m. Some were so tiny I didn't know how they kept awake and some were so action-packed I wished they were sleepy! We played hangman, name cards, Simon Says, introductions round the class, phonics from a paper Mrs. Wong supplied because the parents liked it, relay races to the whiteboard writing days of the week, fruit, clock times etc., but most of all they enjoyed doing the Hokcy Cokey and plays where they could be Red Riding Hood and The Three Bears, etc.("Whose bin sitting on *my* porridge?") I used photographs of my family to illustrate family members and one of the children said my father looked like Santa *CRAWS*!

I was always absolutely shattered by the time the second class ended and will never forget the night I got trapped in the lift, on the wrong floor of the apartment block. It was a Service Area and just a concrete hallway with locked doors all around. My pleas for help
On the lift intercom only produced a Chinese reply and it was only when I pretended to cry into it (not hard!) that the lift resumed its descent and the receptionist let me out.

Saturdays were much more fun. I went to PoKok School (Middle) which was a Buddhist school in Jordan. It wasn't a difficult journey there - Bus No. 1 and to get home I caught the tram from King Kwong Street. The girls were 12 to 13 years old and their English was good, but there were nineteen of them and I had to have *plenty* of material to keep them occupied.

We went through the usual introductions and addresses and telephone numbers round the class, drawing and labelling their partner's face, and describing their mothers, etc. They also loved the relay to the Board with days of the week, months of the year, vegetables and clock times but best of all, again, they loved *plays*. This time it had to be parts of Sound of Music or Grease but they bought in the tapes so that helped, and they made a great job of them.

One day I was in a store called Seibu, and was approached by a Chinese man of about 35. He asked politely if I spoke English and I said yes but then he said would I like to hold his hand because he had a problem. He indicated his head and I asked was it a mental problem and he said yes. I held his hand and walked him to the door and said goodbye to him. Then I went up and down several streets before returning to the shop but there I bumped into him again and he said "Do you speak English?"

I don't know if it was this peculiar adventure that unsettled me, but later in the day I heard "Get There If You Can" played in a supermarket and it is one song that my Jane sings particularly well and I had a bit of a cry behind the tinned goods! I then jammed my trolley in the turnstile and no customers could get in or out! Not my day!

SACRED CIRCLE

I re-joined this pleasant group of people who I had met while I was caring for Molto, the Dalmatian. It was good to see them again. We left our shoes at the door and sat around bowls of flowers and candles and incense, looking over Hong Kong harbour. Tonight we were asked to visualise a wise "self" and lead ourselves to a template of a good "self". We could then allow ourselves to ask for whatever we would like in life and all would be given to us, as it states in the Bible.

I met Leo Anant here for the first time and he told us briefly of his work improving sight by exercise and faith.

I also met and talked with two teenagers who had been in school in Harrogate and were having trouble with their relationship with their mother who was also present. They approached the candle and flowers area and asked for help from us all to get through – the girl cried as we joined hands and gave them our loving thoughts.

I was introduced to Sleepy Time Tea for my insomnia problem and had a helpful chat with an Anni who suggested that to help a 'lumpy' teenager in one of my classes, I should give her a pretty bookmark with kind messages on it.

LEO ANANT

I went to a most interesting talk given by this man, entitled "Regenerate Your Near Point Vision". This vision training was introduced by Bates in 1920 and has been promoted more recently by a Peter Greene. They say we can regain - not correct - our sight with exercises. I knew I could not afford to go to the workshop that was coming up soon, but took notes and Jim copied the leaflets for me when he went and I decided to "give it a go". At the introductory seminar I learned that 97% of six year olds have perfect eyes and, when small children rub their eyes it means that their muscles are tired, and that is what happens as we get older. Leo suggested that massage is useful for five minutes, ten times a day. Also it is good to rub your hands to warm them, palm your eyes and exhale, then look again at anything in your vision.

He said acupuncture points need massage and Aldus Huxley had apparently benefited from this. There are some special spectacles called Trayner Pinhole Glasses which are available in a New Age Shop near the Kathmandu Restaurant, which I may get, to be used in conjunction with this Bates method.

24th Feb. I'm still practicing twice a day – palming, acupressing, reading varying print and blinking and tracing the Tibetan chart that Jim photocopied for me. I notice a sharpening of vision generally and I forget to use my own spectacles a lot of the times when I would have relied on them. I get slight double vision – but usually after palming -and certainly no other problems. Wouldn't it be wonderful if it worked? I shall keep practicing. I suspect it would all work better with the group therapy.

MO's Visit

A friend from Ipswich, Mo, with whom I had worked for years, has a daughter and son in law living in Stanley, so when she came to visit them, she bought them all to visit me. They arrived in the company launch, called Isis, which had a French Captain and flag. Mo's family, Will and Sarah and Mike and Annie who live in Stanley, with Luke and Jonty – little fair boys in pushchairs - and Mo, Patti and I made a very jolly party.

We sat down to lunch at the first seafood restaurant we came to and had wonderful prawns, squid, beef bean-curd, whole fish and beer. They were all delighted with the food and of course we enjoyed their company.

They drew our attention to other items on the menu: jelly fish and pig's ear in sesame chilli sauce, fried pork large intestine $38, chicken feet in salt $38, duck's web and cuttle-fish in sauce, steamed fish head with ginger, loofah and cuttle-fish, fish-woman roast crab, gold and silver Egg with Amaranth in broth and Fried Frog!

Mo waved them off and stayed for a few days in the Heart Wisdom Centre. I envied her the ease with which she picked blossoms from the bushes around our jungle home and threw them on the table among the honey and toast and within minutes produced a lovely watercolour copy of the colourful bougainvillea and hibiscus blooms. She could create these lovely pictures in the time it took me to do the scrambled eggs......

FENG SHUI

The "Y" offered a lecture in Feng Shui which I looked forward to for ages but was sort of disappointed to find that it is a very exact science which would take ages to learn, and not just a case of learning where to place your mirrors etc.

A Benny Hill look-alike called Raymond Lo gave a talk in general terms about Feng Shui, which means Wind and Water and derives from Taoism. He described it as a method of minimising negative energy it has been recorded since 250 AD and is still used for locating the best places for graves to enable descendants to benefit from their energy. A woman next to me whispered "It seemed a Rot of Lubbish to her" but I thought there were some quite sensible points.

Raymond explained why a 'hole' had been created in a huge apartment block that backed on to mountain - it was so that the spirits could escape through it. He told us that the water running away from the Lippo building in Central means that wealth will also run away and it will therefore not be successful. He described it as 'haemorrhaging money'.

The Cultural Centre in Kowloon was purposely built like an ugly dense wall with windows on the other side from harbour so that the good energies couldn't escape.

During the course of his lecture he told us that the Chinese invented bank notes and they thought that money bought their entrance to heaven. They therefore bought pretend money to put in graves and burned it at funerals.

He told us there were 15,000 dangerous sites - possible landslips - in Hong Kong, that the Bank of China is shaped like Bamboo, the Lippo Centre has koala bear shaped sides, that there is a shortage of men - 160,000 women looking for husbands - and that the richest man in Hong Kong is called Li Kal Shina and oh, Kowloon means Nine Dragons and dragons mean protection. What about that for a mine of information?

By the end of the lecture I felt dizzy with all these details of but I will surely place my mirrors and bed facing in new directions from now on.

FRINGE THEATRE
It was lovely going back to this theatre - the adjoining café is always humming with people - mostly Westerners though. Today there were three American musicians playing modern music. The harp was played a woman that looked a hundred years old. She had claw-like hands, coconut hair and pearls and hoop ear-rings. She played beautifully and told me they are all invited back to play whenever they come to Hong Kong for a holiday. (Jo remarked "Cruela lives" when she saw her, but agreed she was a real eccentric and fun to know.) There was a Friday feel to the evening when I last went. I watched a meeting of several Brigitte Jones type girls who met, smoked and drank, and a woman called Evadne wearing Edna Everidge glasses.

I was introduced to a woman called Raewin, who had bright pink hair and told me she also wants to write a book. She has just given up her job in UK and joined her husband who has been here two years. Her desire to earn money of her own and find a Best Friend were apparent but she, too, was eccentric and I could imagine her becoming old in the colourful way of the harpist. She told me she had bought a huge, life-size, dirty old scarecrow as a souvenir of the recent hike with "Y" girls, and her husband had been less than delighted with it!

I made friends with a girl called Lesley who worked in the Bookworm Café and she told me of her infatuation with a boy called Jeff, who did Yoga lessons on Lamma. He had been incredibly kind and warm to her but she felt the romantic aspect wasn't coming on as she'd hoped. From various things she had said, I felt it possible he was gay but didn't want to say this to her, so I was just 'supportive' and kept my mouth shut - unusual for me!

SHENZEN SHOPPING on 14.12.00
"Go to Peddar street MTR No 1 or 2 platforms, then at Mon Kok Station change to the opposite platform, then go to Kowloon Tong KCR to Lo Wu. It will be 500$ for a first class ticket to Shenzen." Those were our instructions on how to get to the mainland China shopping centre and all I can say is without Mary Mac. as tour guide, I would still be circling China.

We fell into the first restaurant for sustenance and were offered free jasmine tea. There were no steamed chicken feet but steamed dumplings stuffed with tripe would be possible.... Lice? Beef strips? Everyone was smoking and phoning around us, and I enjoyed the atmosphere while we ate and got to know Laura, who is en route to Singapore, staying in Central with friends. She is an incredibly beautiful M and S lingerie model, with three admirers, all in England. She absolutely loved the designer handbags and stayed on buying them when Mary Mac and I staggered home at 5 p.m. I was measured for four suits and Mary and Laura were a great help choosing the materials. If all goes well I should end up with a green velvet suit for 270$, an orange flowery suit for 400$ and thin, flowery suit for 210$. Add to this cost, the visa to China which was 200$ and train fare to China which was 200$, and I think I will be well-pleased with the day's shopping. The suits are a sort of pyjama style and uncomplicated to make but *so* comfortable to wear in heat or cold.

I noticed a large green fly made of bamboo leaves, being sold by beggars here for $10 and they are $26 in Central.

SHOWS
The Cultural Centre and the Concert Hall in Hong Kong are well worth visiting, just to admire the terrific architecture - all glass and marble and concrete. The seat prices are modest and I enjoyed several lovely evenings including seeing Ute Lempe, who I had admired in London in "Chicago". She entranced us - and amused us when someone's mobile phone interrupted her - she just said "I hope it was urgent?"

Mikhail Baryshnikov was wonderful and his arms were the best I have ever seen. There was no colour in the costumes - all black. The dancers were all excellent and Baryshnikov shone, but was incredibly modest at the end, including the dancers all the time, in acceptance of the applause.

Hamlet, here, was a unique experience for me! Well for everyone I would have thought! The actors were Lithuanian and Chinese, and Shakespearean sur titles were necessary! I coped, but there were a lot of black clothes, ice-blocks being thrown about and huge glass goblets full of water being drunk by men with either bald or punk heads. Ophelia had the only coloured clothes and she lurched about clutching her head and going mad while smoking a pipe – clouds of smoke!

I went to hear the Hong Kong Philharmonic with Mo while she was staying with her daughter and family in Stanley. She is a musician and there were 96 musicians in the Cultural Centre, that evening. Mo thoroughly enjoyed them and commented that the violinist had earned her money that night.

The Royal Philharmonic Viennese night was lovely and I was interested to see a little boy being admonished by a man sitting next to me, for a very small noise he made. The boy and his mother accepted the warning and he sat still ever after! I have noticed that Western children create a lot more disturbance than Chinese children, which suggests the adults' tolerance level here is lower than ours? The singer was memorable for *nearly* wearing a bright blue dress, and the conductor was very exuberant, wearing his hair with a very white middle parting.

I went most of the time to Central for entertainment but several people told me that the football matches televised to Lamma were 'great nights out' and when I heard that my home town, Ipswich, were going to be televised in the middle of the night I thought I might make the effort. Friends warned me that it might be a rowdy night but I thought I would like the experience so went to bed at 7 p.m. and set the alarm for midnight which got me the half mile hike down my mountain in good time for the Kick Off! When I arrived, there was only one 'supporter' - a Lowestoft man! We bought each other a beer to celebrate the win, but it wasn't the outing I'd anticipated!

HOLLY & WILLIAM

I was really pleased with the 'phone contact with family this time - having a phone at the Heart Wisdom Centre - and today was amused by Jane telling me that William had insisted on stopping the car in a layby to get a photo of me out of the boot, "because Grandma had told him to look at it and not forget her"...........

I had also come to Holly's mind when they were all tramping along in mud and pouring rain, with a Japanese visitor, to show the canal in Tring. Holly said, flatly, "I expect Grandma is walking along in Paradise!"

I had asked Jane on this call if she thought I should send a thong for my daughter-in-law, Bel (they were all over Hong Kong in different materials) for her birthday – and she asked what *song* I would send!

DISMAL DEPARTURE

After six lovely months working in Hong Kong and in the middle of one night I got the 'phone call from my daughter that you always dread: my mum was dying in an Ipswich Hospital.

In the middle of that night I scrambled together all my worldly goods (mostly colourful Chinese junky presents) and borrowed an old rickety shopping trolley from the garden of Susan, my only near neighbour, to pile it in, and push it down 'my' mountain to catch the first ferry to Hong Kong Central station, and on to the airport.

There was a hold-up at the Passport Control turnstile and by the time I got to through, they were announcing my name on the tannoy! I ran what seemed like miles to the departure Gate and was crying copiously by then but an official said "Don't worry, there are people behind you", and so there were. It was the saddest flight and ending of a period abroad but in retrospect I must say it was a truly happy trip with lots of new friends and unusual adventures to treasure.

CHINA

JOURNEY AND ARRIVAL
14.2.98

After my adventures in India and Nepal and Hong Kong, I became more restless not less. I had returned to work, after the year off, unpaid, from my work as an Education Welfare Officer, but finally decided to retire for good, against the advice of all my family and friends who worried about my reduced pension!

I kept an eye out for new travel opportunities and soon found an advertisement for teachers in China. An agency offered accommodation in exchange for 20 hours a week helping students to improve their English conversation, plus a small salary and help with fares to Beijing. Once again I put piles of clothes, shoes and my survival kit of teabags, paperbacks and family photographs, in readiness for a great adventure. I found tenants to rent my house for six months and was so excited!

After a normal take-off in the Boeing 747 the other teachers and I were warned immediately of turbulence and the technical reasons for it. However, I was thrilled to be served with my first cup of real China tea - it tasted like weak English Breakfast with a hint of Nivea. Mini bottles of red wine, cognac and beer were being thrown around by camp cabin staff and there was a very light-hearted feel to the occasion. We were shown a Chinese video of a couple doing the tango, which they described accurately as a War of Legs. The couple performing it were a constipated-looking man and a hawk-faced woman, but their footwork was certainly impressive.

Supper included a Chinese fortune cookie saying Sunday would be my lucky day. Several girls in my teaching group involved me in a very revealing discussion about mother-daughter relationships. One mother's huge mistake had been insisting on the daughter *drying* the bath after use, and another had been driven mad by her mum's insistence on tipping yoghurt out of the pot and on to a plate before eating! I was older than the rest of the volunteer teaching party by a quarter of a century, but was to find them the least ageist of any people I had ever lived and worked with.

I was very drawn to a girl called Jo, who gave a hilarious account of having recently been a bridesmaid for her sister. She had to wear a navy, shot-silk dress with big shoulder pads and a bow on the back and flowers on her head that looked like devil's horns. The outfit had all been assembled for her while she was away travelling in Thailand and she maintained that both the dress and the navy shoes were too small for her. The photo of the proceedings takes pride of place on her mum's television! All that was enough to make anyone leave the country wasn't it!

Jo and another lovely girl, Alison, had been friends from working together in Japan. They were to teach University students at a military establishment and were amused to learn that their family details had been investigated by the Chinese authorities. It had apparently been established that Alison's father had been in the Navy but as he was 'not of senior rank' it was not deemed significant to the Chinese.

It was minus 62 over Siberia at 9 p.m. and minus 4 in Beijing at that time. We changed our watches from 12.05 to 8.05 a.m. and were a very happy and excited group when we landed. Twelve of us were driven by minibus to the Da Juan Hotel, in Beijing. It was a very bleak urban area, which looked much cleaner to me than India had, but there wasn't a leaf or blade of grass to be seen. The hotel was marble-floored and multi-chandeliered and our rooms had en-suite bathrooms. The hot water tap came off in my hand but the powerful shower was bliss and there were toilet rolls! Hotel packets of soap, shampoo, razor, shower-caps and lovely clean beds were also much appreciated.

15.2.98
DAY TWO
I shared this boudoir with Alison and together we enjoyed our first Chinese breakfast in the hotel. There was a carousel in the centre of a huge round table in the dining room, which contained cold spinach, scrambled eggs, ham and sweet corn, white and barely toasted sliced bread, 'frogspawn' soup, and carrot cake. Some heavenly tea was specially obtained for me by a waitress with a Suzy Wong split in her skirt. I appreciated her kindness because everyone else was dealing with warm-smelling milk in glasses and I knew I couldn't cope with that.

The view through the double glazed hotel windows was Dr. Zhivago-like, with men in caps biking about in a very grey landscape with slushy snow and ruined modern buildings. There were people living in a derelict row of 'cottages' opposite our window and while I watched a young man dragged an old armchair to the end of the building and climbed up to fix a hole in the roof. You could see his breath and he kept shrugging his jacket up to stop the snow getting down his neck. Another man was cooking in a wok at 7 a.m. and a girl came up to him and accepted and gnawed at something bone-like that he had given her. He was selling different things the next day - inner soles and huge plants like giant celery.

After breakfast we were taken to a Conference Room and the Director of the Council on International Education Exchange (our boss), talked to us about the expectations of the Chinese students, of which there are 340 million in the education system. Education is compulsory up to age 18 but 40% of children don't complete it There are thousands of what are called 'Foreign Experts' in China every year, 28,000 of whom are teachers and many of these are 'closet' missionaries. The director outlined the attitudes we might expect, including the fact that we mustn't get hurt feelings if our students were withdrawn from our classes without notice. He also warned that we would have, thus far, built ourselves up, using outside familiar influences and we might well fall apart without this structure and 'not be ourselves'. We should therefore take care of ourselves physically - our immune systems will be tested. We weren't to take our personal problems to classrooms and should attempt to combine reading and discussions to arouse the students' intellectual curiosity. He told us that understatement is unknown here and exaggeration more common - so I should be O.K!

Our main translator and guide was a tiny Chinese girl called Dongling who became a wonderful friend to the English contingent wherever they lived afterwards. She told me that she preferred British people and considered us courteous. In her opinion Americans were rich and denigrated Chinese ways and customs.

She accompanied us to Tiananmen Square and we saw Mao's tomb. She told us that 30,000 people had filed past before we did, that day - and it wasn't even a public holiday. At 9 p.m. it was hot and steamy and people were wearing luminous necklaces and bracelets. Mao's huge portrait was illuminated and, despite his reputation, his eyes looked 'humane' and his body in the Coffin could have been anyone really. Dongling told us that people thought him 80% good and that he had been hidebound by tradition and then deteriorated in old age, having to sack people around him to 'go forward'. (And kill!)

The Swedish people ahead of us in the queue had a very blonde daughter of about five years old and the Chinese around her were absolutely *entranced*. I bought two silk kites for 18 Y in one of the many shops still open, and watched the ballroom dancing going on under the highway bridges. Dongling tried to explain family responsibilities to me but I was almost comatose with fatigue by now. I only half comprehended that cousins have names that tell if they belong to the parents' brother or sister and there is also a distinction between the maternal and paternal grandparents so that the children know which granny is which........ Or something!

I am getting to know my fellow teachers who seem very friendly. They are all about 24 years old - and I am enjoying hearing about their lives and they seem very happy to talk to me despite my age. I think they are young enough to need a surrogate mum in some cases, and they have all invited me to visit them in their various schools as soon as possible. They are mostly doing their 'GAP' year and most, to me, seem incredibly posh.

I have now learned that Tom went to Eton and absolutely loves *languages*. Although he thought the roller blade in his rucksack would intrigue and interest his students, he was also loaded down with dictionaries, translations explaining the tones that are part of Mandarin speaking, and tons of other books. He was thrilled with the hours of Mandarin lessons which were compulsory and which tested me to the utmost!

Graham was a twenty-two year old with a sore throat. He would have looked a big boy in England but here in China he looked like Gulliver. I was to become appreciative of his kindness and humour, which were also apparent in

Neil from London. Neil - a black guy with round glasses - was in a muddle when I met him and his Caribbean mum, (a nurse), at Heathrow. He was feverishly transferring some of his luggage to his hand baggage, because his main bags were well over the allowance. He had a soft, kind smile and the word Cool Dude came to mind.

Clare was a very pale, slim girl who wore a pencil tucked into her long hair, like a Japanese hair ornament.

Anton was a law graduate with a lager lout image. He was waiting for his African girlfriend to send for him to go to the Maldives when she could find him work as a VSO. He invited us all to Shanghai where he would go after our compulsory language course.

16.2.98
FIRST SHOPPING EXPEDITION
We all went on a shopping trip - mainly in a supermarket. The goods were very odd things like whole pigs' feet and chitterlings, a baby 'dinosaur', ready-cooked little old birds - hundreds of them, marbled eggs, ordinary eggs, cooked duck eggs in wicker baskets, Spice Girls posters and a Lady Di poster entitled Crazy Princess. There were books for teaching English in schools but we don't know what ages our children will be as yet. There was a whole aisle full of Nescafe goods and I bought a huge jar of Gold Blend with great relief and had a 'fix' on my return to the hotel! While paying I saw a man having his hands examined by the check-out girl, who then prescribed some stuff for him to take on the strength of her diagnosis.....

17.2.98
HARD ROCK CAFÉ, BEIJING
I can't tell you much about this café, except that it was, of course, identical to others in this chain that I have seen in other countries. My memory lapse is because I was so enjoying the company of James. He told me his life story and offered to proof-read the book I was writing about India, when it was ready. I overdosed on a giant salad - the first since I left home - in a peanut oil dressing and then went back to the hotel in a taxi with another granny who is Australian and wasn't ashamed to admit she was tired out by China already! Apparently I got Brownie points from the youngsters for going out to a café the other night and returning to look for Anton who had not returned to the hotel. It had been his birthday and, at the end of the celebrations, he had become detached from us and I helped find him.

I asked a Chinese student what was the significance of the pairs of lions at the doors of most hotels, offices and homes, and she thought it was to stop people parking! I have since heard they are to ward off the evil spirits so you can take your pick.

18.2.98
GREAT WALL OF CHINA
I took my green tea to the open window of the hall, as our bedroom was so

overheated, before boarding the bus to the Great Wall. When I joined the group in the lobby before leaving, I was in time to hear the Director coldly denying knowledge of where to buy hair conditioner. Apparently Alison had asked him this important question but she had overlooked his shiny baldness......

A minibus collected us for our journey and I was thrilled to share an earpiece on the Walkman of a Brideshead Revisited look-alike. He wanted me to appreciate his Bob Dylan, Paul Simon and other political tapes, and of course I did. On the way home I heard about the Business Weekly (Chinese Finance Paper) from another ex Etonian who could've *been* Sebastian. The lovely thing about these new friends is that they really appear to WANT to tell me about themselves and then to hear about when I went to India!

Freezing on The Great Wall of China

The approach to the Wall was dreary and the snow slushy but when we got to the Wall itself, it was dramatically defined by crisp snow and was absolutely breathtaking. I couldn't see anything either side of the wall that was worth fighting for, but postcards bought from the numerous touts showed lovely views of the Wall in different seasons. I skidded about and fell twice on the ice, climbing or descending the route, and the boys said I looked like a giant egg yolk in a borrowed Chinese cycling cape. The sightseers were mainly Chinese - we only saw two other foreigners apart from our party - and, much as tourists at home, they wore high-heeled shoes and baseball caps! We lunched in a MacDonald's and I must admit it was quite a novelty to eat it after a week of Chinese wonderments, and I always love their clean loos and their coffee, in whatever country I turn up.

We all enjoyed Peking duck on our return to Beijing and this was accompanied by Shark Fin Soup (Ugh), best prawns ever, squid soup, octopus strips, and stewed scallops. The Peking duck recipe is duck rolled in crepes with radish and cucumber and bean sauce. One duck makes up to 108 portions and it is eaten more in groups of people to make it worth the bother - much as Americans eat large lobsters according to my US neighbors.

19.2.98
BEIJING OPERA
A party of teachers was collected for this treat. We travelled for an hour or so through Beijing to a small, beautifully 'oriental' Opera House, completely unlike ours in London. There were dozens of small tables and chairs informally laid out facing a stage, and all the visitors - mostly Westerners - were being served jasmine tea. The orchestra were hidden to the right of the stage and there were lots of lanterns and a Chinese scene as a backdrop. Someone told me that the females used to be played by men but today there were two, large-eyed girls with long, long expressive fingers. Singing was definitely in the wailing and screeching category but the acting and stick-throwing tricks were amazing.

It was snowing when we came out and there was ballroom dancing in the street! Most of the dancers were elderly and I really wanted to join them, it looked so unusual in the soft, settling snow. Lots of the surrounding buildings were lit up with colored lights like those I had seen in India - tiny bulbs, cascading down old and new buildings. This wonderful night out was to be our last social event together and we parted with promises to phone, write, meet etc. and were too excited to be sad but I will never forget how much I enjoyed the company of those young people.

22.2.98
21st CENTURY BILINGUAL SCHOOL
I was driven to 'my' school by a Mr. Lee and Miss Chen who are to be my liaison people in school. We travelled for an hour on a new motorway through cold and bleak scenery but I didn't feel the cold until bed-time in my fourth-floor flat, when I was awake all night being *frozen*! During this night I took the polythene cover off the new mattress and that helped - as did adding Long Johns, socks, dressing gown, etc. to my warm pyjamas. I tugged these additions on at different times all night, and went to sleep at about six and then the alarm set for seven allowed to me to get to the vast dining room for the worst breakfast of my life - and no TEA!

24.2.98
WELCOME PARTY

The Head - Mr. Wong - officially welcomed my new colleague, Elke, and I through a translator who works in the English Department where all the teachers have an English name which is *very* helpful – hers is Sarah. About a dozen teachers sat around in the VIP lounge and were very sweet and sang songs to us. It is apparently expected in China so I wished I knew a little ditty. We were then given a banana and an apple each and all of us talked and giggled self-consciously and went back to our rooms. It was a bit of a shock to be told that we are actually *teaching* classes of about forty children, aged from eight to eighteen - no mention of the sessions of conversational English with half a dozen older students which is what we had happily anticipated.

I learned that the last teacher in my place was a 22 year old American boy called Brent. My informant about all that was Elke. She is a 30 year old German who has put me in the picture about the school since it opened in September. She reckons there were no facilities when she started and now there *is* a huge television and brand new furniture in each apartment, but it is all tiled and marbled and freezing cold because the heaters don't work. Apparently the Chinese teachers are fined if they leave their heating on, but I am allowed to, thank Gawd!

The other blow is that there are no international telephones lines except for during office hours but those times are the middle of the night at home! When I did manage to call by reversing the charges and getting my father up at 7 a.m. it was to hear that my mum was in hospital, my niece has shingles and dad's chicken for his lunch had gone off, so I wished I hadn't called!

27.2.98
ELKE & MY FLAT

I pulled my bed into the sitting room where the heater is marginally better and invited Elke to tea. We examined each others' photos and she told me of her boyfriend who had been to stay but they had to stay in bed all the time he was here, because it was so cold in January. She is awesomely well-qualified - a mechanical engineer with computer qualifications and primary school teaching experience. Her English is as good as mine and before we exchanged any personal information she roundly chastised me for holding the two flasks incorrectly which we collect from the boiling water tap in the hall. Apparently I should hold them with my arms hung down and not using the strength of my wrists - she's *that* sort of German person! I must say, she has already fixed my Walkman, my washing machine, my short wave radio and the lavatory - at least for the time being. Oh, and she's taught herself to play the piano while she's been here. I haven't seen her laugh yet - oh, except for one of my grandson William's stories.

There are no shops, temples, houses or anything nearby and the nearest village is twenty minutes walk away. I was issued with a bright blue padded jacket as uniform in school and I may sleep in it. All the teachers wear them and the kids wear bright yellow ones. They also gave me another duvet to go over the existing one, so perhaps I will survive.

REFECTORY
At 6.30 a.m. on the first morning we were shown into a huge hall with 800 students and teachers tucking into a whole pig's foot each, on a bowl of cut spinach. Day two was a mixture of jellyfish, aubergines, bean sprouts, mushrooms (black ones), tofu, tiny fishcakes and skinny green celery sticks, oh and rice! By then I was happy to realize that   I would be allowed to miss breakfast. Lunch and supper proved to be just as unusual and the worst bit was seeing *how* they ate. The food had always been cooked with bones and fish heads and things left in. They had to be spat out, and they did this on to the table or the floor. The recipes were either delicious or disgusting, and scrambled eggs featured quite frequently so I was always pleased to see the enormous buckets of it waiting at the hatch, where white-clad, dinner *men* dolled it out. I was fascinated to see their white wellies, too.

28.2.981
FIRST WEEK OF TEACHING
The sight of forty children, sitting in a classroom with arms folded and waiting for 'miss' to do her stuff, will stay with me for ever! I muddle through and can only think that being a granny, being a bit 'loud', and enjoying passing on language to shy, non-speaking children, saw me through those early days. We did parts of the body, clock and time-telling, fruit and vegetables, Simon Says, Hangman, Hokey Coke and shouting numbers, going round the room. Best of all was the play-acting. We plumped for the Elves and the Shoemaker and they absolutely loved it. They hadn't really done 'drama' before and this ten-minute play was to be entered for an English Speaking Festival in Nanjing. Our 'slot' is at 8.30 a.m. but if the rehearsals are anything to go by, it is going to be worth getting up early for.

I am to teach twenty lessons of an hour's duration to children who have varying degrees of ability to speak English. I already love it. I think I might have been wasted doing secretarial or social work! I just had a huge success in a class of eight-year-olds with Chinese Whispers. I whispered an instruction to the first child in each of six rows, to draw vegetable or fruit or day of the week. The kids whispered back to each other and the last child at the back of the class ran forward to do the writing or drawing. They just loved the running about. Their little old faces were alight and they really do say Ah So! when they twig what you mean.

28.2.98
Teachers Xmas Dance – in February
In the gym, which is still decorated with Happy Christmas and Merry Christmas signs like Selfridges, they erected a karaoke screen and volunteers sung along, non-stop, in their screechy way, and the rest of the gym was

cleared for ballroom dancing. Well, they do something that is a cross between a waltz, a tango and a quickstep and they only do it if they feel they can do it WELL. Someone came up and grabbed me and it was Joyce Grenfell all over again except that we cantered. I was so pleased when she put me down!

Nearly all the teaching staff were there, including the dinner ladies that are men, wearing their white outfits and white wellies. The Keep Fit man was also there, taking it all very seriously and being a vision of balletic and technical excellence. He declined to dance with me - even when Sarah begged him to - so I won't be sending home for the tap dancing routines and other music sheets which he requested from England either.

I asked for some disco music but the man with the records didn't know what I meant and he told me something like "I'll meet you in the Rose and Crown next Thursday" and shuffled away. When some disco music happened, I strutted my stuff and embarrassed everyone, much as I do at home, and then I went home to my flat. I had a shower and was congratulating myself on having hot water, television, kettle boiling for coffee and a heater warming the flat from sub-zero, when there was a huge bang and I must have blown a fuse. I daren't ask for help at that time of night - 9.30 p.m. so I had an even earlier night than usual.

Fried frogs' legs and assorted insects on the mile-long Beijing Snack Street

1.3.98
FLAG MORNING
At school, every Monday, the whole school assembles to sing patriotic songs and raise the Chinese flag. They then read out 'homilies' about improving themselves and their school. One teacher reported the boys' bedrooms were very 'correct' last week except for the smell of feet in some. Another said that some students had been copying others' homework. One of the teachers whispered to ask if we have this trouble in U.K?

CHINESE TEACHERS
Teachers here get RMB 600 which is the result of Li Peng decreeing four pay rises in two years. They now get four times as much as they did. Government support is 80 RMB. They are also allowed two days off at weekends and this is now universal. There are four weeks school holiday in winter and seven in summer but only three public holidays. The hours of work are usually 8 - 11.30 am and 1.50p.m. to 5.30 p.m. The staff mainly live in apartments like mine, and not many are able to get home at weekends, even though they are off-duty – as we were.

Senior Chinese students teach two or three hours a week in their schools, in addition to continuing their own studies, earning 20- 30 yen. I met several in 'my' school who were willing to help me and were most respectful of my age and experience.

Teachers are examined - Ofsted style - here. However, they take it to heart so badly when they have their results put up in the staff room. One new little friend, Lee May, could not cope with the class competition to find the best teacher - because she was low down on the list, she left the school forever.

2.3.98
SOCIAL DILEMMAS
The position of the school was amazingly remote from anywhere! Nanjing is an uncomfortable 45 minute bus ride away and there few buses and you have to beg for a seat on one. Hotels in Nanjing are expensive and we could not afford them from our meagre salary. Elke and I were therefore reliant on a few teachers and each other for amusement at weekends.

The teachers and students seem to have cut off times, as regards sociability. They are really friendly but suddenly cut off from you. They are at their most flinty faced when you take over their classes. I was enjoying the company of the Computer Teacher and he appeared to be pleased to be helping me. I was therefore a bit nonplussed when I went for lunch, directly after a very personal and even intimate chat, and he completely "blanked" me and took his food from the hatch and went to sit far away from me. Then I learned from another teacher that they are not allowed to socialise with us. What a blow! Jennifer told me that a teacher was sacked at their school for talking to foreigners too much. Apparently we could 'influence' them with our Western ways.

DIRECTOR OF CIEE

We had a visitation from the Director of the teaching Council today. He toured the Western teachers' premises with seven Chinese people, all of whom had a total lack of interest except for photographing our rooms, including Elke's loo. He didn't sympathise with our complaints at all and even confirmed that the promised hotel room at weekends will be withdrawn! Since we have only had one weekend there, due to the snow, we are absolutely fed up. Following this depressing visit I managed to be late for a class, tried to teach a class when it was lunchtime, and lost five weeks' work on my computer.....

I wrote to this Director and confirmed all our complaints and suggested that it would be sensible for them to rejig arrangements here before the next lot of foreign teachers arrived as they will not be as stoical as Elke and I at the lack of phones, post, showers, shops or visitors and no weekend breaks, as well as the fact that we are *teaching* English, not improving students' English conversation, as stated on our contracts.

The good news today was an Art Class where I used lovely paper and ink and paint. The first effort was a copied oriental tree and it didn't look too bad to me but the teacher said "So-so"! Elke had a tantrum with herself because her copied picture wasn't perfect - she is so *German* at times. A sixteen year old "Catherine" says I can have her perfectly executed green and black painting of bamboo. She told me the teacher had done some of it but I am thrilled with it and can't believe she can part with it. I shall give her one of my Suffolk souvenirs. The bad news is there is no water or electricity today and because I washed my black velvet trousers yesterday with a red jumper I now have red fluffy velvet trousers.......

5.3.98

SARAH

This diminutive, friendly (for Chinese) English teacher is always happy to tell me about Chinese customs. I never knew her real name as the staff adopted English names for the benefit of the students. Sarah's own little boy lives in school and goes home with her at weekends. She was disappointed that he wasn't going to be taller but not surprised, as her husband is short too. She says all Chinese admire height. Few women drink alcohol but she told me of her enjoyment of some wine yesterday. She reckoned it was not as strong as usual and she liked it, despite a newborn *mouse* being in the bottle! She told me she couldn't look at it, while drinking, but as this is known to be good for female ailments, she persevered...... We commiserated with another English teacher, Celia, about her granny. Celia said her granny was 'hopeless' - but she meant terminally ill, not drippy!

LEFT HAND ' WILLAGE'

The discovery of "Left Hand Willage" - I am now pronouncing it as Elke and the children all do - was a huge success, and I found it without much difficulty. Not being able to cope with the Chinese name, I called it Left Hand Village because it was the *only* village for miles, apparently on the left.

After a lovely class which finished at 9 a.m., and when it stopped raining for a couple of hours, I walked twenty minutes from the school and found this village. It was like a town in an old Western movie, but there was a *supermarket* selling extraordinary things, lit by a 20 watt fluorescent light and with an earth floor, but a supermarket, nevertheless. I bought four butterfly kites for the walls of my room and some queer, elderly peanuts, some coffee-flavoured chewing gum and two teaspoons, which are a rarity here. It seemed like a huge adventure at the time. More people were giving me curious looks than in Nanjing and there was a definite 'outback' feel to the place. I can go each Tuesday when I don't have classes mid-day, and eat noodles in the only café, and bring a bottle of beer 'home' with me.....Divine decadence!

Samantha and Snow (two of my 'star' teenage students), were amazed that I had actually *walked* for twenty minutes, alone, and unable to speak Chinese. I tried to explain that English people are not worried by any of those things but they were not convinced.

Snow (her English name - she loves the Snow White story) - has asked me to do a radio interview with her every Tuesday at 6 a.m. I graciously declined doing it at that time but promised to tape one at a sensible time of day. They don't know which title to choose for this new School Radio - Radio 21 or Radio School, but Snow will decide later. She is a brilliant English speaker and would love to work in radio or television. She and her friend Samantha also run the English Corner in school and are very demanding of me. We are going to record twenty minutes of English conversation and music, once a week.

BROADCASTING

The first interview that I had recorded with the enthusiastic Snow, went quite well but I was shocked to wake this morning to hear the interview being loud-speakered all over the campus and sounding to me like my sister Jackie talking! Despite sounding like a Suffolk lady, the staff assured me that - to them - I speak BBC English and they quiz me all the time about how to pronounce things. They also wanted to know today if it is because I am *Christian* that I am like other Brits they know, honest, friendly, kind, hardworking and smiley.....nice, eh?

Snow forgot the Beatles tape that was supposed to be my signature tune, and had carefully taped my joking before the session started. I said so clearly "don't tape this or you will have a recording of an Englishwoman chomping on an apple..." and it was piped all over school. At the end of the session Snow and her friend persuaded me to demonstrate disco dancing in their studio and this bought on another session of "You must have been beautiful when you were young/Did the boys chase you all the time? /Is your husband handsome?"

Don't ask me how, but they felt it was the right time to tell me, off air, about a Frenchman who was drying his trousers over a fire when he realised the steam going up the chimney could give him "lift off" in a balloon. He went up in 1870 and was the first to start the tradition of drinking champagne when the balloon lands. Now I reckon that is good - two little Chinese girls explaining this episode, in English.

We then discussed forthcoming topics for the programme and Snow wants me to tell about courtships and friendships between young people in England, *but* I am not to mention kissing or embracing in public. There isn't even an equivalent word for this sort of behaviour in China. This led on to other differences here, including the fact that engagements are made by agreement of the parents not the couple, which contradicts what I had been told by Patricia. Oh, I thought the tradition of giving eggs when your babies are born was good: the new mother gives red-painted eggs to friends when the baby arrives.

6.3.98
NANJING FOR LE WEEKEND!
Alison, Clare, Jo, Lisa, Graham, John and Neil and I have just had such a lovely, companionable weekend. I got the school minibus to Nanjing when school finished on Friday, and they made me so welcome. It was great just to drink beer and compare schools and gain ideas for teaching classes of thirty odd non-English speaking kids! Several of these people had worked in Japan for a year and all of them helped me to improve my syllabus. We then went noodle-eating and sightseeing. We visited Ling Gu Park. I learned how to play backgammon but didn't enjoy it much for myself. I borrowed Scrabble for Elke and me for the evenings, as she is keen to improve her already splendid English.

High spot of the weekend was a Night Club. I had never been to one, here or in England, so I loved getting ready and all the teasing and jokes of the others. The Club was situated in the middle of town and absolutely *crammed* full of Chinese but we were, yet again, the feted guests and objects of curiosity. It was mostly Western music so I was happy to dance all night with the best of them. I made frequent visits to the bar for the readily available Green Tea. It was so hot and I was perspiring so freely, but thankfully I only had to go to the loo once. There I saw an absolutely beautiful Chinese girl astride the tiled open ditch that accepted what looked like months of offerings, *chatting on her mobile phone!* I had trouble staying long enough for a wee , it was so *smelly!*

I digress: the dancing was wonderful and frenetic but in the heat of the moment I demonstrated the Can Can to a row of friends, like you do. We were all linked but I was beside Graham who is built like a barn door and he fell on me. I thought I would never walk again and Jennifer said she saw a look of panic on my face that she had never seen on anyone. Oh, I *hurt* in so many places. I got carried into a taxi with the only other old person who wanted to go home, so that was a bit of an anticlimax.

(This adventure didn't put me off going out again and, after being more decorous this time, I climbed over the University wall with them to get to their home. I've always wanted to be bunked over a University wall in the small hours.)

In a nearby café, called by the girls The Meaty Turney Café because of the cooking system for patrons. You turned the kebabs over very red hot coals which glowed in a channel down the middle of the table. We had eaten beef or fish kebabs, in the tiniest portions, dipped in tasty sauces, followed by fried rice. You could add M.S.G. or chilli from separate bowls. The total cost was less than ten pounds - for all of us! It was all delicious and so *cosy*.

Jo cooked us a huge bean feast the next day and they all went clubbing until 4 a.m. but I stayed home and washed a *bathful* of dishes because I want to curry favour so they ask me again for a weekend!

11.3.98
My Dad's Birthday
I skidded in the office at knocking off time for us and 8.15 a.m. for dad. He said it was just right because he was just shaved and showered and ready to receive! He was going to take champagne into hospital to visit mum. My sister, brother-in-law and a friend Dave were visiting with him. I told him he is greatly admired here because he looks so young at 82. The girl in the office was so pleasant, and helped me make this call so I asked her what her name was. She carefully wrote it down for me - in Chinese characters! I am just going to call her Chowder because that is what it sounds like, and hope for the best. She clicks away with an abacus at the same time as she uses the most sophisticated computer I have ever seen.

12.3.98
SCHOOL STAFF
The *teachers* were all cleaning the classrooms thoroughly today. They were washing windows and swabbing floors like mad. Cleaners are only employed to do the passages and courtyards. I have just found a couple of cleaners (girls of about twenty), fast asleep in the broom cupboard. Sometimes teachers put their heads down on their arms in the staff room and go right off, too. I thought it was just ageing foreigners that felt worn out all the time.

14.3.98
ONE CHILD POLICY
This system is immediately obvious in China. It is really noticeable - there is an absence of kids in shops and cafes and the affection shown to them everywhere is definitely different to home. There are tiny little mothers staggering about with whopping big toddlers and loving and adoring fathers playing with them in public places.

I heard that when a local couple have a second child unlawfully, the whole community are forced to pay hundreds of Yuan each. If a couple were both only children, they are allowed two - so that they can be looked after in old age. Also if your child is handicapped, you can have another or if you divorce and remarry, you can have a baby.

20.3. 98
SCHOOL
With thunder, lightning and six inches of snow, school was closed and there was no transport available for the children so we had to miss our weekend away. I was particularly sorry because I wanted to go with the Clare and Alison to Chengdu to visit Neil, Graham and Lisa. I was so envious when they telephoned to invite me, and I couldn't join them. I also felt sorry for the school boys and girls because they will have had twelve days school on the trot by the time they go home. I was so cold last night that I got chapped lips, and there was condensation on my reading glasses.

Even so, last night was a very pleasant evening in my flat with Sarah and Celia - English teachers, and Elke. We had candles, coffee and biscuits and talk ranged through being separated from your love - Sarah's husband being in Saudia Arabia and Elke's fiancée in Germany. We also covered left-handedness -10%in Europe and 1 % in China, patriotism - Elke doesn't think Germans will ever say they are proud to be German again, and Sarah says the Chinese are told to be proud every day of their lives. I could remember the last time I stood up for the National Anthem in the cinema, and the first time I saw friends *not* standing up and I thought they were terrible at the time. Of course, I sprinkled the evening with "Did I Tell You I Went to India?" stories....

POST
My letters home from home have been returned to England. They were marked from a Post Office here that I have never heard of. I was so upset and it was only when the staff realised I was crying that they stopped laughing about it. Apparently they had been marked Iconnu (French for unknown) and sent back - you can imagine how my mum felt about *that!*

The letters from home to *me* are arriving safely, thank Gawd! An unasked for cheque-book and statement from the Co-op Bank suggests they are trying to make up to me for their poor treatment while I was in Kathmandu. The Post Lady in the Library was as excited as me when I got six or seven letters from home. Another good thing about today was my very successful lessons in four classes. In one class I was even sorry to hear the bell go, whereas I am usually a bit anxious about material to fill the last quarter of an hour.

4.4.98
Life is so difficult for me and Elke because of our isolation in this school. We have complained about everything to everyone who will listen but they don't seem to know what to do about us. Eventually, though, the Chairman said we could have a hotel room in the Leo Yen hotel in - *every weekend!* We were so excited and we headed off to see our 'home' for weekends and were delighted with the facilities. There *was* water running down the walls but it was due to the condensation, and there *was* ankle-deep water in the bathroom, but that was because the Chairman's wife had used the room and she didn't know about putting the curtain *inside* the bath. This hotel was in the middle of

Nanjing and meant we felt we were really in China, and could visit the shops and our friends and eat out and ooooh we were thrilled and felt *alive*!

6.4.98
VISIT TO THE WANG FAMILY
Miss Chen took me on the school bus to stay with her in-laws, where she and her husband have lived since their marriage four years ago. Her father-in-law is ex Army. It was a dingy and dark apartment, full of souvenirs and felt very crowded to me. But they all appear to get on really well and made me very welcome. I was the first foreigner they had had to stay, or even had a meal with. I slept in their student daughter's bedroom (she is an artist in Japan). I had green tea (unstrained) and permanently refilled by someone the whole of the time I was there. There were six or seven dishes for supper, after which we walked along the main street to see the market stalls and fairy lights in a very happy atmosphere. I ate half another sculpted pineapple on a stick and bought red fluffy mule slippers, which are wonderfully warm. I was on my knees with tiredness when we returned but managed the four storeys to the flat. Dear little May Wang (Chen's ma in law) had filled my water bottle and in fact came in and tucked me in!

In the morning, from their balcony, I could see washing lines hung from all the balconies, with dreary, weary clothes and sheets. However the people everywhere were cheery and pleasant and breakfast was memorable. We had figs in dumplings with sauce, lychees, French toast called steamed egg for some reason, cold mixed vegetables, hot peanuts and more green tea.

The family don't appear to drink much at all. They drink water from Nescafe jars when they are at work, to which they have added tea leaves. These leaves float on the top for ages so a lot of straining through your teeth is necessary.

They were very knowledgeable about the star signs and told me in detail about the Chinese Year and the relevance of each animal but I only remember the Mouse (1972) produced leaders, the Horse (1978) meant freedom, and the Rabbit was good for girls born in 1975

BLOSSOM FESTIVAL
Chen and her little husband, Well Hung (honestly!) took me to this Scenic Spot by a taxi, which broke down so that we had to get a bus, which was so crowded I felt as if I was in India again. The park was absolutely beautiful with plum blossom of all shades. There were literally thousands of people being photographed under the trees, a wonderful Bonsai garden, rock gardens, a fountain, a huge music arena with piped James Galway, and a special spot for bridal couples to wander about and be photographed. We saw one couple posing on an enormous guitar, which was one of several copies of musical instruments, scattered about for this purpose. One of the brides we saw wore the most beautiful English-style dress and head-dress red shoes, and black trousers visible underneath the dress. The bridesmaid had a white angora cardigan and warm white trousers. Chen told me that they get

married, leave the relatives and friends eating and go to get their pictures taken in the studio or the park. Apart from the taxi breaking down and Mr. Well Hung's chicken being 'off' at lunch-time, I think they enjoyed their day with me but I am sure they were tired too. I went off by myself to give them a rest from me but first got them to do me a map and write their address in Chinese in case I got lost. I got my bearings by a sign that said Small Commodities Street and a shop sign saying Da VID, but kept in mind the time I had once taken my bearings by a purple apartment block which was demolished while I was shopping...

I saw the usual street decorations of all sorts, including Christmas lights, which are permanent, as in India. I only saw one foreigner all day but the influence of our clothes, music and eating habits are everywhere. Many people called Hello - the only English most of them know - and they were mostly very pleased to see you.

By now my mouth was like two pieces of cardboard because I had forgotten my chap-stick, so I fell on a tube saying Lip Salve in the shop where we bought the roses. It turned out to be adhesive though - a good idea some might say? I ended up with ear to ear cold sores.

When Chen and I returned, Mr. And Mrs. Wang had made 100 little tiny pasties called Jowza or Peking Dumplings. Mr. Wang told me that most husbands cook meals in China. He was certainly adept at creating the little dough pasties filled with finely ground beef, lamb, shrimps and onions, black pepper, salt, cornstarch and egg white. They were laid out in a wonderful pattern in a steamer basket. They later let me have a go at making them and I could see why Chen had been horrified at my suggestion that I take the family out for a meal, since they would have spent all day making these pasties. We ate them with chopped sticks of radish mixed with chopped jellyfish. They served the water that the pasties had been steamed over, as soup, afterwards. Soup is always served as a second course here. We dipped our pasties in soy sauce or chilli sauce and of course used chopsticks to pop them in our mouths. I even managed a peanut or three with my chopsticks today but what stupid implements they are. The family enjoyed my efforts with a fried egg....

The flat is so small that I was part of May's pancake-making. Meanwhile Mr. Wang cleared his throat, cleaned his teeth for ten minutes and spitted merrily (well, merrily for him), in the sink under the new Ascot Water Heater, which has pride of place in the kitchen and is still completely covered in polythene. Chen then bought me green tea in the sitting room where I go to get out of their way from time to time.

7.4.98

Breakfast today was pancakes with specks of vegetables in, plus beef dumplings from the previous day, rice pudding (English style but eaten by shovelling it in with chopsticks next to your mouth, whole boiled garlic cloves and delicious hot, salted peanuts again. I enjoyed one of my expensive little packets of Nescafe which are a mix of sugar, dried milk and instant coffee and, I must admit, gives me the same feeling as a strong liquor - a 'fix' do you think?

The family looked after me so kindly all weekend and want me to return but it was such a tiny flat and I know it cost them loads of money to have me but they wouldn't take money, saying it was not Chinese custom. I could only buy roses for May and cigarettes for Mr. Wang. The roses were ten red beauties done up with ribbon and paper and I think gratefully received but they looked a bit worried by it all. Mr. Wang stands on his balcony puffing away and they all say he has bad health because of it, but it doesn't show. He admired my dad's photo and said he must be fit because of eating apples but I suggested it was exercise - raising his right arm every evening at 6 p.m., and he was well impressed - one of the few jokes I made in China which were appreciated!

8.4.98
INTERNATIONAL WOMENS' DAY
All the 'volunteer' teachers were invited to this gathering held in the poshest hotel I have ever been in. There must have been a hundred, very smartly dressed women, and I was glad I had worn my best black Evans velvet trousers, even with navy shoes. It was wonderful, too, not to be wearing my friend Marg's climbing boots which I have been pleased to wear every day so far, in my freezing school. Today there were beautiful table settings with plates of peeled and sliced lychees, melon, kiwi, pineapple and grapes and little savoury samosas. Each of the English volunteers were placed on different tables, but when I met up with the girls from the Group, well three of them, I cried - it was so lovely to see them and they were so obviously pleased to see *me*.

An Australian woman gave a speech and told us that since 1988 she has watched the role of women change in China. She was at the UN Conference for Women in '95, and has seen a big improvement in the health of women and children and in immunisation and education, particularly for rural children. She admitted there is a long way to go, however, and said there are still women being sold as wives in her country. "When did you ever hear of men being sold as husbands", she asked. She urged us to campaign continuously as our efforts can work - witness the anti-smoking campaign. Our aim must be to achieve our fullest potential, not equality.

Chen commented on the speaker's humour and her Indian appearance - which was true. Chinese people seem very interested in other countries and ask me as much about India as they do about England. One of the teachers asked me if gentlemen still wear hats in England and take them off to say good morning or greet women.

One of the women told me that women retired at 50 and men at 60 here, and there is a financial allowance for OAPs but not much for single parents. I had to hear how fat and unhealthy Westerners are, and how fit the Chinese, and how bad all our teeth are and how good the Chinese teeth. When another woman was telling Lisa and me about dogs and cats not being allowed as pets (I have seen many Pekingese however), Lisa told of a T.V. advert she had seen where a live fluffy puppy was popped into a machine and a scarf came out!

Another woman told of the special permit necessary to show foreign channels on Star TV and I know that the school has been fined in the past for allowing staff to see the foreign teachers' televisions with Star channels on.

9.4.98
THE ELVES AND THE SHOEMAKER
We had such fun preparing for this English speaking competition. We rehearsed after school hours and they were very serious about it all at first. A prompter was a new role to them and after I had explained her job in the play, and when someone hesitated, she read from the script and helpfully provided "a"!

I described the mob cap to the Shoemaker's wife and she assured me she had one at home but when it came to school I could chose between a baseball cap and a sunhat which sprang out of a round frame. A bigger problem for her was the bit where she should 'embrace joyfully' her husband, which she declared was absolutely not on.....

At the competition at the Foreign Language School one Saturday, we were an enormous success. In spite of the hall being huge and the fact that our children had never used the microphones that were necessary, we were a HIT! The Shoemaker was superb, in spite of his speech (and personality) impediment and the two elves stole the show. They wore lovely little green outfits and the fact that they had to whisper and giggle a lot comes so naturally to Chinese children, that they were a joy to watch. The Shoemaker's wife, wearing my summer dress and her spring-loaded hat, remembered all her words. The other teachers and I did nothing at all - the children did it all - and I was so proud of them - cried most of the way through, of course.

While I waited for the children to dress, I was waylaid by an English-speaking woman who wanted to know if, perhaps, I was an English Eccentric? I said I didn't know and thought she would go away but she then disparagingly examined the raised veins on the backs of my hand, asked why I was fat and requested a viewing of my varicose veins on my legs. I felt so relieved that she couldn't find any that I deigned to show her my grandchildren pictures.

24.4.98
SUZHOU WEEKEND
Time is passing but, I can't say swiftly! Life in China is different to other adventures, in that the weather, the unfriendly people, the remoteness of the school from a community and the scarcity of post and telephone calls, create a

more challenging lifestyle than any I have ever experienced. However, I find that 'out of the blue' an invitation or suggestion by friends will lift my spirits and energise me.

My school had suggested the trip to Suzhou, and I invited the other English girls to join in. On the day before we picked up the transport to Suzhou, I went to Nanjing and had my hair razored by a 'Diploma Girl' who looked out of the window all the time she was cutting. I then met Jo for a lovely fish supper - we declined the sparrows on the menu. At their apartment I bathed in the luxury of their laughing at my jokes and slept on their damp floor, surrounded by lovely books and listening to Mozart.

Next day, after an interesting bus journey we booked into the Wu Xian Hotel of the Carved Chamber, in Suzhou. We enjoyed a room overlooking rock gardens and water features. Apparently water gardens are numerous because of the risk of fires in the all-wood constructions. In this hotel there was a carousel of delicacies at meal times, Bonsai plants everywhere and displays of pearl jewellery from the local pearl, thread and plastic components factory nearby. When we visited this factory next day, a Chinese man gave a speech to introduce us to these things but kept mentioning Norwich, a town I visit often when I am home in England. I finally twigged that it was Knowledge, he was saying, not Norwich......

After supper we Hit the Town! We danced in a silver-mirror-ball-type dance hall and after a couple of dances and a very expensive beer, adjourned to the karaoke section. It was here we realised we were in a brothel...... I showered and went to bed even when the others were still nattering, the better to manage the return journey to Nanjing next day.

28.4.98
BIKE AND PURPLE MOUNTAIN TRIP
This expedition was planned by Snow, and I was delighted to join them as I now have a BIKE! School gave me the money to buy a bright red bike called Flying Pigeon, which has a bell, a basket, a front light (no rear one) and a lock, and I have to leave it in Nanjing.

I was a bit squeamish, riding it in the overwhelmingly busy traffic but it is mainly bikes and no-one seems to speed or crash. The most common trauma is if you leave it anywhere, someone will report it and it will be picked up by the police and thrown in a lorry.

On my maiden voyage, Snow was most surprised to see me come flying round the roundabout to meet her. The Flying Pigeon could be bigger but I thought it was better too small than too big, and I could ride it with no trouble. Rust appeared by the following Monday but hey, it is lovely to have wheels again. Interpreting the Chinese map was challenging but, considering I can get lost in no time in England, I was happy to arrive mostly to the point I wished for.

Roger and Gary – about thirteen years old - and Snow and I, walked miles before we got to the foot of the mountain, which is 2km away from town. I was amazed –and pleased - to find that I was fitter than the youngsters and the climb was marvellous, with views and temples and shops all the way up. They told me that they didn't think Americans wore many clothes and that Chinese girls worry about gaining weight. I bought sunglasses on a hair-band for Holly, two wall-hanging drawings in an out-door gallery and a wristwatch like a ring for William. Snow and her friends loved hearing about English students and sang Western songs with me up and down the mountain. A lovely day.

30.4.98
ALISON'S STUDENT'S ESSAY
Mabel - a dear little 17 year old student of Alison's - handed in this essay on Filial Duty which we all found a bit sobering:

In Western countries most of the people are sent to the care-house. But in our Chinese people opinion, if the kids send their parents to the care-house, they don't show filial duty. They abandon them. If the one old people were sent to the care home by his kids, the neighbours would feel very anger and astonished and comment on it. When people have kids they raise them like raise a tree - they put their heart and blood to them, take care of their every step of growing, hoping they can well grow, become good and useful people. When the kids grow up, their parents get old. It is a time that the kids return their love to the parents for the old people need kindness and healing as they are afraid of loneliness.

...........AND TALKING OF OLD PEOPLE!
Elke's parents have arrived. She is happy but sometimes tearful and invited me to her apartment within minutes of their coming to stay. I was invited to eat a special Chocolate Cake, made by the mummy before she left. Elke is *so* pleased with me at the moment because she didn't know I could speak German. Well I didn't either! It must be forty years since I learned a bit at school but it came flooding back! Such a surprise, I was as pleased as they were. They didn't speak Chinese or English and Elke had been worried about keeping them entertained. We agreed that our fathers fought each other in WW2 but that fact didn't seem to spoil the tea party. I offered to teach Elke's Reception class for her so that she could stay with her folks, and that was fun - they are such delightful children. It gave Elke a chance to cook up some German delicacies for their supper.

1.5.98
A NEW FLAT IN NANJING?
Elke and I heard of a new flat in Nanjing which we could afford. We had been offered this accommodation by School after they denied us use of the hotel.

After the parents had gone back to Germany, Elke and I continued to try to like this new flat we were offered for weekends. It is freezing cold but has a powerful shower, a tiny kitchen and new furniture so we agreed to try it. We knew we had to share with it least one 44-year old, non-English speaking man. It was impossible to find it, though, either because the taxi-drivers were ripping us off or getting lost, or the buses took different routes to the one they should. The final misery was on our return from a lovely meal out, we found two Chinese men had left unfinished food and a bathroom full of dirty laundry. We had a big row at school about it all and told all the reasons we couldn't cope, so keep your fingers crossed....

By means of a lot of crying by Elke and I, a meeting was arranged between Mrs. Li, the Chairman, the Head, Mrs. Chen, Sarah, John and Biology man (I never could say his name). The Head was half an hour late and then sat and inspected his ear pickings while Mrs. Chen inspected her pop socks and then there was a fair amount of blah, blah, blah about our wonderful service to the school. Then they offered us 300 Yuan to find ourselves something that would suit us. Telephone calls are to be allowed *by appointment with the Head!* We aren't very optimistic about finding accommodation for that price, but I have suggested to Elke that we share the cost of the hotel from time to time. I went back to my room, kicked the furniture, said f*** out loud a few times, ate chocolate and felt better.

The television signal has come back after a week of no reception. I am so pleased because on Tuesdays there are four British programmes: Chef, Absolutely Fabulous, 2.4 Children and Dangerfield. After the first three programmes my eyes were on stalks from all this fun, but I thought I'd just see what Dangerfield was like and there was Hazel Douglas! Hazel is a very dear actress friend and I was so surprised to see her, I yelled out and laughed to see her flashing her bad leg for the doctor in the series. What a lovely surprise!

2.5.98
MY BIRTHDAY
I'm 58! Assorted presents from home and friends here made this a lovely birthday. I was staying with Jo and Alison and they enjoyed Snow's present which was a wooden spatula with Chinese writing on it which translated into Be Quiet and Get a Better Body! I am told this is Wishing You Peace and Health, too! We all went shopping and to McDonalds and then - special treat - a boat ride up a canal in a very lurid, oriental styled boat - through untreated sewage.....

The dear family in the 'Meaty Turney Café' (so-called by Alison and Jo because of the method of cooking) said that their small son shared my birthday and they had therefore invited us to join them for supper. The owners are very fond of Jo and Alison. After snake, chicken, peanuts, hot cashews, cake and wonderful company which included another granny, we left to join the other teachers in café up the road. Unfortunately, I was so busy thanking and waving to our hosts, that I fell in an open drain/sewer and broke my toe. Neil came home with me to help clean me up - (greater love hath no boy I think?) - but the water in the flat had been cut off! Well this *is* China.....

We met up with the others again, at the White Horse Cafe, where the waiter did the tea-pouring with a watering can from a long way away trick, but I had a very green looking toe which throbbed so I finally went home. I slept on the floor while the others boogied the night away at Tequila Night Club. Next morning Claire and I had a nice breakfast, watching a video of "Fried Green Tomatoes", while the rest slept on.

5.5.98

I thought I would go and stay with the girls again– to cheer myself up - but I found the loo blocked there, the dye had come out of my new rucksack and stained my clothes, there were mozzies biting me all night and my sheets were blood-stained where I had killed them. Also dear Alison was in tears most of the time, because her beloved Neil is going home, and what with the damp bed and the water being turned off, I was quite glad to go back to school this time.

I thought a walk to the Willage would lift my spirits and the wild flowers picked on the way did help. I was further cheered when I came across the pond of stagnant water in the middle of the village, which the students told me is known as The Sparkling Waters of the Incandescent Oasis!

**The "Meaty Turney" café owner's small son and I
enjoy a joint Birthday celebration supper.**

Long distance Green tea!

7.5.98

I hope my natural energy returns when the better weather comes because at present I am absolutely whacked by ten p.m. and I suppose it is because of the four flights of deep stairs that I have to manage, what seems like dozens of times per day. It is so cold, too.

We were snowed up in school last weekend but I now hear that we get two Mondays off in lieu of the time worked on the Saturday and Sunday of the snow. This would have been good news except that, since our lovely hotel room for weekends has been withdrawn and the shared flat with two Chinese men in Nanjing is the only alternative, we tried to find it to give it another try, but when we did get there, trouble finding it, the key didn't fit, so we are going to give up trying.

We were waiting for a bus home when a road-cleaning lorry came along, playing All of a Sudden A Bloody Great Pudding Came Floating Through the Air - do you know the one? Well it shot past us, spraying all the queue of people in filthy water! The Chinese just carried out staring into space as if that was a normal happening, while Elke and I got hysterical laughing......

10.5.98

SNOW'S BIRTHDAY

Snow met me and, on our bikes, we set off shopping. She was a bit disappointed that more of her friends were not able to come to her party in a

111

café. We went into clothes shops and she reeled backwards at the sight of a woman trying on a normal vest-top summer dress - *so rude* she thought! There were lots of pink plastic bosoms on sale at the bra counter, and pyjamas with Poo-Poo written on them.

We biked to buy her cake and watched it being iced with her name and birthday wishes. She then cycled off with it in a box hung from her handlebars and we met her friends Jake, Irene and Kiki in the European Flavoured Restaurant. They were all very pleased with this restaurant because they could have pasta and pizza and bread rolls and chips. They tried using knives and forks but ate the birthday cake first even though they had asked me when we would eat it in the West. They were amazed at my drinking a can of beer at the party. Snow admitted to tears and unhappiness on her birthday morning. She said it was because of friendship difficulties but I guess it was a bit miserable without her mum being there. Her mum goes to Wimbledon frequently on business, and her dad has business in South Africa.

One of the boys did all the ordering and payment and we left for a department store called Tea Gallery. Snow has been banned from going there but we drank green tea or coffee in a very innocent area and they played the record player machine. One of them decoyed me away to look round the shop while Snow and the boy with no teeth in front could have an illicit chat, and Kiki and Jake could wander round the store together. Apparently all this was allowed because I was with them, but I left them all in the store and went home at about 9 p.m. - what lovely kids.

Pupil 'Snow (White)' (third left) on a shopping trip in Nanjing

11.5.98
HANJO WEEKEND
Elke, Jens, Claire and I set off on the 9 p.m. train from Nanjing which had no sleeper available so we had seats with softish cushions, called Hard Seat Carriage. With hundreds of other people in suddenly hot weather, we slept fitfully and between naps we were given bananas and talked to by countless passengers. They queued up to practice English and by 6.30 a.m. we had worn ourselves out!

At the train station one of the many women 'touts' suggested a hotel which was lovely. Elke was wonderful with the route and hotel arrangements - I would never have found it. We saw a huge notice saying "There is Paradise in Heaven and Hanzhou in this World. We saw a Bonsai Garden, a Pagoda Park, and several Temples, including the Temple of Inspired Seclusion, 326 AD, which had been destroyed and restored sixteen times. We seemed to be having snacks and meals every five minutes. We took a boat on West Lake in the twilight and sang the Cornetto song and others to startle the bats.

The meals were usually chicken and peanut sauce because Jens likes that recipe and knows how to ask for it. When we didn't choose it once, we got pork fat in water! The beer and the company were lovely and relaxed but Claire admitted she would have had a fall-out every few minutes if she lived with Elke.

Claire talked to me of her mad mum, Atlantic rowing, houseboat living and a midwife adventure, and I do hope I meet her again when she visits Nanjing next month.

She and Jens had to leave a day before Elke and me so they missed the climb to a beautiful camphor wood pagoda. Due to the unseasonable weather - it has turned *hot* - I had completely the wrong shoes and looked as foolish as the Chinese girls in their white stilettos. We met an American called Denise who considers London her home now. She joined us for oyster beef rice and minutely chopped mushrooms when we came down. But we had left ourselves too little time for the journey to the station. We got stuck in a traffic jam on the bus, so hopped out and into a taxi and Our Hero the taxi man drove 'like an Indian' and got us to our Nanjing train in time. Elke was in a state and told me she appreciated my calm attitude to this crisis. (This was such an amazing admission *from her* that I didn't let her see me cry with relief when we got there. We had no money so if we had missed the train.......

20.5.98
SHANGHAI WEEKEND
It was lovely to see Alison and Jo again. At first I found they had forgotten to meet me, as promised, because they had to take some of their college students out to supper. I was a bit nonplussed as I was locked out, but another of their students took me to their dormitory and showed me the 'shelves' they sleep on and the cramped rooms that dozens of them share. They were quite content with their lot, though, and chattered to me about their lives. One

wore pink, high-heeled wellies, and another an 'I Love Jesus' t-shirt. There were live fish in the sink which they would have for their tea......

The pleasant Dean of this University called in and offered me a room from time to time, when I visit Jo and Alison. She seemed pleased that I wasn't being so well looked after at my school as Jo and Alison are here. When they turned up we all went for another supper in the Meaty Turney café with the wonderful channel down the middle of the table where the charcoal is glowing and you can choose your favourite foods to cook on it. Jo and Alison described Snake's Blood and Snake's Bile which they had consumed during the week - like you do! I slept in a sleeping bag on two chairs in their flat and it was great to have a giggly-going-to-sleep night with them. Their floor and furniture is incredibly damp and dirty, but the sleeping bag they lent me was the most expensive and luxurious one imaginable.

We took the 9.30a.m. bus to the train station and the 12.30 train to Shanghai which took three hours instead of two. We talked non-stop to Chinese people dying to practice English and I tried not to stare at a very beautiful Chinese woman who was tucking in to chickens' feet for her lunch. There were a lot of Hong Kong Chinese on the train and they all look much more sophisticated than the local people.

Shanghai - meaning Awake All Night City – has sixteen million people and is one of the most densely populated countries in the World. The Waterfront is known as the Paris of the East because of the European architecture, which was marvellous, as were the shops if you like clothes and antiques. Jennifer, Lisa, Graham and John joined us. We talked our way round Shanghai on the Tourist Bus and saw Bridge Tower, KFC!, Markets, Pin Jian Hotel 1860 (the first modern hotel in China), the Tung Fen hotel which is the old Shanghai Club, The Grand Theatre which was the only modern building to my taste and the Oriental Bright Pearl Tower of 468 floors. It is built on the spot where the East Sea meets the Yangste River and the Huangpu River divides Shanghai. A Chinese passenger on the tourist bus told me that concrete rafts are often necessary to solve the problem of building on the mud flats in Shanghai. Amid all this sophistication we still saw the bizarre Chinese sights like a man pedalling madly with his wife on the back and a Hoover on the front of his bike. There was just as much spitting on the pavement going on, too.

I was tucking into a hard-boiled egg and a sesame cake with almond paste inside when I got talking to a nine-year old girl, wearing a party dress, tights, knee-high socks and woollen knickers. All that would have been fine but it was 30 degrees according to her father!

Graham was his daft and amusing self and I heard Lisa say "We're not laughing *with* you, you know, Graham......" She had a saucepan of hot water to soak her poor feet when we got back and feet were a problem for all of us. At one point in the carriage coming home, the smell was so bad that a Chinese passenger declined her booked seat with us. I absolutely loved being with these people from home, I revelled in their jokes and humorous take on life here.

We caught up with Anton who had flown out with us. He was a London lawyer and he told us he is now getting very rich giving English lessons, has lost a stone and a half, has no social life, and was apparently thrilled to get our call and to meet up with us again. I certainly felt the same.

On my return to School I dragged my weary limbs up the stairs to find no electricity or water in my flat and Snow didn't turn up for the promised recording session which I had rushed home to make. Elke had a tantrum with me for closing the computer incorrectly - she was *raving* at me. I felt about five years old. Later she called in to demonstrate how much better a waist-strapped rucksack would be for me and left to meet her parents in Suzhou. What a girl!

22.5.98
GREAT NIGHT OUT – NOT!
I went out on a 'date' with an Australian professor last night. I had met him with Jo and he was keen to 'do the town'. I bathed luxuriously in my hotel room and enjoyed the anticipation of a night out with a *man* but the novelty wore off pretty quickly. He practically sat on my lap all evening and I realised, too late, that he was *deaf* and had to be near to hear. He insisted on singing to the karaoke machine - Auld Lang Syne! The illuminated list of songs included Smoke gets in your eyes and Nothing's Gonna Stop us Now. I felt he begrudged the couple of beers he paid for and he didn't seem very surprised when I declined his invitation to go to his room. I can only describe the evening as a Relate Session, overlaid with Chinese men singing their impression of Frank Sinatra doing it his way, at the top of their voices....

Today I had a more enjoyable evening at the cinema, even thought it was a blurred version of Titanic in what felt like someone's front room. The Chinese sound track was incredibly loud and the sub-titles practically illegible but of course it didn't matter as I could follow the plot fairly easily!

23.5.98
WEEKEND WITH PATRICIA & JACK
Patricia (another Chinese English teacher) had invited me for the weekend and I accepted eagerly, since she was very pleasant and easy to talk to, her English being excellent. She told me that her husband's political activity had precipitated her separation from him – his actions being a danger to the family. She added that he also had 'another liaison' and that had 'put the tin hat on things'. She also sweetly shared the fact that "Someone has always 'followed me', but there has been no bodily touching, just friendship". She told me that, in China, a marriage partner is selected with the thought that "they would be 'o.k'd ......".

Ma An Shan, her home town, has one of the top ten iron and steel industries in China, and is 45 km from Nanjing. The name of the town means Horse

Saddle Mountain and Patricia told me it was named for a general who left his horse saddle behind when his army was overcome in a battle there.

The town was miserable in a depressingly stark way, and was obviously dependent on the many iron and steel works we saw on the journey, by bus, to her house. I was intrigued at the sight of three men on a building site, with a long iron rod each. These rods were joined together at one end and had a heavy metal ball attached where the rods joined. They all raised this ball and together they struck huge rocks to break them up.

Jack was Patricia's ten year old son, and he ate steadily all weekend. He is an only child, and is allowed anything and everything he desires, which I found to be the norm. in China. Chocolate 'puffs' in a little tray and assorted delicious biscuits were offered to me within minutes of my arrival at the flat and Jack would've kept me eating full time if I hadn't realised this and declined sometimes.

Patricia and I went to a colourful market which was full of cheerful, poor looking people who stared at me but were much more relaxed towards me than my colleagues in school. At a stall next to one selling live snakes we bought a huge, live fish. This was put into a plastic carrier bag but very soon jumped right out and appeared to fly up the aisle between the market stalls. Talk about the One that Got Away! We rescued it and put it back into the bag and made for a beef stall with an ancient mincer on the counter. Several butchers were sitting with their feet on the counter, smoking cigarettes but after washing their hands in what Patricia explained to me was 'rented water' from a nearby tap, one young man served us. The beef we bought was later cooked and served by Patricia, with baby aubergines in garlic and cloves. It was sold to us by a smiling man with Big Elephant written in English on his t-shirt. I asked Phyllis to tell him that I didn't have to wait so long for attention in England and he said that he had purposely kept us waiting because the sight of a Westerner in his queue was good for business!

I was intrigued to see a girl carrying a live chicken under her arm. She paused at the exit and had the chicken killed by a man who I suppose was standing there for that purpose. Patricia told me it was more usual to take the chicken home and kill it when you were properly ready to cook it.

Jack continued to feed me little goodies to supplement the tasty meals that Patricia prepared and I started to feel like a cuckoo in their "nest". I explained this feeling to Patricia and included a detailed description of the cuckoo's habits in England, including of course the cuckoo call, and Patricia just said " Oh, we *eat* them!.......!

Patricia did not appear to be worried about money and, on reflection, I realised that all the teachers at 'my' school seemed to be satisfied with their 'lot' in life. She told me about the four pay rises and said she was able to have a good life, teaching at home too as often as she could.

As well as the teachers, I thought the petrol pump girls looked content with their lot. They all wore frilly party dresses as their uniform and were certainly happier than the female bus drivers, who wore frilly dresses but *very* miserable expressions. They drove really badly and seemed hell bent on making life as difficult for their passengers as they could!

At Patricia's flat on a Saturday, six or seven year old girls came for English lessons. These students worked really diligently in Patricia's main room for two hours. Their mums picked them up and perched them somewhere on their cycles to take them home in pouring rain. While making lunch, Jack played Western tapes including The Blue Danube. We enjoyed jowza dumplings with a fried egg which was shared between Jack and me. I attempted to use chopsticks while Jack had a spoon.

Jack and I watched Basketball - Indiana v Chicago at 7 a.m.! "Anfernee" (honestly) was the most popular player, and Jack's favourite, and he explained tactics and I got quite enthused about it all. We watched from the bedstead allocated to me for the weekend. Patricia and Jack had the mattress from this bed, on the floor beside me. I was spoiled with the bare double bed base, and velvet pillows. I was very much the honoured guest and neighbours and students and their parents called all the time to welcome me and be interested in anything I had to say - a novel experience.

LEE BAI PARK, NANJING
A visit to the Lee Bai Park was fascinating. The Park is named for a poet who was popular in the years 701 to 762. There was a Disney-type open carriage to take us round the Park and Patricia and Jack and some friends jumped into the empty seats. I waited to get in because there seemed to be some disagreement about me riding in it. I hovered while the Driver kept pointing at me and when I joked about paying twice as much because I am fat, Patricia told me the driver was asking three times as many yuan for my fare for just that reason!

Two girls, who were friends of Jack and looked like twins, came with us for this visit and bought me gifts and vowed undying devotion and perpetual correspondence to me forever! We ate bean-curd together, admired the Yangste river and wandered in the caves lining it. I admired the clever paving – all stones and small pebbles in pretty designs set in concrete. There were more trees than usual and everywhere was very clean and well maintained. There were several Buddhist shrines in the caves and a WC called 'Lotus'. I saw several firms' outings in this Park and the men (no women that I could see) said they were from Nanjing.

Lee Bai the Poet was poet to the Emperor. He apparently got drunk a lot but he used to travel as well and did a poem about every town in China. It was said that he tried to catch the moon by leaping on the reflection in the water, but unfortunately he drowned in the attempt. He was sixty when he died. He had written all his poems while drunk. 1200 years later his memorial park covers 13 hectares. and tourists flock to the Park bringing wine and other goodies to leave as offerings. His ink slabs are on display in a museum in the Park, among bamboo groves. Another story told about his 'passing on' alleges that he flew off on a whale when he died.........

Someone else's tomb from the year 222 was discovered in 1984 with lacquer-ware still in it, and this is displayed in the museum. The girls and I were also fascinated by the Green Snail Verandah which was a gift shop selling Caishi rock, bean products, wine, almond pastry, sesame cookies and chrysanthemum milk sweets. A nearby hall housing ink slabs and poems by Lee Bai had been moved and renovated thirteen times. I would have loved to have had the poem about Princess Lychee translated for me.

I was practicing singing on the way home from the Lee Bai Park, as there have been frequent requests from the Chinese for songs. I had tried to learn the words to Titanic's theme song but Patricia agreed it is too high for me - I thought she agreed a bit too readily.

One of Patricia's neighbours, who told me he was a grandfather with great pride, also told me that he had been to America and loved it because it was CLEAN......

I had noticed Patricia's interest in profound and thoughtful sayings and mottos, and I enjoyed several 'sayings' from an American book given to her by another volunteer teacher, who had been Patricia's guest.

"May you live all the days of your life" - is good isn't it? And I thought "I am born happy every morning" fitted some people very well. I totally agreed with "Interesting people are those who are interested. Boring people are those who are bored." "Does it get much better?" didn't come to my mind here, very often, but after six months in China, I was to relish "I'm so glad to be home, I'm glad I went".......

I think the Chinese must love these little gems of sayings - there is advice on most of the columns that surround the school quadrangles but often the English is a bit 'off'. I never did persuade them that Get a Good Habit was probably not a good idea.

After a shrimp supper with dragon leaf tea, Patricia told me how to make some nutty little flapjacks, using honey, margarine, brown sugar, and cinnamon. You mix those things and then heat cashews and walnuts until they are brown - not too long – and mix them in and glaze little dollops of the mixture with a five-spice glaze. She also made Egg rolls and cubed and deep fried them, tossed in the same glaze and placed them on a baking sheet and sprinkled them with sesame seeds.

Sunday
Fish soup was proposed for Sunday dinner, and I was asked to make it "English style". I happily took all the bones out (so that they didn't need to

spit) and everyone enjoyed it very much but, while I was preparing it, Patricia galloped into the kitchen and pleaded that I retain the head for her to eat, as it was the best bit!

I had told her how disgusting Westerners found the endless spitting out of bones that goes on in China for all meat and fish dishes. They do it in homes, restaurants, school refectories, and all the delicious fish and duck dishes still lost something for me by the sight of the spewing out of entrails and bones.

Patricia cooked leafy parcels in the kitchen all Sunday night in her tiny kitchen. She had no surfaces to speak of and hardly any pots or utensils as far as I could see. The parcels were opened in the morning for me to taste one and they were like mini steak and kidney puddings, cooked forever inside the strong, fibrous leaves. They were made to give to her teaching colleagues and were to travel back to school with us on the bus. I hung out of the window of her flat while they were cooking and watched the incredibly heavy rain falling. It made the hydrangeas and honeysuckle crammed in the tiny garden look a little less dusty, but the chickens scratching around the ground floor flat looked very bedraggled. The falling rain hammered depressingly on to corrugated sheets overhanging the downstairs flat and I was very pleased when we were invited out the following evening to meet Patricia's sister Ming back in Nanjing.

26.5.98
Patricia's Sister
Ming lived with her music professor husband in a similar flat to Patricia's, but the couple were obviously a little better off. They had a piano and the professor played things like Country Gardens and Greensleeves, which set my emotions jangling. I admired a photograph taken at their 25[the] Wedding celebrations, and remarked – sincerely – that it could have been taken on the day of their wedding, they looked so young still. Wedding photography is very 'big' in China and I was to see countless pictures like these during my stay. Bridal couples go by themselves to studios or local parks and are photographed from all angles in terribly 'staged' positions, with no supporting bridesmaids or family and friends to alleviate the focus. Marriage is only legal at age 20 for girls and 22 for men, which they say cuts down the family sizes.

Patricia told me that parental agreement is only a formality for a wedding, and you can go to the Registry Office any day and do the business, and then have a party for relatives and friends and do the dressing up again for photographs on another day to suit you. She reckoned that a 'good enough' pairing is accepted as normal here. Divorce is on the increase and couples just turn up for it at the Government Registry Office any day with 200 Yen and a signed Form of Agreement. If there isn't agreement, then there's the same hassle with solicitors as in Britain. I was intrigued to learn that successful matchmaking in China ensures a happy after-life for the match-maker.

At Ming's house Patricia sang another Chinese song at the top of her voice and I was glad there was no other Westerner present because the music is *so* different to ours and so giggle-inducing. I was, however, ashamed, yet again, that I had no musical offering. We were given excellent coffee made from a huge selection of tea and coffee in their cupboard which they said were presents from the husband's students. We ate little fortune cookies with notes like cracker messages, inside.

At a nearby restaurant called *Lun-Chun*, we had a tasty Luncheon, which included Bombay Duck and a delicious locally- brewed beer. The food was served from the, by now, familiar central carousel. I enjoyed a green salad, chopped egg, assorted shellfish, mayonnaise (or mustard and veg. oil), poached and sliced onions, peppers, carrots, beet, potatoes, yams, sweet potatoes and other delicacies. Conversation flowed because everyone's English was good and we were all equally interested in each other's quaint customs. (Are you wondering how I managed conversation *and* eating all that stuff?)

27.5.98
THE DIPLOMA CEREMONY
On our return to school, we were immediately involved in rehearsals for The Diploma Ceremony. My friend Pong May was in charge of the dance routines, which were more like physical training demonstrations but accompanied by trumpets and taped music played very loudly. The girls wore three layers of filmy, different coloured, dresses, which were edged in Velcro so that they could dramatically change in seconds from spring-like yellow to summer-like red etc.

Diplomas were given for Thoughts, Health and Morals. All of the five hundred plus children competed for them and all appeared to enjoy it hugely. The boys wore lipstick and rouge, which looked so incongruous to English eyes. The Speeches given by the teachers were amplified so much that I feared damage to my eardrums. A parent sitting beside me translated from time to time and I was impressed to hear that several teachers swore Oaths to Work Harder. Jingle Bells was heartily sung by some dear little girls (which sounded odd in May) but a recitation of Fryaway Peter, Fryaway Paul would have got my vote as the best rendering. I also loved the (fairly proficient) violin playing and hoped that I could take some of the credit for Do Re Mi, sung by my previously rehearsed pupils.

28.5.98
NANJING WITH MISS CHEN
My 'minder' Chen, supposedly my permanent adviser and assistant while in China, was never visible when I needed her but today invited me to go shopping in Nanjing. I enjoyed the day, buying necessities like an electric kettle, a biscuit jar, a teapot, milk powder and two cups with lids (Chinese style) and Coffee-mate. How about that for granny priorities! I also found toilet rolls, story books for the "littlies", and some peanuts.

In the Post Office Miss Chen had my letter home weighed, bought the stamps, glued them on with the communal glue at a sort of Lick and Stick Station with brushes and liquid glue provided. However, when she returned the letter to the counter, the witch lady in charge weighed it again and told her the glue had made it too heavy! Honestly! We had to take it to the Glue Station, remove the stamps, scrape some glue off, re-stick them and submit to her for re-inspection. It passed! Whew!

Back in school we had stewed duck for tea and Elke and I were offered anti-fever tea to ward off the illnesses likely in winter.

29.5.98
KEEP FIT
At 6.30 a.m. I went to my first Keep Fit session. Mr. Chung arrived, late, and quickly taught us an incredibly complicated and intricate routine. I felt better for a jump about I must say but the hall of mirrors did nothing for my self-confidence. Twenty or so Chinese striplings and a German string bean just accentuated my reflected girth.

30.5.98
MORE ABOUT TEACHING
I lost control when I ran out of material today. I used up all my ideas and was very glad when the bell went. The hour passed quite quickly because the Juniors are adorable and very keen, but I need more ideas for the non-English speakers, and they are so enthusiastic and eager at this age. The older students are bored, rich and not prepared to talk freely in English, even though the standard is high.

Each of the children has an English name but they include some very unusual examples: Coco, Baggie, Bark, George Washington, Third Eye, Coffee, Anfernee and New. 'New' caused a bit of confusion for me, because I thought she meant she was new to the school! One boy wanted to change his name from Frank to Sea Wind - why not, I thought?

I heard my Joyce Grenfell voice saying "Don't write on his arm, please", and - in a Senior Class - "I didn't come all these miles for you to do your homework in my lesson!" One day I tried a somewhat querulous demonstration of singing Twinkle, Twinkle which erupted into their own, already known, Two Little Blackbirds - one named Jack and one named Jill - all sung with gusto to the Twinkle Twinkle tune. Ah well.

Another day I prepared a lesson which entailed a lot of writing on the board and on their desks. When I arrived in the classroom it had been rearranged for a special event. The desks were round the walls and the blackboard had wonderful Chinese script written on it so, I couldn't use either. Panic! I nervously suggested they pass a parcel round and when it stopped they had to sing a song. Well! I was treated to the most unselfconscious and entertaining concert you could imagine. (I couldn't bear to correct that Fryaway Peter, fryaway Paul, could I?

121

30.5.98
ENGLISH CORNER
I've tried to start a "Drop In and Speak English Corner" in the quadrangle near me. They have one of these Centres in most towns and I thought staff as well as children would enjoy the informality of it. However, on Day One I only got a man who wanted to know how to set up a laundry business in a hotel. I don't think I have got the message over, do you?

LIFE WITH ELKE
Elke has kindly told the authorities that I must have somewhere to go at weekends, or I will 'defect' like my predecessor, American Brent, did. She is such a remarkable person. I suspect that in spite of her disapproval of most of my ideas, she does like me. Today she taught me about the computer here which is a miraculous version that plays music while you work. I can use it whenever no one else is, but before 5.30 p.m. I also met the librarian in the library today and she explained she will be dealing with post distribution and I got wobbly just thinking about receiving some.......

Elke has a fiancée called Andreas who lives in Aachen and he visited her here last year. After all these months with her, her intelligence and skill, added to my admiration of Jo and the others, and their knowledge and experience, made me do a double take on one of the Chinese sayings written on the walls around our quadrangle: "I am tormented by my own Mediocrity!"

I had supper in a Nanjing café recently with Elke and her German friend, Jens. He is a relaxed 22-year-old who had lived in Moss-side at one time. He took us to his favourite café and told us about the mugging when he got his only black eye in life while studying in Manchester. We had a lovely meal of mange tout with garlic in oil, chicken pieces - gloriously free of gristle and bone - unlike at our school. There were also hot, salted, huge peanuts, and tomato and egg scramble with *glorious beer!*

Stalls along the nearby streets revealed live turtles, live scorpions, toads, frogs, eels and rows of big, pointy, brassieres alongside knitted dresses for children. I bought one of the latter - a red and white monstrosity that is outrageously awful, but which Holly my grand-daughter, will love for dressing up. I also bought a pair of maroon angora baby bootees with sunflowers knitted on top, for my niece's expected baby - she will think they are very trendy for Finchley! There were duck heads, bamboo feather dusters, and huge pretend golden galleons with light bulbs behind, mangoes piled in baskets - all of these on poles - ready for carrying off on the sellers' shoulders. I indulged again in a sculpted pineapple on a stick, and don't worry any more about the fact that they are kept in water. Someone has told me that, unlike India, all water is boiled here and none of the Chinese would think of drinking it otherwise. There were sacks of nuts and seeds everywhere - some nuts coated in a crispy covering. I saw great slabs of meat which looked awful to me following years of cooking only vegetables at home. Elke was telling me she buys one cabbage a week that she chops and cooks at home in her room, and covers in an instant sauce she bought from

Germany. There were lovely cauliflowers the size of your fist, really sweet little ones, which I shall make a cheese sauce for. The Chinese don't really believe in eating *raw* vegetables or salad.

Alison and Jennifer (the friends from my original team), came to meet Elke, Jens and I at the Post Office building, which is like a wonderful palace. We walked to Jens's place in Nanjing Foreign Languages School and ate beautiful buns from a bakery on the way with some of his excellent home-ground coffee. He then took us to an art exhibition nearby and Alison was particularly interested, as she wants to learn Chinese styles while she's here. There were typical Chinese landscapes, calligraphy, ancient people caricatured, cranes (a lucky symbol) and many horses and blossom on trees. The artists were so keen to show us their work that we dare not ask prices for fear of disappointing them.

The girls and I met Elke and Jens again in a café called 'Sprites' which served our favourite peanuts and chicken in a spicy sauce. Elke admitted that German people would find difficulty in sharing from the carousel in the middle of the table because they would not be confident of getting their fair share!
It was absolutely marvellous to get away and to be independent of the school and meet up with my English friends who I now know will be 'there for me'.

4.6.98
OPERA IN A TEAHOUSE
First on was the Emperor! With chrysanthemums on his head and a long grey beard, he was dripping with sparkles and absolutely *screeching*. He was joined by an assortment of overdressed singers who were so loud it made your fillings hurt! There were other teahouses surrounding the stage. The Tea was poured into little white mugs with lids and the audience were either enraptured or asleep. Anyone awake was fanning themselves and a youth next to me was clipping his chin whiskers with nail clippers. His mum was next to him with a sponge-bag on her head. I couldn't say I enjoyed the singing, but I certainly enjoyed people-watching and the jowzas and cornetto on our walk home.

6.6.98
SICHUAN
This trip was arranged by CIEE for teachers and VSO people. We met up with about thirty people in Nanjing and travelled by bus for a couple of hours through arid countryside.

We first visited a food additive factory which was a bit depressing and then had noodles in a wayside café and had a big *row*. The waiter had asked us for 10Y each for the tea and a VSO chap called George said he would throw the vendor in the ravine before he would pay! A wonderful diplomat, Marie, offered 5 Y and this appeased the waiter but we noted George would rotate his eyeballs at anything he didn't agree with and Marie's skills were more than useful, several times during the trip. She was telling us of her first visit to a KFC recently, and her first taste of Western food for a year. Her school made mine sound like a throbbing metropolis. Her co-VSO worker at school had been travelling on a bus, when a mum next to him drew her boy's attention to his hairy arms (the Chinese seem hairless) - and he went mad with fear! Marie taped messages to her parents in Suffolk and we all contributed a bit. I told them of how Marie had got a rebate for my bus fare, when she agreed with the driver that I was the old woman that talked a lot.......

In the new-to-me shops I bought a huge wooden kitchen spoon and a splendid plastic crocodile for William. We all enjoyed our breakfast bun – pork, beef, dates or figs in different dumplings. The humour of the group was in the "What do you call a woman with one leg shorter than the other?" category. Answer: Eileen! - so I was a happy girl for this weekend trip.

From the Xi Ba Restaurant we sat and admired the largest Buddha in China. You can picnic on his toenail, and he had a nice face with a single eye above the normal ones. This apparently is an all-seeing eye that resolves problems. He had plants in his ears and a nice smile. He was 71 metres tall and the peculiar knots on his head signify the problems of ninety nine people but whether they are alive or dead, I never found out.

We were encouraged to eat chilli with our lunch of lotus roots, potato slices, white boiled radish and quails eggs. It dispels 'wet' illnesses which are bought about by damp humid conditions which we were certainly experiencing. The aubergines were braised with chillies and the hotpot which held bubbling chicken stock and cardamom pods was also full of chillies. Most of us enjoyed it but I must say it raised the roof of your mouth into 'bubbles'...........

10.6.98
JO's UNIVERSITY WEEKEND
I was invited by The Girls for a weekend in central Nanjing. All the other British volunteers would be coming too. Jo and Alison had been 'posted' to the Jiangsu Academy of Agricultural Services in Nanjing and were teaching students who lived in the grounds in awfully cramped accommodation. Their apartment had two-bedrooms and one large sitting room which all sounds lovely but it was damp and dirty and only their high spirits and sense of humour, *and* a profusion of their books, made it a haven for me. Jo had booked a visitors' flat next door for me, and the boys said they would sleep in their newly acquired tent. However, after one night the police called and said no more foreigners were allowed to sleep on the grass. Could they stay if they kept awake, we wondered? And they said definitely no sleeping in That Tent, or coming home late either! Apart from the blocked loos in every bathroom I tried, I enjoyed my weekend - the Guardian Weekly in my damp bedding next door to the girls and, as always, their light-hearted company compensated for the grizzly accommodation.

11.6.98
POOL PARTY
Elke has been depressed lately because she and her boyfriend have fallen out - by post! To cheer her up I put an invitation under her door to come to my Pool Party. We had recently been asked by students what a pool party was, but I had explained that Americans have them all the time. They certainly wouldn't be allowed here. I told Elke on the invitation that bathing costumes were to be worn. I lit candles and very generously supplied a bottle of beer from the village, and she duly arrived after the Simpsons. I had put a washing up bowl of water on the floor and nibbles around and we had a laugh but then students knocked at our door! They had never been to our apartment before and I could understand their confusion at the sight of us in swimwear at 7 p.m. eating and drinking with our feet in a bowl!

Elke had written a letter of rage to her boyfriend, which she gave me to post, so I wrote stuff on the envelope saying she didn't mean it, that she had been hung over from a pool party where she had smoked ciggies and drank beer.... It must've done the trick because she had a sweet letter by return.

20.6.98
XIAN TRIP
There was a definite feeling of 'winding down' in school and permission to go on a last trip before going home, was welcome. This trip was to take twenty-two hours on the train and cost two to three hundred yen (about £23). It was primarily the Terracotta Army that drew me but I never knew how much more I would get for my money!

At 8.30 p.m. our poorly lit carriage drew out of the station, and I faced an unsmiling, vicious-looking woman and her friend, having a row. They eventually calmed down after being served steamed beef porridge, 6 soft boiled eggs, and cooked sweet corn, brought to the window of the train. I had a Nescafe packet in a mug of water bought out of the same window – divine! I feared needing the loo and my other anxiety was the lack of cool air. I plucked up courage and asked a railway man if he could do anything about three roof fans not working all night – but if looks could kill! I think it probably was the most uncomfortable trip I ever made, until the sun came up over the lovely scenery and I got another Nescafe fix......

I saw people working in the fields, goats, donkeys, fruit trees, flat open country and high clouds after the rain. There were buffaloes, small patches of sunflowers, women doing what looked like Tai Chi on a building site, white geese and sheep, maize groves, six blue tractors on a lorry, brick works and coolie hats, children doing their homework on a camping table under the trees, old men sitting on a bridge and I was amused to note that the notices showing names of the stations we passed through were too close to the train to ever recognise! Is this just in line with everything being much more difficult in China?

Inside the train, the grumpy couple and I were joined by a man who exercised his neck and head muscles before connecting his Walkman! The carriage was clean and dry and everyone had put their shoes tidily under the bottom bunk. Everyone enjoyed pot noodle breakfasts, courtesy of flasks of hot water bought to the carriage and, joy of joy - the loo was not only Western style, it was *clean* .

At Lil Young Station, a nervy girl and another I will call Trouble joined us. Trouble let me keep my window seat, even though her ticket was the same number, and we enjoyed the lovely scenery, and everything was tranquil. By Di Li Piping station Trouble had put apple peels and other litter on the floor and a sweeper made her clear them up, and throw them out of the window. There was a big row between a platform seller and a customer on board. Five people joined in the fray, and a very noisy argument continued. A Western student called Matt introduced himself and joined in my fascination with all the people standing on the seats to share in the row which went on for ages. Matt left and I hoped he hadn't noted my disgustingly dirty bare feet. My beer, bought from the platform seller, was uncapped for me by a policeman.

One fellow passenger gave me a handful of green tea-leaves for my tin mug of boiling water which was filled at intervals through the route. She made her face up, read magazines, and generally seemed very modern in contrast to the women in my life over the last six months. The grumpy girl who had been so unfriendly so far, curled up against my back in the middle of the night to get comfy!

Xian!! I was thrilled to arrive and found the recommended North West University without too much trouble but it cost 160Y per night. I was too tired to find alternative accommodation and it had cost 20Y to get there so I settled in. I went out of a side gate to find supper and it was locked when I returned so I had to ask four people and the ice-lolly lady to get me back to bed! I ate supper with a teacher who looked like Leigh, my son, and who talked - in poor English - while I ate. We then talked World Cup with the help of pen and paper – and agreed the need to hurry home to watch it on television!

On Sunday my eyesight improved 100% when I cleaned my glasses, a rickshaw man gave me a yellow balloon, a Sweeper swept the dust into my sandals and I bought a yellow clock shaped like a cat for William.

I booked a trip to the Terra Cotta Army and had a look round Xian. I found the Muslim quarter to be disappointingly dirty but the fish market was very colourful. I meant to find the Bell Tower but mistook it for the fish market, and thus enjoyed the hundreds of varieties of fish and crustaceans. There were crabs tied, alive, by green ropes, and loads of turtles, prawns etc. I walked in the rain before bed and saw a beautiful sunset but a river full of turds spoiled the setting. Oh and the advert. For Jussborn Condoms was a bit worrying, too!

In a café called Carp Café I drank a beer. Men from a nearby building site had their tea shaken and poured into their glasses from a glittery tin pot while they smoked and waited for it. A family party wore polythene gloves to eat their meat course with their hands. The waitress told me it was beef, but it looked like huge portions of duck. Soup followed the main course on the carousel and I hope they all now know what it feels like when someone stares at them! They were all very smartly dressed and I enjoyed a man taking his shirt off – no vest – half way through his meal, when he got hot.

The owner came and "talked" to me – paper and pen mostly – about his being a dentist for his day job and how he had been to Nanjing University for two of his dental years. I called at a shop on my way 'home' and watched two *dear* little boys dancing outside a locked park where hundreds of people were dancing inside. One had the shoulder movement and the clapping off to a T, and he twizzled his little friend and they were so rhythmic and co-ordinated. Their mums enjoyed my granny pictures but I *thoroughly* enjoyed their two childrens' dancing.

While on this Xian Trip, another tour was offered and I happily visited the waxworks where Chiang Kai Shek featured largely. A nice little Chinese woman had adopted me and translated quite a lot of information. She showed me a new and realistic mock up of Chang Kai Shek's flight and arrest by his own troops in 1936. He was forced to sign an alliance with the Communists. The Japanese were invading China while he flew to over-see an exterminating campaign and he was caught behind the Huaging Pools in his pyjamas and without his teeth. He was after allowed to control China as long as he allied with the Communists against the Japanese. We visited a Jade Emporium and a pottery sale in the Banpo Museum.

There was also a fascinating Neolithic village which had been discovered in 1953. This village had been occupied in 3750 by a matriarchal community and the children knew their mothers but not their fathers. All the houses were round and the people tilled the earth, lived with the deer, and 'knew no strife'. They farmed, fished and kept domestic animals. The graves were incredible, the women's graves having many more skeletons in them than the men's. A sign read 'Single Persons Grave' over a single skeleton and I was informed that children were pureed and put in pots with lids on. One little girl was in her jar but with 76 objects around her - jade ear-rings, stone balls. Another three year old child was placed beside her.

By the time I got to the Army site, and the 7,000- life size soldiers, standing guard over the first Emperor Quin Shi Huangli, I was almost too tired to look. They were incredible and wonderful and, as promised, their features and expressions were all different, but I soon had to leave the mass of people and sit with some Good Friendship Store people and accept 2Y worth of boiling water for adding to my teabag. I offered biscuits to a beggar man with a hole in his head and a little girl who looked like Holly. I bought a Mandarin hat and a sunhat for 40Y and gave an English lesson to a girl who was "honoured to take a photo of herself with an English lady". She led me to a Western toilet which had been buried to make it a squat one!

CHINESE MEDICINE

When the bus driver offered to take us to see a Chinese medicine centre, I wasn't at all keen but went anyway and it was fascinating. A girl in a white overall (not very clean) stood on a stage and burnt her hand on purpose by gripping a chain which had been heated by gas flame - before our very eyes! She showed us the burn and then applied a paste made of aconite and ten other flowers. Well there it was - healed - within five minutes! We also saw 100 other pills which would ease arthritis, wind etc. No one bought anything but it was a pretty amazing demonstration. The paste only cost 100 Yen but t it would need to be kept in a fridge so I didn't buy any.

TRAIN HOME

The station was not as horrendous as the Chengdu one had been and then the friendly people in the train insisted I had a lower bunk instead of the highest one I should have had. Then I felt I ought to swap to another carriage so that a family could be together. When I eventually settled in I asked everyone about the details of this trip but ended up not knowing if I was going to arrive home at 12 today, tonight or tomorrow and then someone said that the train wasn't even going to Nanjing! All I now knew was that it was going to be twenty-four hours on the train. By this time I had the blackest finger nails and feet bottoms you have ever seen, and they were being scrutinised by my fellow passengers but I was so tired I didn't care. There was so much condensation on the windows that I contented myself with chatting to everyone. By the time I reached home I was weepy with fatigue, and my clothes were fermenting in my rucksack. Even my apartment at school looked welcoming, and, after a lovely clean up of everything, I was ready to meet up with some of the girls in Nanjing the next day.

4.7.98
CHENGDU ADVENTURE

Jo invited me to join her in a visit to her Chinese friend Tony and some other Chinese friends in Chengdu, which is 1500 km and 39 hours away from Nanjing. The train journey was an adventure from the minute we saw the Signal Woman standing on the platform in the station, wearing a huge peaked cap and saluting every train. I did a bit of a circus trick getting into the top bunk of three, but slept very well. I was greeted by a woman who I had talked to in the ticket queue for, who worked in Nanjng Library and was wearing an unusual bonnet. She called out "Good Morning Teacher" and offered flasks of drink and noodles. All the other passengers were making short work of their breakfasts with flying chopsticks.

We passed drier terrain than the very wet Nanjing, and there were terraces of rice, people sleeping on the roofs of their houses, people washing clothes on rocks, plantations of vegetables and corn and goats being taken for a walk. The smelly industrial areas alternated with rural villages that looked hundreds of years old. The back yards of the houses seemed to be where the old people and the babies sat all day. There were 'holes' in the cliffs, which were houses for seasonal workers or kilns for brick baking, and we saw collections of gravestones where paths crossed but miles from towns.

Baoji was the last big town before Chengdu, and after this there was mist, mountains, and probably 200 caves. We played card games with three packs of cards and an assortment of fellow passengers. Some fascinating lycra-clad legs, finishing with pink ankle socks belonged to a charming Chinese– *man*. At one stop a girl hopped out and obtained two drumsticks for Jo and I and promised us that we would be at our destination in two or three hours. We both voted the toilet the worst in China - it was totally 'flooded' by the morning. However, two beers called Cherished Chicken, cheered us up and kept up our fluid levels. There was no boiled water for ages but eventually some tea came along and Jo promptly burned herself on her metal cup! There was a manacled man in our carriage, but our librarian friend didn't know - or couldn't tell us while he was listening - what he had done. Jo did stirling work translating Auld Lang Syne for the librarian - and writing the musical notes on the special sheets! It seems it is most Chinese peoples' favourite Western song.

At the Station Hotel in Chengdu, Tony, his brother-in-law and Spring, another friend, met us and took us to a Lonely Plant recommended hotel where we had a blissful shower and cups of tea. A toothless pregnant woman was selling yellow marrow flowers or columbine and there were ducks everywhere outside the hotel, but we were too tired to explore further. The next day our hosts took us to teahouses and restaurants and were so obviously delighted to be accompanied by Westerners that we were embarrassed.

The first traditional teahouse I had ever visited provided very fine tea bowls with a thimbleful of different teas for us to taste. We found that the tea mysteriously changed the colour of the pattern on the outside of the bowl. You could buy the teas in small golden packets costing hundreds of yen. We enjoyed a tall glass of iced honey tea, accompanied unexpectedly with pumpkin seeds.

Tony kept promising that the best bit of our visit was to a Snake Bar. I wasn't ever so excited about the prospect and it was a huge relief when the *Snake* turned out to be a *Snack* Bar and the offerings were really Western style!

Another teahouse contained an Opera Theatre. The theatre was closed but the tea was served in a very oriental area with attractive wicker furniture, and people sitting smoking and talking. A Head, Arms and Back massage was offered for l0Y and included your eyebrows and fingers, done with flat of the hand and much nipping and chopping and circular pressings. An old gentleman had an injury 'sandpapered' and his legs and feet massaged, after removing his trousers! His female friend or daughter helped him reveal his bright blue long johns, which were then rolled up. He was treated with great reverence and respect and I vowed to treat my dad differently when I get home!

Here the tea was provided in bowls with lids and was supplied from a filthy old battered kettle by a woman with a very tranquil expression. The stage and windows of the theatre were visible but there was to be no performance that day. The customers, sat separately or in groups, and there were couples with and without children and it was all very 'sociable'. Some sat with their feet on the chairs, some were shoeless, and they chewed melon seeds and smoked 'cheroots' and generally had a very relaxing time. I thought I would have the head massage and overheard Jo telling Tony that 'Jenny is having her head felt - and about time, too!' It was thoroughly beneficial, if a bit more 'brutal' than I anticipated.

8.7.98
Next day
We enjoyed a fried egg breakfast after a night disturbed by our alarm clock which we had set at some ungodly hour in case we wished to get up for an important football match on TV. but it didn't seem so vital at that time, after all. Then we set off on further exploring of the area.

At the Temple called Wen Shu which means hollow wood, we admired the mirrored gardens and water lilies and met an interesting, yellow haired French woman who told us that Chinese medicine is very expensive in France. She had therefore made an appointment with a specialist doctor in Chengdu, and had bought some students with her from France.

We walked among the small and tall pagodas, trees shaped like pagodas, and one Buddhist temple after another. We refreshed ourselves with beers and Lonely God crisps and again marvelled at the menu. Look away now if you are of a nervous disposition: "Crispy fried newborn dog – whole or half?" Can you believe it?

27.7.98
PSYCHING UP FOR FAREWELLS
I called in the Nanjing K.F.C. and thought where else in the world would you see girls wearing party dresses, hold-up stockings and miniskirts, in the rain, and dipping their French fries in ice-cream sundaes? Inside K.F.C. they were playing We Three Kings of Orient Are, and outside I noted that the World Cup song had overtaken the Titanic theme and was blasting out of most shops.

I had been offered Jo's room while she is away and, after leaving my bag there, I wandered down the road to the Meaty Turney café and enjoyed their welcome and their food. I shall miss this dear little family – and their delicious food cooked over the indoor 'trough' of charcoal. They are still giggling about my fall outside their café – on my birthday, so I don't think they will forget *me* either!

I met Alison and Neil who had been on holiday together but I was sorry to feel that there might be cracks in their relationship. Alison had climbed a mountain by herself during their time away, and they had both been ripped off and hassled because they were tourists. Despite his sore throat and her homesickness, they were absolutely lovely to *me* and I am going to be *very* sorry to leave them.

28.7.98
MORE TEARS!
Time to leave my dear English friends and head for home! We did lots of hugging and address-exchanging and I went off to meet Dongling - our kind liaison person of so many months ago. It was lovely to see her again and she insisted on taking me to several tourist spots, before catching my flight home!

Dongling's cousin and aunt met me off the train with a huge cardboard sign saying JENNIFER! They fought to carry my bags, but they were both half my size, and my bags were bigger than they were. We went to Dongling's flat, which she shares with several other students who arrived with two big water melons that they sliced up and shared with great hilarity and affection for each other.

I've thought a lot about the nature of Chinese people and though there have been several men and women who have been kindness itself to me, and showed affection in some cases, I am not confident of meeting up with anyone another day, as I usually am. Of course I shall be pleased to see Patricia and Snow and know that even if we never meet, we will be able to continue our friendship via e-mail.

We then went to Beijing Snake Street - you guessed! Snack Street it was. Well I wrote down most of the stalls because I couldn't believe the variety and number of foodstuffs in what must have been a mile of stalls.

Octopus spring roll
Pigeons on kebabs
Sparrows on kebabs
Pork, mutton and beef fillet
Chicken cubs
Fritter balls in sugar
Coconuts drink offered in their husks
Pineapples, halved and filled with sweet rice
Vegetable parcels, fried, or steamed
Scorpions, alive and dead (good for colds!)
Cicadas on sticks
Pigeons' eggs
Fried ice-cream
Frogs on sticks
Sweet corn, boiled and roasted
Gwenchai soup (?)

Noodles
Mao's favourite - Snow to explain
Battered shrimps
Bamboo filled with rice and meat and steamed

There were crickets in baskets and squirrels in cages, being offered for sale as pets and several Reflexology Chairs and Foot Massagers.

Dongling met me at the Beijing University Refectory for my first Korean meal. We sat on crocheted mats on the floor, and ate egg plant in peanut butter paste, cucumber and cold noodles. While we were eating this course, the chef walked about with a sort of pram loaded with whole roasted ducks. Dongling was invited to comment on the ducks and pointed out a duck's head, sliced in half, which emerged under the pile of whole ducks but I never did know what were her thoughts or her comments as I had disappeared to avoid looking any more. I did however enjoy eating the chopped duck with its crispy skin which was mixed with shallots and sauce and spread on round pastry slices and rolled up to eat with your fingers. Delicious!

SUMMER PALACE, BEIJING
Dongling accompanied me to see some of the 8,000 individual paintings hung in 728 metres of corridors - the longest in the world. (So says the Guinness Book of Records). There were numerous notice boards mentioning that the Anglo/French had destroyed *everything* at some time. The Hall of Diligent Governments had been renamed Hall of Benevolence and Longevity, after this Disaster, so I bet they wished they had been diligent enough to prevent it.

Dongling suggested a trip on the Dragon Boat, which was a lovely oriental passenger boat. The lake was calm but the sky was low and what with the pollution and my chapped thighs (first and last time, but I found this condition very inhibiting and it made me walk funnily), it was a bit of an ordeal. On the bus back to the hotel I noted that sometimes seats are given up for children, but never for women or old people, and for the first time ever, I needed one so badly!

1.8.98
DEPARTURE DAY
I woke early in Dongling's flat. I was plunging about in my luggage looking for the English cash and card that I had put in a safe place ready for my taxi or bus when I got to Heathrow, when it hit me that I really *was* going home.

It had been thundering and lightning all night and was still pouring with the torrential rain that I had become used to. The girls were all cleaning their teeth for what seemed ages after I had boiled a cupful of water to add to my welcome Leptons teabag. They didn't appear to *need* tea like this granny did....We all set off and the road was like a river until we paddled across to a reluctant taxi. The driver remained in his seat and gave Dongling a huge bunch of keys to enable *her* put our luggage in the boot, and then complained that she had bent his key!

I was already tearful about leaving them but they insisted on waiting at the Airbus Station where there was no protection from the rain. Dongling went off at one point and came back with fried pancakes and a tin of drink for me - such a kind, generous girl. After leaving them - they said the rain was Beijing crying at my leaving them - the time flew in the airport and I enjoyed talking to an English couple returning after two years in China. While speaking to them I found myself praising many aspects of my Chinese adventure and overlooking the physical challenge it had been! I realized how valuable the teaching experience had been but most of all I appreciated how *age* had been such an advantage in other aspects and how many of the adventures would have been enough to send me home, had I been young!

We flew over the Gobi Desert, South of Siberia ("Good Morning" the Captain said, at 1 a.m.), over Mongolia, St. Petersburg, Sweden and Amsterdam. The hostess - who was black - said it had been her first experience of China and shared my feelings about many aspects of the China experience. She promised to wake me up in good time for landing, but first I enjoyed the Chinese pork lunch, with *salad*, which was a lovely novelty, as was the butter with the roll. We had red wine and cognac and two coffees but I noticed that the Chinese women on the flight weren't eating or drinking.

My Chinese neighbour expanded about the health-giving properties in the *skin* of fruit, particularly pomegranate, and told me that Beijing is known as The Cradle of New Democracy. He confirmed Dongling's assertion that the rain was Beijing crying because *I* was leaving, then went to sleep until we landed.

While he slept my thoughts ranged over the whole Chinese experience and I find that, having wept at leaving many of the *people*, of all nationalities, that I had met, I am not weeping at leaving *China*. However, I really appreciate the experience I gained here, and have benefited personally in many ways from the hardships and emotional ups and downs. I am certainly a better teacher (the Chinese headmaster offered my return fare if I would go straight back!) which is gratifying, and the 'girls' promise me that I am a very fortunate 'granny' in that their mothers and grandmothers wouldn't have managed to last six months in this country, so it appears my physical and mental health are a bonus I hadn't appreciated before this time. Another warming revelation came to me. I don't think I am the only granny in the world who has the feeling that their prime time is past when their children leave home or they retire from their working life. I now know, from the respect, admiration and love given me by Chinese and Western people here that our life experience and various abilities are valued more than I realised. A lovely feeling to be coming home with!

A MEXICAN ADVENTURE

23rd October 1998

Well it certainly hasn't been boring for me since I came home from my Chinese adventure! In September I went to my nephew's wedding and my parents' Diamond Jubilee Wedding Anniversary and at both celebrations my front (capped) tooth fell out! I am now known throughout the family as the Gappy Mad Aunty who was full of champagne, and they think this is my party trick. My grand-daughter Holly kept trying to find the elusive tooth, which had fallen among a mound of tastefully-scattered sugared almonds - saying "We must find it, Grandma, because the tooth fairy will come!" (I wanted to find it because it cost £120!)

I had a lot of trouble getting temporary work on my return to England, having given up my regular social work, to go to China. There was nothing except the jobs that no-one wants - for 58 year old women anyway - and I tried for 27 without success. Then I lied about my age and was employed filling sandwiches in Rumbles Sandwich Shop from 5.30 a.m. until 10 a.m. when I cycled home with a huuuuuge sandwich of my choice and about £20 which made me very happy.

This wage was the reward for my Tuesday job too. On Tuesday nights I sat still for 20 A- level Art students who were really pleased to draw my curves. They said I was more like a Rubens' model than anyone they had had before - I think they meant I was the First Fat Lady sitter! I was shy the first week and there were many paintings with my four very red cheeks and a sort of pinched-in bottom but I soon relaxed. Nobody actually *laughed* and the boys and girls came straight in and got to work with the charcoal flying. I enjoyed the company of the teacher and the students for a term and then I found the ad. for work in Mexico.

A company called Teaching Abroad offered food and accommodation in Mexican homes, in exchange for twenty hours teaching per week. You paid your own fare. I booked the flights, spent a little time each day learning Spanish, bought some suitable clothes and found a family to rent my house here for six months. I sold my Peugot to pay for the return flight - and have managed without one ever since.

The excitement of these plans compensated me a little for the fact that I missed China! I continued to enjoy everything English - the weather, comfortable beds and chairs, continuous hot water, flowers and trees, family and friends, the Library and Sunday papers, but I still thought often of my Chinese friends and English colleagues and the fabulous food (when it wasn't animal innards it was delicious!) I wanted to *hug* some Chinese people I saw wandering about in town yesterday.....

I prepared another small photo album of photos ready for Mexico. My grand-daughter, Holly, is seven now and William is five. They continue to amuse and amaze me. William is now at school. "Would you like a sweet?" he said the other day. "If you'd like two I'll cut it in half....." Holly has learned what fun it is to make other people laugh - her jokes and puns and 'wittiness' are showing promise of a really great companion and friend.

It was just as difficult as before to leave them but my luggage-full of colourful junk - presents I brought from China has confirmed their affection for me. They certainly don't think I should sit and knit things and be a 'normal' granny, which has been suggested by others. They appear to be as excited as I am about this next adventure.

7.12.98

I stayed with my mother and father (both in their eighties), prior to departure and dad overslept even though he had insisted on having the alarm clock. However, I had been awake all night, not trusting the taxi driver to pick me up for the ride to the bus stop in Ipswich, so I crept out and left without waking them. I had an uneventful journey to Gatwick and I skipped up the ramp - I was so excited. I 'cast off' a warm anorak and thick socks to a worker in the airport loo, and looked forward to being WARM all the time in Mexico.

The ten hour flight to Houston - which is pronounced Euston according to my fellow passenger - passed quickly because he was a Jewish restaurateur who told me about his sister who was weird, his English girlfriend who was too happy living near her old school-friends to marry and move in with him and more about his colonic tumour than I needed to know. This conversation didn't detract from the lovely G and T and wine that perfectly preceded the Frank Cooper jam and clotted cream we had for some meal or other! In Houston there were dozens of really BIG American women walking about, and at mid-night I had my first experience of an efficient and professional U.S. waitress - she earnestly asked what I would like to drink and said "Thank you, sweety" for the dollars. We could learn a lot from their attitude. I walked about humming "I like to be in America" - and I meant it.

After two hours flight to Guadalahara airport I was met by two hunky boys. One was Mexican - Luis - and one called Elliot who was a Jewish volunteer. They made me tea in a cafetiere, in their flat which was attached to the Teaching Abroad Office, at 2 a.m. and showed me photos of 'my' school and its swimming pool and dozens of smiley staff. Luis gave me his room (he is the co-ordinator here) and promised to deliver my post, introduce me to 'my' families and schools and generally look after me during my six months here.

10.12.98

The terms of my employment in Mexico are a bit different to the way I had understood them in the literature. I earn 72 dollars per month - about ten pounds a week. There is no hint of philanthropy though - I work my twenty hours in a beautiful new high school with rich kids everywhere and am accommodated with families who are similarly well-heeled. I am going to be rather the Poor Relation, with no sight of the needy people I anticipated helping

My first host family, the Gonzalez, are charming and seem very pleased to have me with them. There are three children, 15, 10 and 8, an Amazonian mum, Estella, - glamorous but a bit scary - and a father, Jose, who comes and goes. It is quite common to have a second family here because of the divorce laws, and the family members seemed quite at ease with his coming and going to his second home.

I have been here long enough to settle in with this delightful family, keeping up my dependency on my own Punjana tea while eating tortillas, avocados, spaghetti, potato cakes, and jimaca!

Their home is somewhat chaotic. The cold water just ran out as I got the shampoo in my hair in the shower due to a plumbing mistake by the contractors who are making another storey above the girls' bedroom. There is no garden and they keep the windows closed because of burglars. But apart from my feeling that they needed me staying like a hole in the head, it is fun.

Mexico has a Spanish feel about it and I love the weather! It is absolutely gorgeous - sparkly, wonderful, clear blue skies and lack of humidity. The streets are lined with ficus trees cut into shapes, and there are cultivated flowers and bushes and trees everywhere. It is *so* different to China and I am really glad I came!

12.12.98
I visited a sports centre today with 'my' family, but I wasn't invited to use the lovely pool (there was no-one in it) so I just enjoyed the palms and tropical feel of it and contented myself with buying a Noche Buenos (poinsettia to us) on the way home. They are being sold cheaply everywhere for Christmas and grow like weeds apparently.

13th December, 1998
Email from Jenny in Mexico to family and friends in England

Hello All English People! I have only been here six days and it seems as if I have been here all my life and it is like being on holiday! I am learning Spanish as quickly as I can because not knowing what everyone is saying is so frustrating - they are all so friendly and nice and want to speak to you so badly, but they would rather practice their English.

My first family took me to a lake in Mexico, which is infested by water hyacinths and reduced to sludge by the demands of Guadlahara. We had such a lovely day - all crammed into a white VW Beetle and eating whitebait and drinking cans of very weak beer and looking round the tourist shops, which have wonderful, tacky things but also incredibly beautiful wooden, ceramic and metal things - I will need a 'plane to myself to get home.

I have started teaching and the 720 children in my school have quite good English and I have been asked the usual funny, introductory questions. The teacher told them to prepare three questions for me about England, and they said: 'How old are you? What is the strength of the pound? Have you got a boyfriend?' Most of the Mexican people are beautiful and all the children are gorgeous - three inch eyelashes and treacly eyes. The food is the most exciting I have ever experienced but I haven't tried the booze yet.

My first job is to help with a production of the musical "Vaseline"! I was a little dismayed but feel better about it now that I know it is the musical, "GREASE!" Like the Chinese, the Mexican English teachers feel a bit threatened by the English volunteer teachers because we are the first they have had. I am doing the reassuring bit but it makes it a bit difficult. I suppose they think we will make them redundant. The school and playgrounds are immaculate and discipline good. I was a bit amazed to see unborn babies in jars in one classroom, very pinkly rubber, and complete with umbilical cords. Oooerr!

There are nativity scenes in every classroom - each class competing for the annual prize for the best one and using different materials. Religion plays a bigger part in school here than at home.

There were prayers going on in my house last night. They were mostly women relatives who came for a special Saints day. I saw a man in the street, struggling home with a life-size plaster Mary under his arm. The streets are decorated much as ours - it always seems funny to see sparklies in summertime, doesn't it?

Can someone tell me the population of Ipswich and London - (aren't I dim?), the prediction for the strength of the pound and what Prince Charles is going to do next. It is said that a boy who was in school with Prince Harry is coming in January to teach with us, so perhaps he will be able to throw some light on this last domestic matter! There is only one other volunteer at the moment and he is at the Teaching Abroad H.Q. making me spaghetti bolognaise at the moment and filling me in with all I needed to know about life Up Mexico.....

Thank you so much for all the emails. They say the post is slow but reliable so keep the letters coming, too. I have had a couple of 'emotional' moments - promoted once by the music at the party and once the sight of someone looking like Holly, but otherwise I am on top of the world and so glad I came. Adios for the momento - take care of yourselves and miss me very much - lurv, Jenny

15.12.98

My clothes are so dreary in comparison with the Mexicans. I fell with great relief upon an outfit my sister Jackie insisted would be useful, the other night, and it was commented upon by all! I think I am a disappointment in the fashion area. The Mexicans are SO smart. They all had sparkly jumpers and fitted suits and high, high heels and we all mamba-d and salsa-ed and rhumba-d and line-danced all night - it was super. Mexicans certainly know how to enjoy themselves. Right from the minute we got to the school (it was a Parents' Evening and the Band were parents) and from 10 p.m. until 3.30 a.m. in the morning there was supper (creamed potatoes, chicken stuffed with eggs) and music and singing and dancing - wonderful! The Head of English says he is going to kidnap me, he is so pleased with me, but it could have been the accumulation of guitar playing, tequila, poinsettias, bougainvillea, tequila and more tequila speaking.......

Gifts of Teabags from England, to keep a Grandma happy!

The children happily steal exam papers and condense them on their computer and use them in the next exams. Their parents approve! Many children get paid work and in the supermarkets they have uniforms and pack the shopping for you, and they are all totally non-plussed by my explanation of my last job - chasing up truants who work. One boy wasn't expelled for bad behaviour in school <u>because</u> he worked outside. This shows good character they said!

Parents here are more generous at Christmas in regard to presents to the teachers. I saw one teacher stagger home under the weight of parcels containing best quality shirts, bottles of drink etc. and he told me this is normal practice.

16.12.98

The Gonzalez family moved out of their house to wait for the new floor to be added and when I cried after a phone call from home, they thought I was crying because I was leaving *them* and insist I must return soon....... I left them in utter chaos, with a picture in my mind of a crowded hallway with granny Gonzalez asking where should she pack a huge plastic tomato held in one hand and a terracotta dinosaur in the other!

I moved to my second family, the Zavalas, who lived about twenty minutes away through a modern development. They are just as mad and lovely, and this time there are two teenage girls and a younger boy. I sleep in the girls' room and am sworn to secrecy about their smoking habits in there. They have internet for my emails but the girls have to boot it up and save it for me, and since they are mostly waiting for messages from boys, it is a bit erratic when it comes to letting visiting grandmothers using it! One day someone tripped over the wire in the electric supply and we lost all the typing from that day. They all speak perfect American and laugh and shout at each other all the time - sometimes until 5 a.m. They just love their families *and* visitors.

17.12.98

I am over the homesickness bit that the Christmas messages and letters to me provoked, and am thoroughly enjoying these "Darling Buds of May" type people. They are without a maid at the moment but the mother and girls sweep even the grass outside the house and spend hours cleaning the garage and two enormous cars, as well as the house. I am teaching more French than English to the girls and the father of the family, since their English is excellent.

Yesterday we all went to a 6 p.m. mass in a round, very modern church. The Priest led the service and there were two lessons read by women. Communion was taken but there was no singing and the people were very 'ordinary' and there were hundreds of children, well not hundreds but ever so many. After church the family went visiting and I read and drank tea by myself for the first time since I left home - lovely. When the family returned the only son got a smack for the first and only time during my stay - for jumping on beds with a nephew who looked like Dennis the Menace. This only boy is treated completely differently to the girls, but they don't seem to resent it.

19.12.98

Teaching in this Mexican school is more fun than in China in some ways but not at all as it was described to us initially. I am disappointed that the groups of six or eight sixth formers that were going to benefit from English Conversation – just my cup of tea – are not on the 'menu' at all. We are expected to take thirty or forty pupils to cover the syllabus being followed by the Mexican teachers. As this involves a lot of subjunctives and conditionals and other mysterious grammatical adventures – I have to bone up on them at night!

The staff meetings – for coffee and for business meetings – are fun and the people are really friendly and interested in things English. They are very hard on my young colleagues though, and accuse them of being standoffish. I have questioned how they think their 'children' would cope at 18/20 years old, entering a foreign staff room, and they now look at it in a different light I think.

My first proper look-round in Guadalajara was a sightseeing trip with the family and "Dennis" (the Menace), who informed me that the town was 458 years old on 14th February. We all travelled in a huge Buick and breakfasted in Café Uruapan, which offered (along with the guitar players) pork-filled baguettes or tortillas (carnitas), and tacos with pork. There were plaid tablecloths, painted chairs and tables and even a huge air-duct was painted in bright colours. Opposite the cafe was a reproduction medieval banqueting hall with coats of arms and goblets everywhere. The outside wall had a mural of Romeo and Juliet's balcony and even the ivy was painted on the mural. Refreshed by our most - to me - unusual breakfast, we walked on to another interesting building nearby.

Hospicio Cabana had been an orphanage for 150 years, housing 3,000 kids at one time. This building had also been a church, an asylum, military barracks and a jail. Hidalgo planned the revolution here and signed a proclamation against slavery in 1811. Between 1936 and 1939 Orozco painted marvellous murals in the main chapel before he had his hand blown off in an accident at some time.. He had cleverly drawn optical illusions on walls and ceilings and I was particularly impressed with a doorway, two horses and a man in a fire in the cupola. People (including me) looked very odd lying on benches or the floor, looking up at the murals.

In the Plaza Tapatia there were modern sculptures and brass statues of humans. These latter had been made into seats which just asked for people to pose in them for photographs. I noted that my Mexican hostess preferred the plazas clear of people and the father enjoyed them full and lively. This accurately reflected their personalities.

In the magnificent Cathedral, a plaster Jesus could be seen with bleeding knees and heart in a glass case. A visitor stroked his child and then stroked the case holding Jesus and then the child kissed the case. There was also a statue of St. Jeronimo, and spectacular white and gold columns everywhere. I kept my opinion to myself about the most tacky nativity scene I had ever seen - it didn't hold a candle to the school ones. I tried not to look at a girl in the confessional box who had tears pouring down her face and into her neck.

21.12.98
Jesus, an uncle of the family, is a plastic surgeon and he visited and told me it was two thousand five hundred pounds for a face lift, surgery only. I offered to baby sit to cover cost and he said it would take twenty years – does he mean he is expensive or would it take him so long? He returned to the grandparents bunker design house where he has been exiled, to discuss his

marital problems in the garden, with his sister. Another sister lives there, too. She would like a husband and was very interested in my son, Leigh, but I explained that he is promised to another.

On Sunday there was a family meeting to plan the Christmas food and drink. The grandparents, two brothers (one on crutches), two sisters, "my" family of five, Dennis the Menace, two other chicos, and a sister in law who was the "scribe", and a man who no-one spoke to, all arrived and found chairs somewhere and noisily made their preparations.

I followed most of the conversation and heard mention the following for the meal: turkey, mushrooms, apple salad, spaghetti, carrot and pineapple in aspic, guacamole, vino, tequila, Blue Nun something, Indian nuts, asparagus, champagne, cake called Monique, Herodes, something brown called Masoquista and something yellow called Montezuma (the Emperor). I don't know what the last three will be but they sound promising, don't they?

24.12.98

On Christmas Eve I bussed into town by myself, and was interested to see that they have T.V. in the buses. It took about twenty minutes and was through a mainly residential area. My companions on the buses were never keen to practice my Spanish but delighted to try out their English. The housing was reflected by the passengers – mainly middle-class and all well-dressed and made up.

I thoroughly enjoyed rediscovering the Orphanage and the bronze statues of Illustrious Figures in the town centre. I bought odds and ends to send the grandchildren and had piña-colada and quesadillas with beans and guacamole in the sunshine. A man was miming outside and there was another more grisly performer, showing a snake and vegetables and books in his bag and then tricking us with evidence of what he suggested was his blood from an arm bitten by the snake. I guess the blood was cooked beet.

I peeked into a cemetery and saw a dog's grave marked with the inscription, in English, "More faithful to me than my three husbands". On the journey home, I was intrigued to read in an American newspaper that there are classes here for Overeaters Anonymous, Papier Mache, Jehovah's Witnesses, Women's' AA, or Percussion classes. No need to be bored here.

During the evening I was told that Mexicans may drive at 13 years of age, if accompanied by a teacher, usually their mother or father. Then they can drive when they are 16 years old with a provisional licence, which is renewable until they are 18 years. Then it is o.k. to drive without passing a test! After this information had been absorbed, I was not surprised to learn that there have been 165 people killed on the road by bus drivers alone, this year! Apparently there is a twenty pound fine if they kill a pedestrian but even more if they are injured, so there are rumours that the drivers reverse to finish the job off.

Every day feels like a holiday here but there are undercurrents which cause anxiety. New cars are not seen as a particularly good idea because gun point 'requests' to drivers to get out and go, are frequent. The car owners are left without possessions in the streets. Wrong cars are often brought to the doors of restaurants after being valet-parked, and the correct car is never seen again.

31.1.98
NEW YEARS EVE
Attempted to get togged up and, looking in the mirror, I think I'll ask the Plastic Surgeon to give me a price. He arrived with a disposable nappy filled with his contribution to the midnight feast: oyster filled cheese. He was such good fun and didn't go home until 9.30 the next day. It was another host of friends and family and we ate grapes at midnight – one for each month of the year – in a champagne glass.

E-mail from Jenny to everyone on 31st December 1998

First of all a Happy and Helfy New Year to you all from Mexico! At the risk of repeating myself, I am having a ball! Mexico is the most amazing place I have ever been to and I am living the life of Riley (who-ever he was).

I am enjoying luxuries like racks of expensive perfume in the bedrooms and bathrooms, huge speakers and music in Chevrolets and Buicks as well as every room, and visits to wonderfully restored houses with courtyards full of fountains and ficus and avocado trees. There are whole towns full of beautifully crafted glassware, metalwork, rope things, paintings, wooden treasures. No tourist tack, just lovely cheap things.

Yesterday the boys in my volunteer group and I went to Tlacquepaque (pronounced clackypacky). We nearly had to visit the next town because Luis, the co-ordinator was so busy admiring the Dutch girls on the bus that he forgot to tell us to get off. However, we jumped off quickly and within minutes I was dribbling over a huge French iron bed in the heavenly revamped room of one of these Spanish-styled houses. It was covered in coffee coloured linen and satin and a bath-tub-sized terracotta pot was suspended over it, with cascading convolvulus type flowers.

When I left the boys and met up with my family they dragged me away to drink chilled beer from a cognac-shaped glass filled by a handsome waiter. A dear little Mexican man with a 'gran corpulancia' like mine played The Entertainer on an antique grand piano - honestly I was in heaven!

Christmas Eve and Christmas Day were celebrated with food, drink and people, much as we do but multiplied by ten! One of the grannies, called Maria, (they all seem to be called Maria come to think of it) and I, had a quiet weep because she has lost two young adult children through road accidents this year. Then I had a weep because, having suggested no-one phones me from England except in case of trauma, my hostess said there was a call for me. My legs went to jelly and I had to do a very forced laugh when it turned out to be a teacher from my school here, pretending to be calling from England to have a joke with me and to wish me a Happy Christmas.

However, I recovered enough to enjoy dancing and singing - they are all completely uninhibited here and do it all the time. I will probably be remembered for my rendering of the song that goes with the Bodyguard film - you would have been proud of me. On The Day, my hostess just enjoyed everyone and didn't have to work at all really. They all bowled up with whatever was on the list. They used plastic tableware for the first time. Everyone dressed up and No. 1 son was particularly beautiful in a suit which he had requested as his Christmas present, and a gleaming white shirt, looking just like his dad. (I was pleased to see that he later played with a dumper truck in the dirt outside, though). I had presents from all the family here, and from my own family, and everyone kept saying how much they loved me so I wasn't too homesick at all.

We went to bed at 5 a.m. and the pattern has been repeated several times since. Mexican hours are different altogether - bed at 1 or 2 and rise at 11 and back to bed after a whacking great lunch at 3 or 4 o'clock. Breakfast is usually scrambled eggs with diced ham or sausage or tomato in it or a heavenly baguette filled with double cream, Dijon mustard and ham. I could go on about food but will control myself and tell you about the people.

Mexicans are the most pleasant, smiling, relaxed and attractive people I have ever met. They hug and kiss and sit on each others' laps and absolutely adore babies, old people, foreigners, toddlers, and children. I am going to copy them forever, so look out! They laugh and talk to everyone they meet or sit next to, in cafes and they even play guitars to you while you eat breakfast in a cafe. I asked about the symbol of a horn seen hanging in most homes and cafes and it seems Mexico is shaped like a horn and these symbols are given as gifts.

There are, however, horrendous stories of kidnappings and belongings are stolen from you or from your house before you can turn around, if you aren't careful. The houses are enclosed in protective cages, so the people can't all be as wonderful (or rich) as the people I am mixing with. But I must say, I am overwhelmed with how well-behaved the kids are, and how loving the families to each other, and how polite in queues and buses etc.

The family love telling me horror stories and revel in the soaps on television, where I saw thirteen people crying in one half hour episode! (Big tears and nose-runny crying, it was, too). Oh, the stories they have told:

A woman in the rear of her own car was shot and killed by police while she was being abducted. Apparently the public were very 'cross' about this.

A man who had been kidnapped and put down a well, was being rescued, but was dropped by the rescuers and died..

A bomb at a 50th birthday celebration killed all the drug dealers at the party.

An explosion at a petrol depot destroyed a whole housing area.

A drug dealer's daughter, who goes to school with one of the girls in my house, has a bodyguard and is often off school to go to visit relatives in jail.

Children's' organs are sold by kidnappers.

A boy, who was kidnapped and then returned to his mother, had been blinded.

I have to endure shopping in Harvey Nichols type shops with my hostess. Quelle horreur! I look like something the cat bought in, in all the mirrors in the stores. Of course I have no money to spend (or interest in) clothes, even though everything is of wonderful quality and cheaper than at home. However, I did enjoy spending my Christmas present money from home on a pair of navy suede sandals and denim Bermuda shorts yesterday - sincere thanks to all who sent money!

Yesterday the Head of English took me to the Plaza del Mariachi and I was introduced to this famous Mexican trumpet playing which reduces their men to tears. There were about a dozen in each group and people hire them to blast out trumpetty songs as a serenade. People were paying a hundred pounds for 20 songs or an hour's worth! Tossing up for the price is customary and we had two playing different tunes, one on each side for different customers. I felt physically abused by the end but the beer and scenery helped - there were old buildings and arches around us and grilled windows, old yellow paint and pigeons asleep on ridges on the buildings.

I am still on holiday and school is going to be a bit of a shock next week - well the 7.30 a.m. start will be, for starters....

Oh! Yesterday was April Fools day (and All Saints), here) and I got completely taken in by a front-page spread announcing Clinton's resignation because he has Aids! I was so disgusted when I translated it and asked to see the US channel on television, only to be told it was a joke! I fell for it even though I had looked up SIDA (Aids initials in Spanish) because I couldn't believe it, and that just said Cider.....

Two English volunteer teachers have returned from their first visit to a supermarket and called to see me, so we are going to try Mexican teabags. I will close now and Elliott (from London) will copy and send this for me. I'm typing it in the Teaching Abroad office because the one at 'home' seems to cause havoc of varying kinds. I have my own Hotmail address now and am as excited about it as I was getting my driving licence! Isn't modern technology wonderful? I have had my first 'real' post today, too, so I will send some proper letters back from now on, as well as those with this magical system.

Take care of yourselves and keep warm! Love Jenny

5.1.99

On thinking about the crime rate here and comparing it with my information in China, there appears more kidnapping for money here than the odd posters on walls in China which pleaded for information about "Disappeared" children. They were written in English and Chinese and were heart-breaking. The parents seemed always to have 'lost' mentally and physically handicapped children and Chinese friends said they were never recovered. Whereas the Chinese had little money and no evident crime, the Mexicans lived with constant stories of horrendous kidnapping crimes and burglaries and hit and run traffic.

I was longing to know how Christmas went for everyone at home and needless to say I thought of them often. I keep seeing VW camping vans like we had while our children were growing up and funnily enough this was enough to bring on the tears, as does hearing Western songs that the Mexicans play on their fantastic car radios and in their homes.

I feel that I am having a more relaxed and interesting time here, than the young people. There is definitely an advantage in traveling abroad if you have been to other places, are not *lonely* but only *alone,* and have experiences to enthrall the people you are staying with! They give me the happiest, warm feeling that Grannies are not Has-Beens, but the source of stories and adventures of countries they know little about.

I hear that twenty more volunteers are expected in January and that they are all under 23! So much for my feeling that they would be retired teachers. I like to go to the Teaching Abroad office in a far-flung area of Guadalhara to use their computer and to have a chat with English folk. It is about two miles to walk but walking is blissful in this lovely climate.

I thought not having contact with anyone English would affect me, but it isn't too bad because the Mexicans are SO friendly. I had to explain Do-Gooder to a teacher yesterday and I overheard him telling another teacher Jenny is a Good Doer.......

8th January 1999

Worrying news from home - my father needs a small operation in two weeks. I e-mailed to wish him well and got enormous sympathy and offers of prayers from the Mexicans. They are all amazed that someone my age has a father alive! I wrote this to home on hearing the news:

Mexico Calling:
Dear everyone I know on the Internet. My hosts' internet facility is ok only for Receiving emails and I am today in the Teaching Abroad office where, courtesy of the wonderful Elliot, I can Send as well! At home, where the teenage girls can nearly work their computer, they merrily tell me that I have Messages Waiting and then go out or get on the 'phone to their boyfriends so I can't read mine. Also I've typed a

couple of foolscap pages of email and then they say the equivalent of OOPS in Mexican and I know the message has gone into space......

1,600 Catholic children included you in their morning assembly prayers yesterday, dad! I had mentioned my anxiety to a teaching Head, with whom I work. He quietly arranged these prayers and after the kids had prayed, he went on to tell them that Saddam Hussein had asked them to listen to their God and join him fighting the U.S. and the U.K! My teacher friend says I needn't worry because even if Mexico joined Sadam in fighting us, their Forces are useless!

I am still reeling from the life of luxury I am leading compared with former lives abroad. Mexicans here are far more sophisticated than us, but I can't persuade them that we aren't all rich and living like aristocrats. Their impression of us as a race is that we are serious, unfriendly and superior. They think we are all "up ourselves". I keep saying I am a typical English granny but they won't have it because I don't fit their impression. Well hopefully these young people will prove my point. Snobs are apparently called strawberries and the students reckon there are a lot in the United Kingdom! They thought that all Britons looked down on Mexicans, as they think the Americans do.

On Sunday I went with three English boys to Tonala - a market town, and it was the most eye-hurtingly colourful experience. We ate pancake pockets stuffed with chicken and tomato or cactus and cheese, and drank melon juice. I gawped at the population which included a girl wearing I Love Jesus braces, and at the amazing gifts on sale. There were plaster cherubs, a life-sized Arab with a huge red handbag, leather baseball caps, (leather everything actually), a t-shirt with a collar and tie realistically painted on it, wonderful artificial sunflowers, and arum lilies, candles of all aromas including coffee, and metal and ceramic and wooden items to die for.

The kids in my school have beautiful clothes, faces and attitudes and I love them. They are called Israel, Pablo, Xavier, Oscar, Cesar, Gladys or Begonia. The young teachers from England are going to be absolutely LOVED by them all because their questions are often about Oasis, Progeny et al, and the girls' hormones are absolutely FIZZING.

"Keep off the Grass" is one of the few Spanish phrases which I can remember for some reason, and they all tease me about it now and it is my password on the answer-phone and entry phones. They are in fits about the mistake I made at first: I said keep off the pisto, instead of pasto, and that means keep off the strong drink.....

Love and Adios from Jenny XX

10.1.98
REUNION
Theresa, my current hostess, took me to a reunion of her classmates - from 25 years ago. It was held in her friend Alicia's huge house with poinsettia trees in the garden. A 'girl' called Vicky had studied in Boston and translated for me all evening, so that was nice. We drank Punch made with tequila but

innocuous, and had cold pickings including a cheese made by one of the guests. There was also fruit salad with walnuts and tequila poured on top.

All the guests seemed to be married to politicians or medical people and came in huge cars, Buicks, a Chevs, and Japanese monsters and Claudia told me that all the families have at least one car. They all own masses of clothes but she herself liked fewer but expensive ones. She noticed in England that we have one coat for ages, not one every year. She was surprised that I didn't have the same standard of material goods and fashion items and cosmetic surgery as all her friends and family enjoy.

I found this meeting one of the most uncomfortable as far as fashion and appearance were concerned. The difference between my families here and former families in China and India are stark in material form, but the contentment levels are much the same.

12.1.98
Theresa's Cafe
My hostess told me, over coffee one day, of a cafe that she had opened in 1994. This was only one scheme of many I heard about from men or women in Mexico. They have great initiative and often do two or three things - one of the teachers at my school was a dentist as well as teaching. I loved hearing about Theresa's cafe on her garage forecourt. She started with one table and two 'coca cola' chairs because their house was opposite the University, and she knew there would be demand for snacks and breakfasts. She ended up with fifty customers daily and she made a mint. She simultaneously did school meetings, PTAs and her kids' meals and had the garage clear and the cars back in by mid-day!

Alfredo and Lisa
These relatives of Theresa are like film stars to look at and were up to date on the English political situation - being pro Tony and anti Margaret! Lisa was so elegant and her home so beautiful that I wasn't surprised when she opined that she agreed with Herod, (most unusual for a Mexican), and they wouldn't be having children.... I had a most interesting visit to Lisa's house. This was set in particularly lovely garden with a mandarin tree, avocado trees (the fruit are so big they dent the car when they fall), orange and banana trees, ferns, Busy Lizzy trees, ulstramaria, and jicama which is a white, apple-tasting fruit, eaten with lemon, chilli and salt, as an aperitif. There were squirrels and birds eating the burst avocados. She pointed out a sleep-inducing, hanging convolvulus flower while we ate crisps and drank rum and coke and listened to a Lionel Ritchie CD. She smoked Marlboroughs and we had a thoroughly good time.

16.1.98
My family all turned up again for piñata bashing today. A huge effigy, containing small gifts, is whacked at by blindfolded guests until it breaks. It used to be made of terra cotta but it is papier mache these days. Alfredo broke

it ahead of the kids in spite of hearing Theresa warn me not to break it so that the children would enjoy it! She was cross with him.

The children are well-behaved here but I was interested that the only boy in the Zavala family had a tantrum with his sister over breakfast and when I put a plastic crocodile in his scrambled egg, he had a tantrum with me!

20.1.98
Language
Everyone seems to understand my English better than my Spanish at the moment but I will persevere. The girls sometimes test my vocabulary. I am teaching them some French or 'English' as opposed to 'American', but have given in at school and bend to demands for U.S. English - 'doncha' and 'woncha'- but it definitely goes against the grain.

28.1.98
My lovely 'boss' Temo collected me to go to his house for a Carmi Canada – BBQ to us. It was lit by filling eight tissues with oil and making a nest in some coal. The guests comprised two Begonias - one large and one small - one Xavier and a Mathilde, Jose, and Granny Maria Cognac. They told me during the course of the evening that their monthly water bill is one pound, gas is five pounds, electric ten pounds, phone ten pounds, 2 litres of milk are 60p and a kilo of meat is two pounds. House rents average 200 pounds per month.

Colour Prejudice
I was intrigued to learn from one of the teachers at the BBQ that their colour prejudice was not considered as bad as that of Americans, and they think that excuses them for their undoubted prejudice. One teacher maintained that Germans like brown-skinned persons best and another says the lighter the skin in Mexico, the more acceptable. It is a constant subject of discussion and I heard one man who understands, but resents, the fact that one of his own children is favoured above the other because he is blue-eyed and fair-skinned. This attitude was demonstrated by an unfortunate episode that had happened recently to one of our volunteers from London. He had accompanied one of the Mexican teachers' wives to the supermarket. When the check out girl enquired, in a light-hearted way, if they were related, Paul laughed and said "No, look at our different colour skin" and showed his bare arms to compare them. The Mexican wife is now not speaking to any of us, she was so offended.

It's Sunday today and, on a cycle ride around a housing estate with the children of one of the teachers, I listened with them to Mariachi music in a communal terrace. There was a lovely relaxed atmosphere with many women lunching in a nearby cafe. My hostess had made a Spanish omelette and pizza and salad which were delicious.

Dogs
I am a bit worried about the dog situation here. They appear to be either guard dogs or status symbols and not family pets as they are at home. I never

see anyone actually walking these dogs and they often live on the roof of the house – often in strong sunlight. They don't have kennels but I did once see a bulldog in a cardigan. I was telling my teacher friend about my anxiety and relating the story of the Chihuahua that had bitten one of us, but he just asked if the dog had died......

10.1.98
Volunteers
The Teaching Abroad people have arrived and they are an amazing bunch. Apart from seeming so wobbly, homesick and young, they are fascinating in their diversity. There is a Belfast Spice Girl look-alike, a baron's son and several little aristocrats who 'went to a party at the Parker-Bowles, just before leaving'. One of the boys told me he played jokes on the Princes at school, and another thought that all girls drank only gin and tonic, not beer. They believe they are telling the Mexicans the truth when they say it is usual to have a marquee and 250 guests for a 21st Birthday party and that the average wage is forty thousand a year. All in all they are typical teenagers in many ways but very, very posh! They all loved me instantly because I am a surrogate mummy and of course I sympathise with their wobbly feelings and initial nerves, having had them myself. One boy told me he always asks for champagne as his free drink on the flights - why didn't I think of that? I can see I shall learn lots from them!

30.1.98
Chapala Expedition
I have been to many parties and outings with the Mexicans and they are so good at enjoying themselves. They love me to tell them how much more fun I am having than when in China but it is certainly the truth - I am having an absolute ball! Picture this, for example: Sunday afternoon, about four-ish, and I'm picked up by three dashing Mexican teachers, Salvador, Temo and Miguel, in a flash car - a Chevrolet. I sit in the back (to balance the weight they tactfully inform me!) with my elbow on the open windowsill, the wind streaming through my what is left of my hair, 'Fifties rock and roll music on the stereophonic radio and we are all given a can of beer and go screeching off to the lakeside! I am still persuading them that I am a typical English grandmother, but I did begin to doubt it myself today.

We then went to the biggest lake in Mexico, which revealed a bit of a tragedy really. It was lovely but is shrinking so fast we may be the last to enjoy it. We watched horse-riders race along the shore and the dramatically wonderful sun setting behind the mountains. We saw cranes, cormorants, and egrets pottering about and soon the stars were incredibly brilliant. A useful discussion about homosexuality enabled me to suggest to the teachers that they should start re-education about this topic in their school. They still insist it is sinful.....

Christine and I went for a walk in the dark some way away from the boys to have a private wee, but when we retraced our steps with them, we got the giggles at one huge puddle in the dust, beside her delicate little puddle.

We then went to another village and saw a firework display in a courtyard below a neon-lit Catholic Church. There were Foot Searchers as a finale - sort of bangers that shot about on the ground. Then, when the fireworks finished, the bells on the Church started and we all came away with the bells and the Mariachi bands playing. Thousands of Mexicans, mostly in Stetsons, milled about eating things and smiling. Everyone thought we were *all* Westerners, which pleased the Mexican teachers no end.

Oui Cafe
Another lovely outing was to the Oui Cafe which turned out to be a restaurant where they take your car away and park it, even though we only had coffee. There was a six-piece band, including a grand piano, a blind pianist and a black guy playing tom-tom drums. A violinist strolled between the tables, playing and singing romantic songs like 'Begin the Beguine', 'Bewitched, Bothered and Bewildered' and 'You'd be So Easy to Love'. I admired the tasteful paintings of nudes, and real water falling down one wall and plants and a real pigeon in a bird bath!

Conversation flowed - mercifully in English - and Cecilia told us all about a recent visit to the theatre to listen to the Philharmonic with 'cygnets' in the orchestra, and about an ex boyfriend of hers who had become incredibly rich and got kidnapped for three months last year.

The talk continued and before I left I heard the details of an Irish volunteer teacher who had been arrested for indecent exposure within days of arriving here. She was in the front of her Mexican friend's car with no clothes on and the police fined her escort two thousand pesos and his Rolex. After all that he took her back to his hotel for the night!

1.2.98
School Teaching
I love teaching the little children and they ask lovely questions like: Are you a grandfather? Do you have a Mexican boyfriend? How much do you weigh? Are you afraid of the dark?" and "What does your father do? One of them was so desperate to speak to me he looked up a question in his book and asked me "How many apples can you get in a bowl?"
I assisted the English teacher for most of this week. We are getting on much better now that they feel reassured of their role. I suggested we teach parts of the body by singing Hokey Cokey and we were shaking it all about when the Head visited to see how I was getting on!

Their knowledge of England is a bit sketchy - they know a few football teams but their maps of Europe don't show Britain at all. The staff names are romantic - Alfonso, Angelica, Ricardo and the Head is Geraldo.

I struggled in the class of about 30 when we needed to use a strange black tape recorder with no indication of what the knobs were for. I turned quickly at one point and made a boy's nose bleed and mopped him up while explaining to Angelica what 'piss' was. Another time I was talking to six children at once and getting good results from them when a boy joined the group and proceeded to ignite his jeans that he had dowsed with lighter fuel. He had burned the hairs off his legs underneath before I could get to him!

All the staff hugged each other this morning because two staff members had been absent for the Annual Christmas hug! They had all given each other beautiful gifts, too. The Pope was the other topic at coffee time as he had been visiting Mexico and two million people had tried to see him. They talked of their tears just seeing him on television.

The older students are less than glad to know us, following our marking of their examination papers. They pleaded for higher marks - one of them on his knees.

Food
Food continues to be an amazement here and since it is rude to refuse anything and they can practically tell you the weight of anything you once left on the plate at their house, I am rocketing into a Very Big Girl. Breakfast today was chicken and crushed crispy tacos in a spicy sauce, and yesterday's outing with The Boys (volunteer teachers) meant pretty well continuous consumption of things like caramelised crispy pancakes, chilled whitebait, hot chick peas, beef and onion parcels, pure pineapple juice and ice-cream, and avocados with everything.

The list of Things Declined almost matched my Declined Chinese Delicacies: cow spine tacos, intestine tortillas, pig's lips - honestly! The other morning we were allowed to leave school and go to a street stall with tables and chairs for breakfast. The piece de resistance, declined by the three other Brits and I, were 'Pork skin' tacos which we were told translates as 'Foreskin Taco'.

2.2.98
Maria, last hostess, is an artist. There is a terrible sense of loss about her as her 26-year old eldest son died in a car crash four years ago at Christmas. I liked Maria very much and am now looking forward to staying with her. I was allocated this home *after* Christmas as she knew she would not be much fun at this sad time

About this time I drove to the airport with my the Zavalas see them off to America. Their plane was delayed until the morning and so we all came home to a fantastic take-away paella and tequilla lunch! They are so relaxed and happy, whatever the circumstances and make every occasion a party here. Think what we would have been like if we had got to Heathrow and then been told the flight was delayed until 3 a.m. the next day. They are so smiley and adjustable. The take-away party included a couple of grandparents and Jesus the plastic surgeon. I am kippered by Marlboroughs smoked secretly by the teenage girls in our bedroom, but it is worth it to be included in their high spirits and jokes.

3rd February 1999
VISIT TO PUERTA VALLETA

Hello Everyone in the World on the old Internet. Isn't it a wonderful invention, when it works? This letter must be all about the most heavenly weekend I have had for ages. It was at Puerta Valleta, north of Acapulco, and absolutely divine. I can't find words to describe it actually.... It was at the invitation of Maria and her family and a lovely getting-to-know-you time.

The journey there - four hours in a pick-up truck with six headboards in the back and four people in the front (one of them a six month pregnancy actually) - was wonderful. Claudia, the expectant mum, told me on the way that she was having a girl according to the scan but they both wanted a girl, which is unusual in Mexico. She also told me that our infant mortality rate is the highest in Europe but that one in ten mothers die in childbirth in Mexico - strong stuff.

It was an air-conditioned pickup, and we were sitting high up with views of mountains, cowboys in cowboy country, extinct volcanoes with lava, jacaranda trees (large orange flowering shrub), coconut trees, crops of pineapple, tobacco, papaya, agave - the cactus that tequila is made of, cinnamon and, best of all, we had a lovely driver and I wasn't scared to death of the other terrible driving I witness all the time here.

We stayed with Maria's sister and her 80 year old American husband, John, who was sweet in an elderly American way. He was a health freak and living proof that you can live a long time if you are thin. In his youth he had making the bomb "bay" for the B29 that dropped on Hiroshima and then worked for Boeing for years. They now have a Christmas tree business and his Mexican wife is the successful co-ordinator and personnel controller, John said with pride. There is a twenty year age difference and he told me he married her because she promised to produce children right away. Their three sons are embarrassed by her poor English but I certainly enjoyed talking to her. They have this wonderful house with a view of the sea which has to be seen to be believed, a garden full of horticultural exotica and a barbecue platform serving slices of beef (well, half a cow really) and prawns in delectable sauce, and salads to die for.

We ate at various cafes and restaurants - there were many and various for the hundreds of tourists - mostly American. At the Fuenta de la Puenta they played Mariachi music and Roll out the Barrel and the song Guadalahara, while we ate cheese nachos and drank pina coladas. The palm trees and clean roads and comfortable driving made the whole experience pleasurable and the most amazing aspect for me was the number of absolutely enormous American people!

Lunch one day was at Zacualco, which was a very Mexican cafe where I ate giant prawns in butter and had in depth talks with Rose Alba, Hilda and April, about cock fighting - like you do! Anita told me that her brother in law breeds cocks for betting on. Loads of money is involved, especially when you buy your own cockerel. They cost 200 to 500 pesos and can win 600 pesos a time for their owner. They are about two years old when they are ready to fight to the death apparently with blades on their legs.....

We lurched from one wonderful restaurant to another all weekend, eating bean and cheese nachos, huge tall glasses full of prawns, tostadas - crispy pancakes covered in shredded fish, tomato or peppers, and a nasturtium omelette which was breakfast in a millionaire's restaurant under time-share condominiums in the marina. Oh, and of course chilled beers on the beaches and pina colladas in cafes where you are serenaded by bands playing Roll out the Barrel as well as Mexican favourites - am I making you sick? There's more!

The swimming was from a beach in view of the house in clear blue water with rolling white tipped waves, pelicans circling pairs in a clear blue sky, and the most delectable HEAT - sun every day.

We left John reading the paper in a little park, and drove slowly round the lovely coast road. It was clear to see why it had been used as location for films. We enjoyed beers with squeezed lemon and salt licked from you hand, in a cliff-side restaurant surrounded by pine trees and reached by paths made of slices of wood set in cement and edged with bamboo handrails.

Maria's sisters were smart and immaculate and had delicate gestures and manners but earthy humour of the "Can you smell fish? Close your legs, girls" type. Maria was a different person when she was with her sisters and just laughed when I said she looked years younger. She says I should be there when there are five sisters present.

All good things come to an end and I returned to a pretty hectic week at school. It was called Cultural Week and there were competitions and concerts all the time. We (the English teachers) had to organise English productions to prove that pronunciation, team effort, humour, standard and content were good. 'My' team rehearsed Hey Jude (Beatles are still the tops here) and took my advice on hippy outfits, roll-ups, incense etc. for props, and went off to rehearse. However, on The Day, they did a completely different song; there were only two hippies and only two English sentences!

Today we had to ask groups of four at a time to answer five quiz questions in English. It was a scream. Apart from 'What is your mother's brother called? Answer Alfredo, or My Grandmother, they thought that the English Queen's name was Freddie Mercury.....

Will close now and send you all love and hugs and please don't let your envy of my life-style stop you writing to me, will you? I promise not to go on about it so much next time.
Jenny

I went to an open-air cafe called Green Brolly in the centre of Guadalahara yesterday with two of the volunteers and we got talking to a man called Lars who had the first digital camera I have ever seen. He told us he would e-mail the pictures he had taken, and showed us on a tiny screen what they would be like. I thought him very friendly, but Tom said he should leave the L off his name, and wasn't impressed with his camera. Tom had a sore throat and his host had told him to strip off and had plastered him in Vick but he still felt poorly. He was also distressed because his credit card had been swallowed by the machine one night (when he was tipsy) and they hadn't been able to find it when it was opened up in the morning.

5th February, 1999
Have only just stopped crying, Mum and Dad, having received your letter about The Christmas from Hell! I just couldn't believe what I was reading - what a terrible, awful experience for you dad, and how absolutely unlike anything that usually happens to you two. We thought it was the end of the world when you had your heart attack, mum, but that was quite well-organised compared with all the lurching about the hospital that you endured in the night, dad. And then falling behind the door and getting temperatures and Oh, I can't bear to think about it. I would certainly not have had such a good time at Christmas if I had known all about it. It was certainly blissful being ignorant.

My little E-Mail operator has arrived to send this message to you. She is a beautiful girl, a secret smoker, 15 years old, but absolutely on my wave length in all aspects of life - brings me cups of camomile tea in twos, laughs at my jokes and tells me when my feet smell, etc.

I can't wait for your Friday Fone call and news of your Unmentionable Organ, dad - hope it stood up (!) to the operation and of course I wish you the speediest of recoveries and send all my love and hugs to you both. XXX

20th February 1999
VISIT TO TEQUILA
Another lovely trip with the volunteers - this time to Tequila! Had to be good, didn't it? The bus ride to the town was only the beginning of the adventure. Picture this: most of the passengers were Argentinian polo players who knew lady polo players in teams from London. Mariachi musicians played trumpets up and down the bus while Mexican Luis (Teach Abroad co-ordinator), Luis Trellis (Gorgeous) Francisco, looked deep into my eyes with his very brown ones and explained at length how my popularity in Mexico is due to my reflected positivity. I had trouble with this because outside the window were Mexican horsemen in Stetsons, fields of cactus and volcanic eruptions and similar excitements. We went to a Tequila factory and saw the whole fascinating process. It was explained to Irish, French, English and Mexicans by a trilingual Nancy. She told us it takes about eight to ten years to mature the agave plant. The outside leaves are chopped off with an ancient tool, which was demonstrated by an ancient man. They are then cooked in a huge oven but prior to this we tasted slices and it was lovely. We looked at the fermentation tanks and were told that the bacteria is produced naturally and then fought off by other bacteria introduced by someone swimming in

the tank! Ten kilo of cactus makes five litres; the 'babies' are planted just before the rainy seas; only one weeding is needed per year and no watering ever needed.

We were then asked to sing a drinking song, and the French did very well but we English couldn't think of one. After visiting a shop or two for tastings we all had a jolly 'getting to know you' session with the Etonian, Cheltenham, Amplethorpe-type, aristocratic, rich children that are my fellow volunteers. They are all going to do maths, three languages, physics and worse at Cambridge!

En route to Tequila (hic!)

27.2.98
EXTRA TEACHING WORK
I am feeling very uncomfortable about having no money and called one day at the Canadian English School nearby.
A U.S. (less) woman gave me the 'don't call me, I'll call you' bit but gave me a quiz/application form which a charming Rodrigues (Mormon) helped me with in the waiting room. He even knew about past participles and present subjunctives . In the space where it asked about phrasal verbiage or verbal phrasing, I put "I don't have a clue" and the Boss Lady said she didn't either - she'd change the form! Several other promises of private tuition came to nothing and I found the Mexican people very lax about appointments and I suppose that is why they find British people very punctilious and pull our legs about turning up on time for anything.

12.1.98
THEATRO DEGOLLADA
Lovely night at the theatre - a fifty piece Philharmonic orchestral concert. We gained entrance for nothing and couldn't sit together but that didn't matter of course as the two hours just flashed by. There were soloists, choristers, a pointy-toed, very enthusiastic conductor, a hair-waving solo violinist and lots of pom, pom, pom 'down in the forest' type music.

After this treat we met up with Luis and the others in the Green Brolly cafe in the main square, but they all looked miserable so some of us went to find another recommended cafe which turned out to be a Gay Bar! They served chitterlings and sausages and popcorn free with their very nice beer. The clientele looked miserable here, too, but the waiter was lovely. He played something for us on the nickelodeon and gave Christine his telephone number. He was a part time policeman and worked there when he was off duty. We found it all very enjoyable and shared a taxi home in a giggly mood.

24.2.98
SCHOOL
At school I had trouble remembering who wrote Tom Sawyer. I was struggling here but bravely refuted their insistence that it was Oliver Twist and resorted to asking if Anyone knew? Happily someone did, and the next question was "What is your wife's name?" One pupil told me he has 63 cousins because his mother has ten brothers and sisters. Several pupils say I am known as the "English who said Happy Bum to everyone instead of Happy New Year". Well apparently it should have been Feliz Ano instead of Feliz Anyo - an easy mistake?

Today being Ash Wednesday we had tuna-filled puff pastry because we mustn't eat meat. They were called panadas. Other delicacies to date: crispy baguettes filled with diced cold meat and drowned in tomato soup - these are called Hogarbadas. Followed by coffee-flavored tequila, I can recommend them. Salsa Geubona is called Lazy Sauce because you don't cook it - just dice tomatoes, onions, chillis, and peppers and douse it all in lemon juice and serve like chutney on top of tasty cheesy baguettes.

1.3.98
NATURE
The poinsettia was pruned today in our garden - savagely and brutally attacked is more like it, but they just flourish in spite of it. Rosamanrada - a tree with pink AND purple flowers on it, and pallofiero (Ironwood) grow in this garden. This last takes 200 years to grow and has huge yellow flowers . The hard wood is used to sculpt anything and everything and you see dolphins, lions etc. made out of it, everywhere. Colibri are little humming, hovering birds which aren't much bigger than dragonflies and there are several in this garden. The Burrowing owl is one I can't claim to have seen but an environmentalist here was thrilled to have seen it yesterday. It is rare, even here, and she said they would measure where it had come from by the

isotopes on its feathers. She mentioned that hedgehogs are endangered here too.

Walking about is fascinating . You pass things like a man sitting on a giant plastic woman's hand-shaped chair, at the corner of my street, mending something to do with cars. Then a van overtook me with a man painted on the rear of it with a brake light on his head and the advert written underneath him was CONSTIPACION? There are little piles of rear lights at each intersection in the road and a music man plays several instruments and bangs on windows up and down the streets, begging. The maids of each household sweep away every leaf, branch or litter, and wash down the pavements before it is light.

3.3.98
VOLUNTEERS
I accompanied one of the new volunteer teachers, to a Lutheran Church service, where we were made very welcome. She had been a bit weepy but I think the service helped her. I was pleased to introduce her to Angela the organist who, to my surprise I discovered had taught at my own Grammar School in Ipswich, years ago. She loved meeting the Minister and his wife Rebecca and their babies. I couldn't believe that I actually stood and sang "I am Jesus' Little Lamb" but it was in a good cause, wasn't it?

A lovely volunteer, called Hadley talked his mother and father into bringing me a huuuuge packet of PG tips when they came to have a holiday with him. Yesterday that gift coincided with the Director of Teaching Abroad bringing me a packet from Harrods! I was photographed with a box under each arm, looking VERY happy.

I recently boogied the night away in two fantastic nightclubs! They mostly played salsa and the Western music was all sixties and seventies. I met a boy from Ipswich who was ghastly posh and insisted he was from Henley. He was most anxious to tell me he went to Amplethorpe School and his actual words when I said I was from Ipswich were "How embarrassing!" So I don't know what to make of that. That was before he saw my dancing display too! Drinks and admission were free for women and it was a wonderful old place and the temperature and atmosphere were superb.

E-Mail message to the World from Jenny in Mexico:

Imagine this: bougainvillea, jacaranda, avocados, papaya breakfasts, smiling people, brown-eyed babies borrowed for a hug, three weeks' post from you all (thanks so much), oompah bands, brown-eyed, long-eye-lashed men saying nice things, kiwi fruit, dancing in night clubs to Beatles music - mucho decibels - while explaining the differences between Protestantism and Catholicism. Add sunburned ear tips after my rather unusual haircut, mangos, Busy Lizzy TREES, poinsettia hedges, humming birds the size of dragon-flies, Mozart Requiems in a cathedral-like theatre and you'll get the flavour of life here. I waited for a bus home from the theatre with four or five ladies who turned out not to be waiting for the bus and my host explained what they WERE waiting for...... I digress: more lovely things: pineapples, coconut trees, banana trees in flower and, and, and....!

All replies welcome - love and hugs from Jenny.

5.3.98
FAUX PAS
Oh dear, I have offended the Pavarotti look-alike Temo that used to love me! I returned a t-shirt which he had loaned me for a sports event. I didn't wear it because I felt it would look partisan with only one of the school team colours on it. And also it was too big by far. Well, this was apparently the worst thing I could do and he took it very badly and told everyone he was going to throw it in the rubbish. I did a letter explaining my reasons and went round to apologise but I hated not being in favour with him, I must say.
He kept giving me cold looks for ages and then came round a bit and admitted he has trouble controlling anger when riled and looses his cool easily. My cause was also helped when a Canadian told him that anyone from their country would do the same as me.

I only discovered my second faux pas months later but apparently the teachers all gossiped about my inappropriate dress at the Posada (PTA) because I wore a loose clothes and sandals. Ah well! I always feel slightly on edge about offending people in different countries - one has to gauge their reactions to our humour and practices and you only realise the extent of anxiety this imposes, when you come home and flop.....

6.3.98
POZOLA
All of a sudden the other evening a Pozola (Mexican dish) cooked by my hostess's mum, was announced by telephone and we all leapt into the car to go and share it, even though everyone had been tired, ill or something a minute before. Only Son wasn't allowed to go because he had failed to deliver two home-works. Everyone else tucked into the pig's head cooked with onion, oregano and stock. You broke off pieces of meat and it was served with lemon, lettuce and salt. While waiting for it we all watched Marlborough ads on the TV. and coughed together - very sociable. It occurred to me we were all hogging a hog.....

It is interesting to see how the 'youngies' are settling in - or not. One girl, who is a rowing champion - 25th in Britain - was delighted to find cheap contact lenses on sale here, and
a very good gym with rowing machines. Several are pleased with Spanish lessons. They are SO bright and quick at picking it all up.

Sarah and Alice are fed up because their host families imposed curfews, and they thought they had finished with all that. One lovely timid boy is agonising because he found three shotguns under his bed. He is rather 'camp' and has a hard time with the Mexicans, they are so 'anti', you wouldn't believe it.

7.3.98

I am moving to Maria's house soon. The girls want me to continue to visit even when I move away, and it isn't far from them, so that will be nice. They wanted to come to a Teaching Abroad BBQ because they love two of the boys, but they telephoned me to say that unhappily for them, their grandfather was coughing up blood and they all had to go to see him! Their staunch sense of family never fails to amaze me.

Today the younger girl lost all her sister's work on the computer but she didn't berate her at all, and even when there *is* a noisy altercation, you can bet they will be smoking and playing cards on the computer together, within no time. One of them NAME just grinned at me, apropos of nothing, and said she loved the duty-free cigarettes that one of the UK volunteers gave her - much better than her usual make. She was telling me about the wedding she had just been to: there were 1, 200 guests and 200 bodyguards or chauffeurs outside. There were candles both sides of the road to the reception and ten bridesmaids wore varying shades of purple. There was a mass held at 1 a.m. and the celebrating went on until 3 a.m.

7.3.98

SARAH's BIRTHDAY

Sarah had a birthday so we all met at Hogarcasa, which is a lovely Taverna. There were jugs of beer and tequila and a birthday tradition was a lot of fun. A quantity of tequila is forced down the throat of the birthday person and their head shaken about for luck. Danny told me it is called Shaky-Shaky - I am very glad it wasn't me.

During this evening I was in the loo, revelling in the difference between Mexican and Chinese loos, when a hand came under the door with some toilet paper. Someone, somewhere knew it had run out in my booth. We all drank tequila and I walked - in a very wavy fashion - with Laura who talked gibberish all the way to our homes. The others went on to a night club - even Alice - so I don't know how she squared that with her hostess and the curfew.

10.3.98

MARIA's HOUSE

The girls escorted me to Maria's and I returned to their house after a couple of days with a huge birthday card and present for Theresa. Unfortunately the present dropped out on the way there. I then got lost coming back to Maria's and they were all horrified that a man I asked the way, gave me a lift.

I am installed in a downstairs room and there is a lovely little garden where I can read, learn Spanish, eat papaya and drink pots of tea. There are quails eggs, double cream, home-grown oranges for juicing etc. in their 'fridge and they have a maid. Maria is an English teacher at 'my' school and her husband Hugo is an architect who works in Quertero There are two boys left living at home. Maria is lovely and seems to like having company and hearing about my travels and life, as a grandmother, and "on the road". I think I seem rather strongly feminist to Maria, but we were to have some lively discussions on the topic

11.3.98
AMATITAN FOR BARRELS
En route to this town, Mari told me of her problems getting a good maid, and how the last one had loved her husband. She had come home to find a bite mark on his neck one day. He said he was defending himself! He certainly rules the roost and she has turned down an invitation to work for a friend for six weeks in the summer in Chicago because her husband doesn't want her to. He lives and works miles away most of the time but when he speaks she jumps.

We went to this town of Amatitan, (pop.10, 000) which was miles away from home, to collect some gift barrels of tequila which had to be specially engraved for Maria's husband to give to his colleagues. Well she forgot the paper with the names on, so we had to go twice! It took all day but I thoroughly enjoyed the journey, looking at the cactus (the one that tequila is made from) and sugar cane and admiring the gourds being sold in villages for water-carrying or ornaments. We lunched on chilli con carne - very spicy and nicy - and drank beer and apple-juice and got to know each other. I learned that Mexicans would never be honest enough to pay the cash at petrol pumps - there has to be a man piping it in and taking the money. I was also intrigued to learn that they mostly measure distances to places in hours travelling, not kilometres.

15.3.98
GUANAJUATO
I hoped to meet the rest of the volunteers in their hotel in Guanajuato, where we were doing the tourist bit, but I arrived too early. I found a cheaper hotel for me for one night (in retrospect I think it was a brothel!) and wasted the afternoon away in a nearby café. They provided hot milk with a separate metal jug of strong coffee and along came an old man in a sports jacket who serenaded me with "Because, Because, Because!" He had a plastic bag full of shopping hanging off his guitar.

I watched the television in this café and marvelled at the media offerings - I couldn't believe an ad which showed us a Wings ad which revealed everything except the actual emission, and a horrid one for osteoporosis which demonstrated a rotten old branch in a woman's shape, snapping sickeningly!

When I did meet the boys and girls, they were so lovely and pleased to see me that I drank more tequila than was good for me and they decided I should be escorted back to my hotel. Apparently the police diverted us on the way, to avoid bomb blasting operations in a road-improving scheme but I am ashamed to say I remember nothing of that! Next morning I found a sweet note written in lipstick, by Elli, saying where and when they would meet me in the morning.

I loved Elli - she was from Guildford and going to Leeds University after her Gap year. Both she and her friend were embarrassed to mention their private schooling. She had shaved her head to come to Mexico and it was now a very short crew-cut. She was a confident, relaxed girl, on her first independent journey but it seemed to me as if she'd been born to travel. She booked my coach ticket home when she did the others, and even looked at the screen in the agency and picked me a seat near them. She told me she considered me 'loose' as opposed to 'tight' - I just hope she didn't mean 'screw loose'.

We trekked into three churches and enjoyed weddings in all three. In one the minister looked like the Pope and we saw him drinking from a flask behind a column. In another the bride made very wobbly responses to the ministers and the reading was given by a family member through the microphones which were supplied for all participants. There were 'trippers' in and out all the time and altar-boys in black who swung incense; everywhere was painted gold and there was a golden copy of the altar sold next door to the church as a fire-guard. There were huge green and white floral displays at the altar of one church and twenty huge candelabras lit the ceremony.

This town is famous for its' Mummies and I walked up a mountainside early one morning when all the visitors and villagers were rushing off to Mass. I walked through the first 'rough' area I had seen in Mexico but I found a cafe with a washing line strung between cacti and asked for Nescafe. The owner was beating egg whites and stopped to scoop water out of an unsavoury pot when it wasn't boiling, so I declined it and asked for bottled water instead. Meanwhile another customer enjoyed - very noisily - a soup bowl full of the innards of the most globular intestinal variety I have ever seen.....

I joined an American group (SAGA types) for the tour of the Mummies and an Omar Sharif look-alike told us all about them. It only takes five years to mummify in this clay and the catacomb was built when they realised how perfectly these bodies were preserved. It is 136 years since some of them were put there.

He showed us two German brothers who had died in a stagecoach accident and you could see where a jaw had stoved in. A Chinese lady illustrated on the ticket was in a sarcophagus-shaped coffin, standing up. The Mummies faces looked horrified to me, but the guide suggested that if you were a pessimist you could think all these open mouthed, chest-clasping bodies were in pain but, if you were like him, you imagined they had died laughing....

A female in the case next to a foetus taken from her mother by a Caesarian operation, showed an incorrectly performed operation. One female from the village had drowned seven years previously and another had been buried alive because her cataleptic fit made her appear dead. 78 hours later she had to be buried again as she had managed to get out. She ruined her nails in the first attempt and for some reason tried to eat her arm. You could see that she was mummified with her arm in her mouth.

Omar offered the Americans a speedy exit if they didn't feel happy hearing all this and several of them did look uneasy. I thought the Mummies looked like papier-mache and it was bizarre to see elastic-waisted boxer shorts on one.

17.3.98
HOSPITAL
Yesterday Maria had a coronary in school! Before I heard about it, she had been taken to hospital, tested, been shopping, and gone home to cook the tea! Today I went with her for more tests and during one of them she became very poorly and a consultant advised an immediate operation.

San Javier was a very posh hospital, owned by a drug dealer, who kept the bullet-proof penthouse suite for his own use, or for his relatives. The doctors all wore white and the female nurses had sexy trouser suits and several male nurses had trusses over their trousers, to help with lifting patients. There were cellular 'phones everywhere, babies in little glass 'pods' so that you could see them, visitors watched televisions at every bed, and there was a very busy Interflora section.

Maria was saying her prayers and I was holding her watch and her handbag and trying to guess what everyone was saying. Maria didn't like the Permission to Operate form and wanted her husband to confirm that they could go ahead, and that the operation was really necessary - she thought the medical people just wanted the money! She said she was ever so pleased I was there with her, and told me the operation had been found necessary due to the tests showing that she couldn't cope with stress.

Another doctor was called for a second opinion and Maria's husband telephoned that they should go ahead. He then set out for the hospital by road. I had persuaded Maria to sign by then but her poor son was rushing about, white-faced, and other relatives sat with very sad faces and made no attempt to tell me what the doctors were saying.

It took about an hour -no general anaesthetic - to find that her 'tubes' were 75% occluded and her cholesterol level unbelievable. She was told not to eat or drink anything nice ever again but allowed to go home. Her son dressed her and she appeared clutching flowers and a video of the procedure, and smiling - what a star!

I got brownie points for supervising everything but it was nightmarish because of not knowing the language and all that I have said about 'getting on well with learning Spanish', is lies.

She is now home and I am eating her grapes and chocs. and telling her to keep her feet raised, and what not to eat, and how she should give up the stress of work. She currently has three teaching jobs but cannot face the thought of retiring. Lucky for me, I can do all her classes and hopefully go on holiday with her next week.

I have reflected on her life-style and whether I could cope with knowing my husband had another family – which is so common here. Maria was apparently maintaining all those teaching jobs with the fear that if she gave them up she would not ever be able to be independent of her husband, should he 'dump' her. Her sons were obviously comfortable with their father's role and I felt that they would happily copy his example.

I feel so happy that my own amicable divorce was achieved by simply dividing our goods and chattels in half. (Friends asked how this would be managed – "Who will have your pine dresser, your grandfather clock etc.?" I assured them that Bob and I were not materialistic at all and there would be no problem because I would have everything.....! How contented I am, on looking back, that we didn't even fall out over this sometimes acrimonious area of a divorce, leaving us free to enjoy our new lifestyles – me Town Mouse, he Country Mouse.

Mothers' Day
Maria had a fridge/freezer delivered for her Mother's Day present. It was as big as my kitchen! The deep freeze is from floor to ceiling on one side and the normal 'fridge on the other. The doors contain an ice-making gadget that spills out cubes into your drink. I can't imagine my dismay at having to be pleased to accept *furniture* that everyone in the family needed – for Mother's Day! People here even give other peoples' mums presents. A neighbouring mum had a full Mariachi band serenade her at 2.30 a.m. - six songs trumpeted up and down the road beneath her bedroom! This is quite a normal custom apparently but I thought they were in my bedroom when they first started up, and definitely would *not* have enjoyed this offering for myself.

10.4.98
MELAQUI
Three English girls and I have been offered work in Melaqui and it sounds more like the sort of work I anticipated when I came. We had completed our school work in Guadalajara and many of the teachers went on to do projects with environmental aims, and I liked the more philanthropic ideas offered for this period.

The Education authority in Melaqui were going to offer our services to the poor people of the village, from a van with a loudspeaker on top - free to anyone who would like to improve their spoken English. Marianne, Lisa and Mary are agreeing to come only if I come too, as they have had no teaching experience. I am very happy to concur, since it is four weeks on the beach. They are rather 'precious' girls but make me laugh, and I knew right away that they appreciated my help over the teaching bit.

I was going to leave Maria but to return after this spell 'on the beach'.

E-Mail Message on 16th April

At the risk of being boring, and because I have the chance to e-mail which is rare in this little town, here is another story to make you hate me: the pelicans are still circling, the sun is still shining, the sand is white, rolling waves are green and white, coconut and banana trees still shade me as I lay in a hammock with loads of lovely paperbacks that the three English girls I live with have loaned me.....

The village of Melaqui's Director of Education annoyed (?) the village and the resulting 66 Mexican children and six adults are now repeating "Oi am Noin (years old), this is a Poinapple and Froiday is my next lesson", with gusto! True Suffolk graduates.

Lisa is co-teaching the under-privileged in the village hall with me and ... and .... are teaching in a proper school. We share the cooking and have one eating out day and one de-tox day. This means we only cook once a week and on de-tox day we have the most joyful fruit and veg. to choose from, so it isn't a problem.

Sometimes the water goes off and sometimes the mosquitoes are very bad, but life is generally wonderful. I wake about 9 a.m. have a pot of tea and biscuit on the balcony, looking up the very rural street or out to the hazy, film-set sea, framed by palm trees. A walk into 'town' is a bit like being on a Western film set, then shopping for shells or fruit and vegetables or clothes. The clothes are gorgeous but of course way beyond my current pocket.

I am just off to a beach cafe for Happy Hour with a lot of wrinkly, retired Americans and Canadians and post-menopausal foreigners in caftans, but the cafe is situated in Bounty Ad surroundings and the walk home is along the beach with the sun setting and, and, ooooh I am embarrassed to tell you about it again.
Love and hugs to everyone, see you in June, Kiss Kiss

Melaqui beach belles

24.4.98

Yesterday some children were leaning on the door early with a four month old puppy and a red rose (head only) from someone's garden - presents for us. We have now split the class in two to make it more manageable. Lisa was unhappy about doing this initially, but they love her so much and encourage her, and she is fine about it now. They produce art work about right for their ages, and make us laugh so often - a picture today entitled Walter Melon (a slice of water melon) and another entitled Bog (a dog of course). They love Head and Shoulders and Hokey Kokey - to learn parts of the body. Their names are wonderful - Esmeralda, Ophelia, Blanca etc.

After school we take a tin of weak but beautiful beer to the beach and swim and then we meet the other two girls at home and hear about their day. They are doing twice as long as us in a local school but they have desks and the company of other teachers so manage well, and we have offered to wash up all the time after they do their turn cooking.

The Americans and Canadians that live and holiday here in the winter have mostly gone home now but a lovely American neighbour has just given us her 'leftovers' - food, stationery, toiletries etc., because she is going home - and it was a real bonus because we are very hard up. She told us that Robert Redford flies in to eat octopus from time to time! I hope we get to taste it but I don't think our budget will allow!

30.4.98

Lisa and I have been introduced to an Education Department person called Eloise and she has arranged seating for our class room (no desks) and paper cups and water daily for the teachers. We cobble together a syllabus in the evenings, but Lisa has no self-confidence and finds the whole episode a bit of a worry. The kids love her of course and call out to her in the street and ask to come on Saturdays and Sundays. I feel we are making progress even though we couldn't keep the bigger boys.

I've mastered body surfing the huge waves here - necessary to get in and out of the sea - and I only limp a little bit from a previous rather inelegant exit. I love watching the wonderful rollers but sometimes wish one could walk slowly into the aquamarine velvetiness and laze about in calmer water. I have to brace my old body to undertake the challenge of the waves, they are so high.

One evening in Pipers' Bar, Barra de Navidad - a lovely bar about half a mile along the beach from our home - I accepted a dishy American's proposal of marriage! He said he adored my chapped lips and he found my British accent irresistible. He showed his photos of Activity Holidays, which he plans with his friends, but he declined to see my granny photos. He said he would pick me up for a beach picnic and I need only bring my thong! Anyway, since that night I have been playing hard to get and have been pretty successful of course.....

2.5.98
BIRTHDAY
The girls gave me the happiest birthday imaginable. They prepared a special breakfast on our balcony that overlooks a bird-and-hyacinth-congested lagoon on one side and the Pacific rollers on the other. Mary made a wonderful savoury scrambled egg breakfast with toast and freshly squeezed orange juice. They gave me a red Mexican dress which I'll probably never take off and I was really impressed when a huge cockroach came out of the sleeve which I had immediately tried on, and Eva who is really scared of them, flapped it out of the way. What a star!

In the evening I was given a special Birthday Drink at the Pipers' Bar, which involved igniting Kalua in a glass and then submerging it in brown beer. It was quite delicious and a bit of a relief because I had been fearing the tequila-in-your-mouth-and-wag-your-head about birthday treatment that I had seen previously!

I enjoyed my first octopus fried in garlic buttered breadcrumbs as well as some squid. This was a celebration of the fact that the Teaching Abroad people had reluctantly wired us some money for food because we had run out. Mary and I walked home along the brightly moonlit beach and Marianne and Lisa stayed on to talk to the Americans.

10.5.98
COOKING
The cooking rota is going well this week - Lisa did spaghetti bolognaise. Mary (only 18) made moussaka and fruit salad, and I did onion bhagees, baked potatoes and stuffed peppers. The baked Banana Surprise was more of a shock than a surprise - the plates weren't as oven-proof as they looked, and exploded in the oven......

The next shock was an earthquake in the night, but I didn't wake so it couldn't have been too serious.

12.5.98
I am intrigued with the girls' personalities and the differing opinions that are coming up now that we have settled in to the flat. Lisa had a tantrum when we were late to dinner, Mary is doing Lisa's share of chores as well as her own, Marianne invited two more teachers to come and stay with us for the weekend without mentioning it to us, and Lisa has sort of 'sulks' which we now realise are not personal to any of us, and all leave things like rubbish, laundry, complaints to the management of the holiday accommodation, washing up, and cleaning to me! As regards tidying up, I know that I am what the Americans call anal retentive, so I try to accept it is *my* problem that I hate everywhere looking so squalid because I am the only one who cares about it.

Our social life is not impressive - we are invited to things by Mexicans and Americans, but then not collected or 'phoned when the time comes. This is apparently how Mexicans view life - their attitude to time-keeping is the same. In the course of a long conversation with Luis about Mexicans' unreliability, he had this theory to offer: He thinks that Mexicans don't turn up for appointments and don't mind if you don't follow up invitations, because the intention was in their hearts and they are more spiritual than us. He also thinks that is why they don't mind saying goodbye because you remain with them in spirit and never really leave them, even though you are physically parted.

However, we unexpectedly did get collected for a lovely Canadian Lasagne Party. A trio of drinkers from the Pipers' Cafe, picked us up in a beautiful, air-conditioned car, whisked us to a nearby town, and were really good company. The delicious lasagne had been cooked by a neurotic Canadian who didn't come to the party until long after we had eaten her offering

I went to several hotels, begging to use their pools, but only one allowed it. The Lesbian owners charged us 30 pesos but it was heavenly and we used it frequently.

13.5.98
I have just peeled the skin off yet another nose and I have found the paperback swap shop! So pleased. It is mostly Catherine Cookson and Jackie Collins or Sci-Fi, but I found five that I will enjoy and it was fun talking to Book Bob, who has been there 25 years. He runs a bistro as well and there is no charge for the book swapping. There is a collage of photos of all the tourists that have visited him, on one wall of the shop.

Another local character is a John from Islington, who lives in the Monterrey Hotel. He is 75, dribbly and bald but we talked for ages about Flanagan and Allen and others at the Palladium and he reckons he is 'going to send his car' for me to talk some more. He is waiting for his grand piano to arrive from England. He was very deaf, and I have the same problem since coming to Melaqui. I suppose it is the sand forced into my ears by the ocean but I can only hear loud speech and my posh flat-mates must find me such a dimwit, having to repeat everything. I noticed that the kids' Spanish is easier for me than the mumbled Sloane chat at home!

I am still enjoying life here in Melaqui but must admit the domestic situation is challenging. I sometimes have to go for a walk so that I don't say what I think when I find the sink full of pots and pans used for scrambled egg, porridge or spaghetti burn-ups. Part of me wants to leave it, but the other part says we'll have no clean pots to make supper with... They didn't seem to think my housework rota was a good idea and after only a few days I had to tear it up with a smile and as much nonchalance as I could muster. That did promote a flurry of help but it didn't last.

14.5.98
There had been no rubbish clearance, shopping or fridge or cooker cleaning done, one morning, and one of the girls complained of a smell of "poo". I

suggested it might be the unwashed and overflowing rubbish bin, which was her job, and she glared and said she didn't feel well. I have to admit I did a very evil smile when I heard her being sick....

E-Mail on 16th May,98
Hello Darlings in England!

Thanks for the post, delivered to me by the gorgeous Luis. Glad to tell you I am still loving it here - especially the 'teaching' - but the most dramatic happening was when a party of volunteers came for the weekend and laid about on the sand looking like white, stranded bodies. They got pinker and pinker in the three days and thought we were very lucky to have this 'posting'.

One night they woke me up to tell me that three of them, who had been sitting on the beach talking, had disappeared. There was just an assortment of possessions in the dark, where they had been, and twelve foot waves were breaking on the beach, and shaking the flat. It was so scary, waiting and wondering where they were. Lisa said it had decided her against ever having children. I kept calm. But when she and Luis went searching for them and returned half an hour later, walking slowly down the entire length of the road towards the balcony where I was pacing up and down, without calling out "They're found", I reacted furiously with "Well You Could Have Bloody Well, Told Me!" In my defence I suppose it was like when you find your lost kid in the supermarket and give it a smack. I had been mentally composing telephone calls to their parents to say they wouldn't be coming home!

Another happier story: an American called Colin invited Mary and I to join some friends on his yacht on Sunday. It was called Get Reel, 120 feet long, and twelve million 'bucks' worth. There were gleaming, scrubbed decks and brass rails and we loved seeing all the other yachts in the marina and on the high sea. One of the hosts cooked a waffle, syrup and bacon breakfast and wonderful coffee, but, while I was sitting in the stern, Grace Kelly-like and humming True Love, seasickness overcame me and I had to sidle off to a more private part of the boat and discreetly and voluminously eject it.

Colin (sunglasses and bleached hair) told of his being kicked out by his parents because he was "too smart for his own good". He started selling jeans (three pairs in a cardboard box, he recalls) and is now wealthy enough to give his son a new Harley Davidson for his birthday. He lost a brother recently, aged only 50 years, so he says he is going to live life to the full from now on.

The conversation flowed - mostly about their efforts to translate the Bible into American so that Americans could understand it. I just hope it doesn't include the several dozen instances of the F word that our host considered necessary with every utterance.. To hear him saying "F----Moses was a stud to put up with all those F---Israelites giving him s---," etc. was a unique experience. There were little shoals of flying fish, little flocks of birds, and several good-sized dorado and manta ray were caught - using lures not live bait. One of the dorado weighed ten pounds and Colin filleted it professionally for us to take home. Oh and we saw dolphins!

Well I will 'cast off' sending love to all. The mosquitoes, bus-loads of tourists disembarking before dawn, and a swimming pool being built all day right in front of our flat do not detract from a blissful life with coconuts, banana trees, plump and beautiful children, humming birds, avocados and papaya and, and ...... XX Jenny

'Mummies'- an English class on the balcony at Melaqui

18.5.98

On our last day at 'school' the children were adorable and they are certainly going to miss us and us them. We came home to find that Mary and Marianne had been given - their words, not mine- Shit-loads of Presents! - the gifts from their students covered our dining table. There were masses of ornaments, jewellery and sweets and Lisa was very cross that *we* hadn't got presents too. I commented caustically that I would really have liked one of those Jesus-bleeding-on-the-cross ornaments, made of shells, which we had seen in the shops. Well, within minutes there was a knock at the door and there stood another grateful parent with, yes! a Jesus statue, complete with bleed, made totally of shells! How we kept serious faces I will never know......

We had little sleep on our last night at Melaqui because of a beach party but I must have slept some of the night because the girls heard me snoring. We had a divine last session by the pool with an avocado salad picnic and I finished my Kirk Douglas autobiography and the girls talked to another Lesbian couple from America who described a murder in their neighbouring cafe - the man was knifed by his best friend. We went to their cafe for a chilli con carne but I didn't think it was as nice as my soya recipe. The American friends told us that chilli con carne is not recognised as Mexican!

A lovely Mother's Day present - a telephone call from my son to invite me to his wedding! A complete surprise, since he and Annabel have been together for years without marrying. Leigh was surprised too - he didn't think I would be able to come. Happily I had already changed my departure date to be at home for my mum's birthday. So pleased!

20.5.98

I returned to my dear Maria, who is still struggling with her new eating regime and fighting the suggestion that she gives up work. She welcomed me back so warmly, and reckoned - apropos of my being in hospital when she was taken ill - that I was a present sent by God! Bit over the top, eh? Her husband took us all to a marvellous restaurant - the Plaza - for steaks to celebrate Maria's cholesterol level being normal. The waiters were wearing starched white shirts with pink braces and there were geraniums everywhere, and fountains and sun-umbrellas at every table. I had chicken - tostada pollo - and Maria's husband gave me a lump of his steak to be sure that I appreciated the high standard of meat they have in Mexico. Maria and I shared a wonderful bottle of red wine (which cost twenty pounds) and it was just the right temperature and in a beautiful glass and Maria was confident it was medicinal on this occasion. Her son requested an Irish coffee called The Spectacular, and when they queried the lack of the advertised 'flaming', three waiters bought flame equipment and he was appeased. Maria took us through her operation again, her son and husband remonstrated with her about smoking. The men kindly spoke English to tell me that they didn't admire Lady Di because she should have stayed with her husband whatever he did or did not do. Their opinion is that women are emotionally stronger and can hold families together...... I badly wanted to explore this subject further in the light of Maria's husband's double life and to know if *he* was living with his second partner because Maria was strong enough to cope and he wouldn't be!

Farewell meal.

Another lovely meal was cooked for us by the Head of English Studies, ..., - paella with fish, chicken and pork in it, but the occasion was a bit strained because his wife was fed up with us all talking English which she couldn't understand. I must say I sympathised - I had done hours of nodding and smiling and pretending I knew what the Dickens they were all saying in Spanish.

26.5.98

A final outing to Dolores Hidalago, where Maria insisted on buying me a lovely cream linen dress for my birthday. I was thrilled with it and wore it for the wedding when I got home. She also bought me a metal bird cage which wasn't the easiest item to take on the plane but I am so glad I persevered. It is so Spanish and was admired all the way home.

I was so sad to leave these lovely warm people – my memories of Mexico will be of the paintings, the absolutely fabulous weather, the pottery, and most of all the people who are so passionate and fun-loving.

Although my intention had been to work in Mexico in an altruistic way, the fact that I played more than I worked was a very pleasurable experience. I had had a hard and challenging life in China, but after Mexico I felt rested and relaxed – as one would expect after a six months' holiday. Perhaps it was the best experience a granny could have, considering the lengthy times working in China and India which test people of all ages.

After the flight to England I caught a bus from Heathrow to Tring, via Hemel Hempstead. After being deposited at the bus stop near my daughter's home, complete with birdcage and luggage, I realised, too late, that she had moved while I was away and I didn't know which direction the new house was. A dear little man, who was mowing his grass, heard my story, scooped my chattels into his car and delivered me to my precious family who stood in a row with eyes popping when he deposited me and my possessions at their door!

A SPOT OF BOSOM BOTHER

This was one journey I didn't mean to take - the Cancer Journey. I had been living on an island, off Hong Kong for seven months, teaching English and having perhaps my happiest trip, when I got the 'phone call in the middle of the night that everyone dreads. My mum was dying in hospital in Ipswich. I gathered up all my 'stuff' and caught the ferry to Hong Kong Central and then to the airport and there was a seat spare on a flight that morning.

All went well through the flight and I caught the coach at Heathrow, but at the Ipswich end all did *not* go well! At 2 a.m. there were no taxis and I struggled on to a bus that went near to my father's house but it was full of men leaving a stag party dressed as women! The boys wanted me to admire their eye make up, and their tits, and other unspeakable demands, so I was impressed to overhear the bus driver patiently 'counselling' a boy/girl about his future - very sympathetically in the circumstances, I thought.

There was even a legless man in there, with his wheelchair parked on my foot, and when I thought I was near my father's house, only the help of two party-going *girls* enabled me and my luggage to fall off the bus.

I found that I was still too far from home to attempt to carry my luggage so I begged a complete stranger to give me a lift a couple of streets when he had just locked his car. Talk about a guardian angel.

The house was, of course, locked up and in darkness and I couldn't wake anyone for ages and when I did it was to hear that my mum had died. I am telling you all this because I subsequently read that suppressed emotion, or shock, has been suggested as a *cause* of breast cancer, and with all the questions and reading I have done since about causes, I reckon this was mine.

When, six months after my mum died, I discovered a lump at the base of my right breast, I couldn't believe it. I had lost a lovely friend to breast cancer a year before (hence my regular checking) and when I discovered *my* lump I was surprised at how *unsurprised*, calm and accepting I was, even though I had a feeling it was malignant. I felt very pessimistic about my chance of survival, however.

The mastectomy followed several prompt appointments given by my local G.P. and Ipswich Hospital and was predictably horrible but the staff were wonderful. The surgeon assured me that if I was him, he would have the surgery - it was a "life-saving operation", he said. Going on my theory that in my experience a trouble shared is a trouble multiplied, I kept the whole matter a secret from my family until I came home to my own house, after the appointments and admissions for lumpectomy, biopsies and all that stuff. I think I was avoiding pity and loss of independence and oh, everything seemed better when I shut the door on everyone else.

Another reason was because it happened so soon after my mother dying and I couldn't see the point of worrying family when there was nothing they could do except worry with me. I eventually had a go at telephoning to share the information but cried both times, so I asked everyone to coffee one sunny Sunday and told them in my garden. They all coped in their different ways, crying, going for counselling, being cross with me, etc. My daughter who is a very emotional and anxious person was the biggest surprise. She was an absolute rock right from the start and her optimism and good spirits - even humour - kept me going even though she lived so far away.

I did feel a desperate need to share my troubles with someone early on, though, and I sent off this email to my friends in Hong Kong but didn't say anything at home, because whenever I thought of *saying* the word Cancer, I cried.

From Jenny Hoggar on 18.05.01: Subject: jennymail
Hello Hong Kongers All:

Got a favour to ask of you! Please send me your prayers, vibrations, musings, etc. on 25th May - it is Mastectomy Time and I'm ever so scared but I can't tell anyone it is happening here because they are all either struggling or joyful about their lives currently - and because I find it impossible to talk about it without crying. Hence the email - wot a wonderful invention! Sorry this sounds Drama Queenish now I have written it but I value your friendships so much and wanted to share my dilemma! Love to you all, Jenny

This promoted lovely words back, as I had known it would, and I'm glad I saved them to tell you:

"I cannot believe what you have had to go through this year - annus horriblis? - Please know that we are all thinking of you, especially me as my mum went through the same thing last year. She did really well and is back to her old self with far more life than I will ever have".

"I send my good wishes to you. We've all got our fingers and toes crossed for you. You're such a great person with such a wonderful zest for life, that I'm sure it is just a temporary hiccup!"

"This is a time for nurturing yourself and being completely selfish - our thoughts and prayers will be with you on the 25th"

"From deep within the Hong Kong Government, I sincerely wish you good luck and best wishes for the operation. We will be sure to say a prayer for you and will be thinking of you this Friday. We were very sad to read the news and realise how hard it must be for you to tell your family but we do understand and admire you for it and are sure they'll love you even more for it."

"You are the world's favourite Angel from Ipswich and you are only just beginning your journey. Small comfort for the huge emotional and physical 'experience' that is ahead. I believe 'someone' thought you were strong enough to deal with this in this life, and that is why you are getting this card."

"I am sure the op. will go fine - the scars inside may take much longer but we are all willing you well soon and you will still be Jenny to us, albeit a bit lighter!....."

Weren't they lovely?

Look away now if you don't want to read the gory bits:-

There were two lumps apparently and both malignant so it was a good job I went early! I had no lymph gland involvement and suppose that is why I didn't have to have radiotherapy or chemotherapy and I only have to take a pill each day for five years to hopefully prevent recurrence. I am *so* lucky there.

I was always impressed with the service provided by the NHS - the staff were wonderful in every way and in every department. From the ghastly moment when the surgeon looked at me and said words like "invasive cancer, mastectomy and even *patient*, which have never applied to me before, he and an army of caring and efficient people saw me through what the surgeon had called the Cancer Journey.

On admission to Ipswich Hospital for a right mastectomy, I found the first of the books I had scooped up for company was about Amazonian women who volunteered having their bosoms orf to help them use their bows and arrows more efficiently in battle! How was that for good company? It was funny how many ordinary comments took on a whole new relevance - "making a clean breast of it" and "get it off your chest" were never going to be the same, were they?

The surgery was predictably horrible but the staff were wonderful - the nurses, anaesthetists, stretcher pushers, surgeons, volunteer counsellors, breast care nurses (who were subsequently always at the end of the phone for the black 'mental' moments when you get home), pharmacists, oh, absolutely everyone, were brilliant. They continued in the way of the Breast Screening Radiographers, and my local GPs and receptionists, who did the initial investigations. Fantastic, they were!

My English friends and family were as comforting as my Hong Kong friends had been and, from the minute I got home, and over the next five weeks, I got presents, invitations to go on holidays and forty seven cards! It is the very best 'attention-seeking' ploy you can imagine. This generosity was so warming and wonderful - here are some of the lovely things that arrived:

Flowers (7 bunches),

Sunflower plants,
Eel stew (cooked and delivered),
Wine ++,
Fruit ++,
Premium Bond winnings from friends who shared a recent win with their two daughters and me
Concert tickets,
A fur coat from the people for whom I had modelled big clothes in Hong Kong.
Herbal remedies,
A nude charcoal drawing of myself prior to the operation.
Thick lovely paperbacks from the Oxford Street Waterstones from visiting Americans en route to their home
Invitations for holidays in Ireland, Croatia and America.

Oh and two offers from cheeky men to examine my remaining bosom regularly......

After I left hospital, I wrote to the local newspaper to thank everyone involved in my medical treatment and recovery and tell how grateful and impressed I was. I headed it up A Spot of Bosom Bother and they printed it word for word and sent a reporter to tell more of my personal details - namely that I had lost my mum, my right breast, a nice statue of a pig from my front garden and my bike from outside the railway station!

There was an embarrassingly large photo of me but it was worth the 'cringe' factor to know from several people that it had helped them through their initial 'journey' to know that things get better as you adjust to the fact that *you* have cancer, and it really isn't too bad.

I have now read hundreds of books and talked to many professional people about the possible causes of breast cancer, because I feel I have always eaten and drunken sensibly, not smoked, and had what I thought was a stress-free life.

One autobiography written by an American woman who had the same size tumour as me, listed possible causes she found in her experience and research as:
Repressing emotions, especially anger and sadness
A period of major life change and stress and depression
Being too self critical
Eating too much animal fat in diet when young
Drinking too much coffee
Smoking ciggies
Precocious sexual activity at a young age
H.R.T. and The Pill
Change of structure in life
Divorce
House moves

Well I put my tick against most of those things but she went and *died* so I only think about her on bad days. I certainly made a mess of trying to smoke and as for sexual activity - well you didn't do 'it' before you were married in my day, did you?

I also found evidence from other researchers or sufferers that they thought these personality traits or experiences were common among breast cancer sufferers:-

Worrying about purpose in life
Internal pressure to find calling, work
Feeling lonely and hopeless as a child
Long-standing tendency to be self contained, independent and in control
Failure to vigorously pursue a spiritual path
Not having a partner
Family bound
Putting others before themselves
Altruistic

Perhaps keeping your anguish to yourself is a common thing among people who then have breast cancer, I don't know. I didn't share my fears with anyone and, according to several psychologists and psychiatrists; this secret-keeping could have been a contributing factor to my getting cancer of the breast. It is certainly the way I have always dealt with personal unhappiness or disappointment, despite being the biggest motor-mouth on all other subjects......

As soon as I was allowed to fly, I had a wonderful holiday in America with long-standing Ipswich friends who live there - a few days after 11th September. This trip certainly gave me something else to think about and stopped me being too self-absorbed.

I hated the carefully weighed and measured prosthesis (false boob) that was given me when the wound healed - I don't know why but I just hated it. I eventually threw it away - I wonder where in the U.S. it finished its' life.

On another trip - this time with a dear family to Croatia, I accidentally lost another cotton 'falsie' overboard from a yacht among the beautiful Croatian islands!

When I went for a check up at the hospital, the Breast Care Nurse listened to my complaints and - on spotting that my undies are all black - offered me a black prosthesis! How is that for thoughtfulness? I wore it happily until my second (voluntary) mastectomy, and Nurse told me to bring it back to her if I didn't want it as all surplus 'bits' get sent to India. I liked the thought of that.

I now can't say "That gets on my tits" but then it wasn't a very elegant phrase, was it? I was amused to note the time that friends mentioned something being an 'uplifting' experience, or someone being 'upfront' about something - they went red and embarrassed. Coffee being so strong it would've put hairs on my chest, doesn't get a chance now! A friend has just telephoned and, while looking out of her window and telling of the wildlife in her garden she suddenly yelled "Oh I've got two Tits!" and then apologised to me for boasting ……

In the early days after the first operation, my grand-daughter was anxious for me to have a boyfriend now that I am divorced. I explained to her that I was sincerely happy being single - and *alive* - even but she insisted I should write to the dating agencies in the paper. We both thought it would make an unusual plea - "One-bosomed woman would like to meet……and she didn't think I should put the bit about my *snoring* in, as that could put a suitor off!

So I am continuing my travels - Spain for the winter to write this and other stories - and I am so happy that the Cancer Journey has not stopped me from doing anything I want to do! I still have the cat, big armchair and be-gardened cottage to fall back on but my message to all on the Cancer Journey is "Go For It", whatever you have ever wanted to do - because you CAN.

Signed: Jenny (Breastless and Restless) (64).

AMERICA

NEW JERSEY
18th September 2001

I had been invited by old friends, Anne and Tony, to visit them for seven or eight weeks, to care for Anne who was due to have foot surgery. They have been living in the States for years and their children have taken up citizenship there, and I don't think they will return to Suffolk now. They live between their house in New Jersey and their house and Tony's work in a bank in Bermuda, and I am really looking forward to meeting up with them again and getting to know America on a domestic front as well as the tourist trail. It was, however, only days since the 9/11 tragedy, so my excitement was tinged with fear at facing up to the aftermath of such a ghastly day.

My normal excitement at the prospect of six months travelling in a foreign country was mixed this time with trepidation. I love adventures of this sort, but I didn't know how I would deal with the sadness and grief I would find, following the horrendous terrorist attack on America. I had been warned that passengers with compassionate grounds would take precedence on all flights to New York and so my seat was not guaranteed. However, on arrival at Gatwick I was never questioned and the pleasant tannoy messages asking for our patience at the delays, gave no indication of the chaos that had followed the hijacked flights.

Our flight from Gatwick was three hours late taking off, and it had taken me six hours longer to get through the normal boarding procedures because of increased security. Hand-baggage was examined by airport personnel who confiscated any combs, tweezers, knitting needles, scissors or similar sharp articles. Quite ordinary sized handbags were deemed too large and had to go with the luggage in the hold. Everyone was rigorously frisked but a scary and officious-looking examiner responded kindly to my plea for consideration of my newish mastectomy wound when she 'frisked' me!

The next passenger she checked was a young Jewish man who had to remove his tall black hat for examination at this point, and then replace it on top of a black skull-cap. I didn't know then that at least thirty men of this religion would keep us entertained with their constant removing and replacing of these hats (and long coats) throughout the trip. Since they had a long, lustrous ringlet of hair on each side of their pale, serious faces, and seemed oblivious to our stares, the seven and a half-hour flight passed quickly, watching their antics.

My first view of New York from the 'plane was through a late evening haze and from a considerable distance away as all planes now have to fly well away from the centre. Several people told me that the Statue of Liberty was normally clearly visible, but all I saw was the sun glinting on the glass of tall buildings in the far distance.

After landing, the journey to Mountain Lakes, New Jersey, took about forty minutes, by car, and the highways and signs seemed familiar because of those seen on films and TV. Our driver was my first experience of the friendly and warm welcome given by every American person I have met so far. Since then I have been impressed by how much more amiable and gentle they are. I haven't seen any evidence of road rage; I haven't seen a child smacked or yelled at in the supermarket; shop assistants ask *how you are* before they ask what you'd like to buy - and they wait for your reply! Anyone and everyone strikes up a conversation in cafes. I was not surprised to hear that 300 million dollars had already been donated by the American public for relief of suffering victims, since there seems to be a sincere regard for other people here and they just seem to *like* each other!

The TV film footage I watched here has been much more harrowing than the initial reports I saw in the UK. I have seen close-ups of blood and debris on the streets, people crying and running away, people hugging each other and comforting the hysterical or tearful survivors, and many more personal accounts immediately after the attack. No one could watch all this without tears streaming down their faces.

Flags are now flying outside every home, on cars and lorries and poking out of rucksacks being carried in the streets. Everywhere people are talking about how it was for them. A lady sitting next to me in a restaurant in a Mall told me of her daughter's proximity to the attack site, which they are now calling Ground Zero. She is a student at the New York University, 35 blocks away but when the woman described her feelings before she knew her daughter was safe, I started to cry and we abandoned conversation. On TV there are frequent appeals for money for the Red Cross and other charities and many different renderings of God Bless America which all bring a lump to your throat.

There is such a conflict of conscience around: I have heard of so many Americans in confusion about whether to continue with job interviews, stag parties, holidays etc. or whether to stay indoors and watch and suffer with their countrymen. I myself don't know whether to enjoy America or even continue journeying while there is such grief and suffering.

I must describe the beautiful house and garden where Anne and Tony live. Built in an area of similar, rather grand clapboard houses, it is on four floors, elegantly furnished but in a comfortable way, and with views from every window of huge trees with multi-coloured foliage.

I am cooking and tidying for my friends but there is a friendly, efficient cleaner who comes regularly, and all manner of dishwashers and dryers etc. which I hope to learn to manage and not break...... ooooooerr! Tony comes and goes from work in New York, and from overseas trips, so sometimes I cook for us all, and sometimes we go out to restaurants or to friends of theirs to eat. I am therefore having a very interesting and varied view of American life, but with the background of the tragedy which hangs over everyone.

179

Tributes in New York after 11ᵗʰ September 2001

One day a lady sitting next to me in a restaurant in a Mall told me of her daughter's proximity to the attack site, which they are now calling Ground Zero. She is a student at the New York University, 35 blocks away but when the woman described her feelings before she knew her daughter was safe, I started to cry and we abandoned conversation. On TV there are frequent appeals for money for the Red Cross and other charities and many different renderings of God Bless America which all bring a lump to your throat.

I feel guilty even enjoying the wonderful weather, but my first breakfast in a Diner took my mind off the problems for a while. It was called Westside Diner and a cheery waitress greeted us and showed us to our seats. There were very fat people everywhere and I watched in amazement at the size of the meals devoured by two men sitting on bar stools, wearing baseball caps. The friendly waitress interpreted the menu for me and there were so many exotic options it took ages! I learned that jam is called jelly and they eat it with the most unlikely things. I settled on spinach and feta cheese omelette with hash browns for my lunch and when it arrived there was enough for four people! All the omelettes are THREE egg omelettes and hash browns are delicious fried potatoes. I noted that there was also an egg-white omelette on the menu. It is expected that you take home what you can't eat. I just can't imagine what Americans think of our *normal* portions, let alone nouvelle cuisine. The enormous woman next to me was obviously a frequent customer! The excellent cups of coffee were refilled continuously. The waitress was very witty and Tony told the tale of when he returned his glass because of a lipstick stain on it, the waitress had called out for a replacement "because it was not his colour!'

More impressive food today - this time in a Mall in which we passed branches of Bloomingdales and Saks. There were dozens of Ladies Lunching and the choice was amazing. I didn't regret my choice of frozen yoghurt with about a quarter pound of walnuts covering it, muffins made with cranberries or carrots and raisins and just in case this wasn't enough, you could have butter and jam, to accompany them.........

Today on TV, Oprah Winfrey and a psychiatrist tried to help two survivors to tell their stories. Both broke into tears but admitted it had helped them to talk. One of them - just an ordinary chap who had been in a business meeting on the 105th floor - had survived and ran away from the debris. He said he felt guilty for running, but all he could think and say was "*I want to go home.*" Another woman on the programme - (not a New Yorker) - said she just wanted to remain in her house and keep her family with her all the time. Even a week after the attack, four newsreaders broke down while reading four News Specials in one night. A friend of my hostess has had to go to four funerals this week - all young friends of her 20-something son. One boy had been on the flight from Boston. It seems as if everyone in New Jersey has had to go to a wake, a funeral or a memorial service. There are 2,000 missing from New Jersey alone.

One New Yorker said on TV. he just had to get out of New York this weekend, to look at *trees* in New Jersey, and get strength from seeing them, to carry on. One man told that he had never admired the Mayor of New York in a political sense but his courage and strength throughout this crisis was exemplary. (Mayor Guilani has prostate cancer, too.) David Letterman, a chat show host, has been mentioned favourably to me in several cafes and restaurants because of his sensitive coverage of the tragedy. His careful and caring words were totally different to his normal output. It has been announced on the radio that bomb hoaxers will now be imprisoned – *quite right too!*

NEW YORK
25.09.01
Anne was by now recovering from her operations and being inundated with requests for her to visit, or for friends to call and visit. This American tradition is great: a group of friends arrive at the 'patient's' house bringing baskets of 'cookies', cakes, ingredients for tea-making, and even the crockery, so that a tea-party can be held around the patient's bed! Because of this lovely tradition, Anne decreed that she could manage one day a week and I should have Thursdays 'off' and I used these days to get the bus to New York.

I found that Americans here in New York and in the countryside in New Jersey, were now putting a brave face on their situation, and celebrations were in hand for Harvest Time, Halloween, Thanksgiving and Christmas in a much bigger way than in England.

As a visitor from Britain I was obviously feeling enormous sympathy for the Americans Sadness and shock were more apparent than feelings of anger or revenge. There were still funerals every day - my host's friend attended one at St. Patrick's Cathedral for her brother who perished at the World Trade Centre site, and she still has to go to another for work colleague who died in the Pentagon crash. I read that the average age of those who died was 28 years. Everyone I spoke to had a tragic story to relate about lost friends and relatives and several people told me of the loss of forty and fifty work colleagues in one day. Stores everywhere have sold all their black ties and had to re-order. I read that doctors are getting unprecedented demands for sleeping pills here in Manhattan where one and a half million people live. Today I learned that support groups are being set up for Muslims but that restaurants and cafes run by Afghans and other Muslims are being avoided. Many are empty because fewer people are going out to shows or meals in the capital.

42ⁿᵈ Street

The smell in the air around Ground Zero is still acrid and horrible and although I had decided to be brave and see the devastation from the open top of an 'English' tourist bus, I lost my nerve at the last minute and decided not to go. I cried anyway, most of the morning of my first day walking round New York, because there are flowers and tributes and condolence books outside the Fire Stations, Police Stations, shops and hotels. Many children have written and drawn tributes to their heroes - one was a drawing of a big hand saying "Here's High Five for the great job you're doing!" On Broadway there was a huge bronze statue of a fireman, and a roll of honour with dozens of names on it, parked temporarily by the roadside, collecting donations for the Red Cross appeal. There have been many stories of the incredible escapes made from the buildings, including a lawyer friend who told me that lawyers are among the very few workers who start later in the day and therefore hadn't arrived when the terrorists attacked. Their secretary was there but fortunately ran out and lived.

Tony Blair's presence and the British involvement since llth September is much appreciated here, and the public have been quick to praise the New York Mayor, Rudi Guiliani who was the first spokesman after the attack and has consistently given information and advice in a kindly and unemotional way. I learned today that the 999 call we would make, is 911 here and because the day is recorded after the month when writing the date in America, this, also, was 9.ll.

New York is a wonderful place for tourists and the grid system makes finding your way so easy. Twenty blocks is one mile and New Yorkers are the only people known to *walk* in America, since it is quicker to walk here than to take a cab, because of the traffic. I couldn't help noticing that very smart women wear trainers! They have their shoes in a bag for when they arrive at their destinations. (One woman told me she was now wearing her 'sneakers' (trainers to us) in the office because of the hoax calls and urgent evacuation of buildings since the disaster - she could make a faster getaway!)

I have to tell you: - Times Square isn't a square - there are very few squares as we know them, in New York - only circles and triangles. I was thrilled to "Take a left on 8th on to 42nd Street" (42nd Street!) to find the place where "the bus from England stops." This information was from a huge black man when I asked where the open top red tourist bus left. Before hopping on I was even more delighted to have coffee in Applebee's Broadway Coffee Shop under a poster with Our Ruthie (Henshall), from Ipswich on it! I wanted to point it out to fellow Brits that were tucking into huge plates of breakfast but I restrained myself. The waiter told me that Broadway was 176 miles long - the longest street. (Do you think that is true?). I must tell you that the ladies' loo was the *whitest* I have ever seen - it hurt your eyes.

TOURIST BUS TOUR
The tourist bus was ideal for me, because the temperature was in the nineties and the excellent tour guide gave intriguing anecdotes about the residents of the apartments as well as the architectural and historical information everyone needed. No smoking was allowed - even on the open top deck - and smoking seems even less socially acceptable here than at home. We wove between the 13, 000 yellow taxi cabs and black or white 'stretch' limousines and delivery trucks and were allowed to stand up only at red lights to take photographs - because of low bridges and overhanging branches from the trees lining many streets.

Our tour guide, a diminutive New Yorker called Gwen, told of her fear on the day of the attack - she apparently grabbed her mum from her house in Chinatown at 11 am and walked to her own house, taking until 4 p.m. to get there. She had a very strong accent and lost no time telling us where, how much and when to tip her and the driver, and that she wanted us to know she was in the same working category as a waitress. She pointed out the Pennsylvania Hotel which has the telephone number Pennsylvania 65000 featured in the Glen Miller Story, and the building shaped like an old flat iron, where Cary Grant (when he was Archibald Leach) was a lift operator! We saw the Empire State Building (with Empire Strikes Back written bold on it) and learned that it is now the highest in New York at 102 floors and 1454 feet high. 85 million people have visited the observatories since it was opened in 1931. It was designed for ease and speed of construction apparently and the prefabricated pieces were slotted into place at a rate of about four storeys per week! The landing stage at the top was designed for Zeppelin passengers to alight but this scheme was abandoned and it was subsequently used by RKO for the famous King Kong picture and now for receiving radio signals.

In a building which was built at great expense from allegedly self-cleaning stainless steel (it didn't) I saw a settee for sale which was shaped like a pair of lips − bright red of course − and another like a huge leather hand. The decision as to whether I would investigate the stores with this weird and wonderful merchandise or walk in Central Park was a difficult one. My itinerary was in doubt because of unreliable knicker elastic and so I 'did' another bus tour instead. I said goodbye to a new Dutch friend who had sat with me throughout the trip.

SECOND BUS TOUR
I felt quite at home on my second adventure on an open-top "English" red double-decker now. My tour guide this time is a rather brusque - quite sarcastic in fact - New Yorker. I shall forgive him his chauvinistic tendencies because he *did* tell us loads of interesting facts and figures about a city which he clearly loves. He was amazingly scathing about the residents in the tallest apartment block, owned by Donald Trump, namely Sophia Loren, Steven Spielberg, Bill Gates and more! We passed Macy's Store - the largest in the World, where there are 500,000 items for sale, and the tour guide patronisingly suggested all the women on board might as well get off as we would enjoy shopping more than the rest of the trip! However, within ten minutes we saw the Intrepid Aircraft Carrier Museum which was moored on the river, and Saks store on Fifth Avenue, and the biggest Post Office in the World. On Bryant Park - which was an English-feeling square at the rear of the biggest public library in America - one could picnic on the grass or watch fashion shows and old movies on Mondays and Tuesdays. It looked a very restful oasis among the hubbub of traffic. In passing our courier reckoned that one stop on a London subway costs one dollar ten and for one dollar fifty one could go all the way to the end of the subway here. While passing Central Park the tour guide asked if there were any English on the bus who could tell her which English building Strawberry Fields was named for? Unfortunately the only English representative hadn't got a clue.

Into Greenwich Village now - no grid system here. The random street plan reminds Americans of England but the area is a real mixture of nationalities and personalities. Many gays and lesbians, mainstream and young people live here and have huge parades for Halloween and Columbus Day and there are restaurants and cafes for all tastes. The guide told us of 4 - 5 million dollar apartments in Greenwich but there are never any for sale. Rents for one-bedroom flats range from 1, 800 to 4 thousand dollars per month. To buy a one bedroom flat would cost 900,000 dollars. The Village, as New Yorkers call it, has a very Bohemian feel and famous people, particularly artists and writers, have made their homes in the houses and apartments lining the narrow, old-fashioned streets. I would love to go back to stroll around late at night to the coffee houses and cafes, experimental theatre and music clubs and jazz venues.

The art deco Waldorf Astoria on Park Lane, built in 1895 as the largest Hotel in the world, had a row of limousines outside. The Sheraton Hotel and Chrysler buildings were breath-takingly beautiful, and I had never seen cast iron facades like those on many of the other buildings. Wooden buildings are now not allowed in New York. Cast iron was preferred to other construction material, years ago, because it supported larger windows when the buildings were factories. These must certainly now benefit the residents in the conversions. We inspected the exterior of Madonna's apartment, and Seinfield's Soup Kitchen, and the apartment where John Lennon lived and the spot where he died. We admired an insurance building with a spire coated in 24-ct. gold, (no risk of theft there I suppose!) and the School of Performing Arts of "Fame" fame. Michael Douglas and Elizabeth Taylor have each been married three times in a most beautiful church off Fifth Avenue.

Outside the Plaza Hotel there were decorated horses and carts and a familiar East Anglian smell of horse manure. You could go for a drive in and around Central Park for 37$ per hour, or take 'English' tea in the Plaza Hotel. Designed and built in 1907, it has 800 rooms and 17 apartments for families. Owner Donald Trump has restored the hotel's original glitter but old public areas have apparently not lost their original ambience and looks.

An apartment overlooking Central Park would cost 15 - 30 million dollars! Intriguing shops called Beasty Feast (pet foods), Victoria's Secret (undies), Yellow Rat Bastard (young THIN peoples' clothes), and numerous outlets for live chickens, or fish, made me wish I could get off the bus for an hour or six. The tour bus continued its way with interesting sights and anecdotes and I could have stayed on forever.

With regard to my fascination with assessing the American temperament, I had a funny experience in the bus station here: I was in the queue for a cup of coffee when a man pushed in front of me and demanded coffee. I look surprised and he glared at me and said I had pushed in front of *him*! I don't remember what I said back but he realised I was British, and said "Well I am a New Yorker! I said "Well, never mind!" or something like that and he shouted to the Barman "Give the lady a coffee on me!"

CENTRAL PARK

I went to see the Park another day with my gorgeous guide, Giles – Ann and Tony's son. Giles showed me all the sites made familiar to me by films and I found it much 'wilder' than my local Ipswich Park and very well-used, and it felt airy and spacious. There were joggers and skateboarders and twice I came across a girl trainer on a bike, wearing a crash helmet and teaching acrobics to mothers with babies in buggies. They all ran a bit, then stopped and waved their arms and legs about following her instructions, then ran on! Some of the buggies had speakers in the hoods so that the babies could hear taped stories and songs while their mums exercised! One of them told me she had an electrically heated loo seat for her children........

I saw the memorial to John Lennon in a tear-drop shaped section of the park which was Yoko Ono's tribute, but it was not as evocative as I had anticipated. The mosaic circle on the ground, with Imagine picked out in the centre, was within sight of Dakota Building where they had lived, and a gift from the city of Naples. It is in an international Peace Garden, planted with 161 species of plant (one from every country of the world) - and strawberries.

Nearby was the ice-skating rink featured in so many American films, and a lake with turtles, swans and ducks - all the more attractive because there was no sign of litter. The current Mayor of New York has been successful in cutting crime in the Park and many people told me of their renewed confidence these days to enjoy time in the Park without anxiety about muggers etc. The American people here must certainly feel the benefit of this natural area to contemplate their sad situation.

Giles then suggested lunch and took me to a very Italian pizza restaurant. While we were eating this welcome feast, we watched some filming in the street outside - you really need to be able to concentrate on several things at once in New York - it is *terrific!*

'Home' to Ann and Tony's house in the flame red trees and a wonderful invitation to tea with a glamorous friend. I don't know whether the Englishness of the tea party was in my honour but the welcome, the table setting, the other guests and the conversations were - as they say here - *awesome!* All the women were beautifully groomed and I was fascinated with their hands - expertly manicured - and the rings! Great diamonds and clusters of rubies and other wonderful stones. They all had fascinating stories to tell of their various origins and I had difficulty remembering to try all the delicious pastries and sandwiches without missing a word. They were so interested in my replies about things English and - apart from getting in a muddle about who was who in the Royal Family - I fielded their questions fairly well I think.

Anne is doing well with the crutches and on a shopping expedition to a nearby Mall we managed to see branches of Bloomingdales and Saks. There were dozens of Ladies Lunching and the choice of food was amazing. I didn't regret my choice of starter of frozen yoghurt with about a quarter pound of walnuts covering it, followed by muffins made with cranberries or carrots and raisins and just in case this wasn't enough, you could have butter and jam, to accompany them.........

PENNSYLVANIA
20.10.01

I was to be repeatedly enthralled by the rural scenery in America and the route to Tony and Anne's daughter and son-in-law, Emma and Kevin's house in Millersville, Pennsylvania, was no disappointment. The wonderful trees and rivers and hills, and the rows and rows of pumpkins being offered for sale for Halloween, were amazing..

We arrived at their house in time for Garage Sale Day! It was raining and everyone a bit nervous as to whether to have their goods displayed on the front porches or in garages under cover, or out on the front lawns. It seemed as if everyone was taking part in this sale day and household and sports items were tempting neighbours everywhere you looked. Many people were attracted to my British accent and one man gave me an ashtray with heraldic signs of towns in England. They were so welcoming that I am still mystified why Emma doesn't own to being English, or even that her parents are! She has lived here since her early teens and certainly now looks and sounds like an American beauty.

We went for walks around the Millersville and I didn't see a single Coke can or paper bag anywhere. The well-tended gardens and parks and the grounds of the University were beautiful. Some enthusiastic hockey-playing girls exercised to very loud disco music in an adjoining sports field.

I noticed the Western Red Cedar fences, which are popular here, pale brown when new and then aging to a beautiful grey colour. There are relatively few fences needed, however, since the plots for the houses are absolutely huge, and gardens stretch forever. Individual houses are mainly clad in horizontal white boarding - which is made of 'alooooominium' these days.

Most of the shops here sold goods in the 'comfort food' category - lots of cream wheat and waffles and doughy cakes and pretzels. However, there were also acres of farm shops selling houseplants and vegetables of the highest quality.

LANCASTER
30.10.01

We all travelled one day to Lancaster, where the Armish and Mennonites live. In a cafe there, I was given a portion of Shoo Fly Pie by a waitress who heard my British accent. Apparently it was called after the girls that were employed to shoo the flies off newly baked pies. Pumpkin pie and carrot cake were other specialities on offer. I was impressed with what I was told about the Armish and longed to have a proper conversation with some of them but there wasn't time. The souvenir shops and cafes were full of their craft and were refreshingly simple and made of natural materials – far removed from the tacky plastic penises and bosoms offered to British tourists in Spain!

The Armish do not drive cars and it was delightful to see their horses and carts driven by families wearing Quaker style clothes – even white bonnets. They provided tea and home-made cookies under the trees and it was obvious that this is a very popular day out for all the American neighbours.

NANTUCKET

Another lovely expedition with my hosts – this time to their holiday home in Nantucket. On the journey from New Jersey to the ferry, I felt like one of those pretend Alsatians nodding and smiling in the back of cars. We travelled down highways at 65 mph maximum - in a huge, air-conditioned car – over the Tappanzee Bridge and the Hudson river, and on for about 250 tree-lined miles to the Hyannis Ferry and to Nantucket island.

Exotic place names like Tappan Zee, Pequot Reservation and Mashantucket were interspersed with exits to Norwich or Groton or Bedford! Tempting signs indicated exits to many different, exciting-looking venues. There was one to Wild West Town – a theme park where they stage fights and brawls in the bar where you eat. I would also have loved to explore Mystic Aquarium, Horse-Neck Beach, Gales Ferry and Noonsocket, to name but a few. Signs indicating that only two or more persons were allowed in one vehicle have apparently not succeeded in cutting down the traffic sufficiently to prevent traffic building up for hours, several times during our journey. I loved watching America pass the window, but the hundreds of stars and stripes flats in gardens, and sticking out of nearly every car, kept reminding me of their shared grief and repeatedly made my heart sink. We saw fourteen flags over one bridge alone – including a Union Jack – and on hundreds of buildings there were huge, beautifully made flags, some at half-mast and some defiantly at the top of the pole.

After two and a half hours on the ferry – 26 miles from Hyannis, Mass. – with lots of dogs and smiling holiday-makers – we edged in to Nantucket Harbour. Nantucket was a major whaling centre for much of the nineteenth century and the harbour looks exactly the same as it did years ago – quaint lighthouses and attractively designed houses all uniformly shingled in cedar squares with sparkling white paint and flowers everywhere. The boats coming into the harbour used the sparkling white spires of an Episcopalian and a Unitarian Church to get their bearings or line up. At one time there were 1,600 people -the Indian population being larger than the Quaker settlers. The settlers' influence on the furnishings and architecture here fit perfectly with the simple beauty of the beaches, wild moors and cobble-stoned roads.

There is now a winter population of 5,000 but in the summer there are over 40,000 people – and that's without the dogs! Over 60% of the houses are large, beautiful second homes and I have never seen such a good combination of money and taste. People here are obviously wealthy but not in an ostentatious way. They dress in expensive casual clothes and the shops of are full of tasteful goods. A holiday atmosphere prevails even when the sea mist drifts in and you hear the haunting fog horns. There are many famous stars and business people who spend their summers here.

We breakfasted at the Airport Restaurant – called Hutch's – where the TV series "Wings" was filmed. It was entertaining to eat and watch the small private jets landing and taking off. The larger planes had been cancelled due to a terrorist scare. I ate my 'easy over' eggs and enjoyed the free refills of excellent coffee in the company of tourists, residents and construction workers in immaculate work clothes. A resident told me of the grief felt when Kennedy crashed near here. He was known to be an excellent pilot and, when he died, the emotions this man described reminded me of our own feelings when Princess Diana died.

At another of the many inviting seafood restaurants, I enjoyed the local prize-winning clam chowder for lunch. It is an un-fishy soup, which has lumps of clams and potatoes in it but tastes remarkably like very creamy chicken soup. It can be made with different ingredients in other States, but I highly recommend this one.

Another popular place to eat was Baxter's Fish and Chip Restaurant – full of visiting Brits today! The Sea Grille served the sweetest scallops ever, and the stuffed *'shrimp'* (as they call it)) proved to be the biggest *prawns* in a baked crab 'crumble' with lobster sauce!

Back on the heath the sandpipers ran up and down in front of the foamy surf. They_pecked food from the receding waves and then scampered comically back up the beach again. This section of the beach had been closed for months to protect the nesting piping plovers and they seemed plentiful again. In fact some of the residents must have thought the ban a bit over the top as I saw a car sticker saying "Piping Plovers taste Like Chicken"! The environmentally aware have also imposed a ban on fully inflated tyres on the beach, to protect it from erosion. Everyone has to deflate their tyres before driving on it and re-flate them to get home.

There were several fishermen and women in waders having a wonderful time. They all had a selection of rods attached vertically to the front of their enormous 'jeeps'. No live bait is needed, only cigar-shaped wooden blocks. They were fishing for bass, which is good to eat, and bluefish which swim in shoals and are popular with sports fishermen.

There were very few swimmers but I managed to change behind the open car door and have a dip which was wonderful – clear and cool – and I felt an absolute surge of joy and contentment. This is a bit over the top isn't it – but my operation scar is healed and my fears of recurrence of the cancer are fading, and my friends are spoiling me so I couldn't suppress my happiness in such fantastic surroundings.

In the town the sops offered a mixture of souvenirs and gifts with a nautical flavour. Moby Dick is a popular figure here, since whaling ships have sailed from Nantucket to all parts of the world in search of whales and whale oil. The ships were mostly owned and captained by Quakers and one, the "Essex" was attacked and sunk by an angry sperm whale in the Pacific. The crew sailed several thousand miles in tiny wooden skiffs and some eventually made it back home to Nantucket. Melville based his book "Moby Dick" on this true story. Tempting glass, wooden and porcelain models of whales nestle among other objects d'art. I saw a clock shaped like a highland terrier, with his tongue as a pendulum. I wasn't tempted by this but I loved a shop notice saying "Your husband called to say you can buy whatever you want!"......

Ann and Tony spend weeks in their lovely clapboard house by the sea, in the summer, and their family join them from wherever *they* are living at the time. The winters are pretty cold and wet but Ann and Tony often think of trying a Christmas get-together here some day.

It was time to leave to return to New Jersey and, after a bit more shopping for souvenirs for my grandchildren, I swam again in the drinkable sea, walked on the white empty beach and sunbathed under cloudless blue skies. I went 'home' absolutely Nantuckered Out - as seen on a T-shirt!

BERMUDA
5.11.01
As a thank you gesture, my old friends Ann and Tony invited me to leave New Jersey with them and stay in Bermuda which is their permanent home - well as permanent as they are *anywhere* -, for a holiday! As if the adventures so far, haven't been thanks enough!

We flew into the tiny airport and I loved Bermuda from Day One. You would *all* love it. Imagine sparkling sunshine on blue seas and swimming pools in every other garden. Add green gardens and little parks full of palm trees and flowers, with yellow-breasted kiskadees piping their funny song, and you will start to get the 'feeling' of Bermuda. It was a comfortable 70 degrees all the time I was there. All the houses are painted in soft pinks, yellows, and greens and have roofs that are lime-washed white, which makes them, look like iced cakes. There are lime-washed ridges which collect the rain just before where the gutter would be, to take it to storage tanks under the houses. The roads are lined by sheer walls and blind curves which make it suicidal to walk anywhere, but the hedges and gardens are so flowery it takes your breath away to drive around the islands.

Surveying all this today while eating a juicy apple from the pillion of an l00cc Italian motor scooter I thought I might have arrived in Heaven. Bermuda is 2l miles long and a half a mile wide and the bougainvillea, hibiscus and oleander hedges make a journey anywhere an absolutely wonderful experience. Masses of prickly pear - which I had only heard about in a song -

it is a dramatically purple fruit with thorns - grow at the roadsides. The scooter is the residents' main form of transport here and only one car per family is allowed. The twenty-mile an hour speed limit doesn't seem to slow the traffic as the scooters buzz in and out of the numerous taxis and pink buses in a most alarming way.

We passed over the smallest drawbridge in the world which allows shipping to pass from the north to the south coasts of the hundreds of small islands that comprise Bermuda. A string of coral reefs around the islands make it an underwater paradise for divers and snorkellers. Situated in mid-Atlantic, Bermuda is 650 nautical miles east of North Carolina in the United States, and stands today as the oldest self-governing British Colony. I loved the historical influence of the British, mixed with the modern American feel, and overlaid with the relaxed and cheery Bermudan bits. Someone told me Bermuda is the third richest country in the world with 58,000 population.

There were flowery lanes and roads (no pavements) with names like Happy Talk Lane, Point Finger Road and Featherbed Alley but I was disappointed to learn that a disused railway line which is now a wonderful walkway round the island was not recommended for solitary walkers who would be a target for crime.

A Bermudan called Johnny Barnes waves and smiles and blows kisses at travellers on a roundabout near Hamilton. He has been doing this every morning for 20 years apparently and typifies the welcoming and friendly atmosphere in the town. He is nicknamed The Greeter and is Bermuda's unofficial ambassador of good will. Hamilton, the capital has shops full of expensive gifts and souvenirs and many excellent restaurants and bars. The shops are named for their very British-sounding owners, or things like Hodge Podge Gifts, Fantasea (water sports gear), Bees Knees Gifts, Rum Cake Company etc. There is no indication that this is also one of the most densely populated countries in the world - perhaps due to the fact that most of the population can find work, and there is no tax on earnings. I watched a ferry called Corona dock at Hamilton with people going to work and counted twenty black and twenty white people disembark. I got talking to a Portugese girl with her boy of about three, who shouted to him "What bit of NO don't you understand!" when he was disobedient.

The famous Perfumery was fairly quiet because it was winter, but it 'nestled' in an area full of banana and mango trees, hibiscus - coloured red and white on the same bloom), peach, pink, yellow and orange! Some of these were double blooms, too. I loved the Moongate entrance where you were invited to make a wish but I couldn't honestly think of one desire because I was in such a beautiful place – geographically and emotionally.

I also visited some caves nearby which had been discovered by boys looking for their cricket ball in 1905. At the entrance to the caves were several Match-me-if-You-Can trees - every leaf was different!

Sunday, 11th November, 2001.

His Excellency the Governor arrived at the Cenotaph in a cockaded hat and red uniform, accompanied by a dozen white police motor bikes. He inspected the War Veterans and laid a wreath and the red-coated bands played in the sparkling sunshine and it was altogether very moving - whatever is it about a band that makes you cry? They played the National Anthem and several hymns.

The Last Post was sounded and a cannon was fired some distance away. Some 40 - 50 elderly men and women war veterans had marched to join the dignitaries at the Cenotaph, one in a wheelchair, and I was in a prime position to see everything, standing on the pavement opposite the Government Building. A charming Bermudan veteran standing next to me in the street told his story. He recalled his seven years as a drummer in the Army in the days when there was a Black Army and a White Army. (They subsequently amalgamated). He would have liked to be with the other veterans today, but knew that he couldn't stand for the duration of the service. (One of the veterans did in fact have to be stretchered away - probably the heat as well as the long time they had to stand.) My informant told of his pride in firing the cannon on one occasion. His huge son, sporting a tee shirt advertising his own chiropody practice, was obviously proud of his dad, and of his remarkably well-behaved - and adorable - twin sons of about seven years. Bermudan children are definitely happier, more respectful and well behaved in restaurants and shops, than in America or the UK and I could have taken these two home with me for two pins. Outside an Anglican church there was an invitation from the Minister to fast, starting next Sunday, to respect Ramadan *and* Advent. There was a notice nearby saying "Please Don't Steal the Notice"………

It was strange to keep hearing British accents after my two months in America and fascinating to hear the life stories of so many ex-patriate residents. I met a lady at the bus stop - an ex Finchley resident, 85 years old and wearing a baseball cap and much golden jewellery - and she told me the gossip about the lady Premier. O.K. - I'll tell you because I know you are dying to know. She has a really expensive taste in hats, apparently, and only ever drinks champagne (having had the glass checked for chips each time), and she fell off her high heels last year at the Remembrance Service. No such accident this year - she looked incredibly elegant and dignified

Everyone urges tourists to go to the old Royal Navy Dockyard, and to the Maritime Museum and it was indeed an interesting experience, starting with watching incredible dolphins in the Keep and ending with eating Haagen Daz ice-cream, looking the harbour. The limestone buildings and forts would keep lovers of architecture happy for days, and there were six buildings housing artefacts to interest divers, historians and especially military historians. The largest fort in Bermuda was built to protect the dockyard in the 19th century. The Commissioner's House has been resurrected and is reborn as a showcase of island culture and history. It is similar to houses at British military outposts all over the world but is recognised now as the most spectacular. I loved everything about it but best of all were the Dolls Houses - exquisite! All Victorian furniture and ornaments and dinner services and kitchen equipment - wonderful. The rugs had been made by two women who wore magnifying glasses to create them like a tapestry, and each took eighty hours of work. I could have looked at the tiny details of the rooms for hours.

The top floors consist of elegant dining rooms and Messes. The US Navy and the Royal Navy have two of the rooms. In the latter I saw pictures of Harold Macmillan, Ted Heath, etc. and the most smiley picture of the Queen I have ever seen, in the mass of memorabilia there. I think our Royal Family love Bermuda as much as I do. I saw evidence of their visits all over the islands. There is a lovely chatty letter displayed in the Bermudan Perfumery, from the Queen Mother thanking Bermudan friends for a gift of lilies sent from here every Easter and Princess Margaret had visited and unveiled a statue in the little park in St. George.

At the bus stop for coming home I talked with a nine-year old from Nova Scotia who had Jesus says Love One Another on his tee-shirt - he wanted to know where exactly England was?

St. George is the oldest settlement in the Western Hemisphere and houses and churches date from 1612. The cemeteries were a fascinating reminder of Bermuda's long history. In the Naval Cemetery I saw the graves of 24 and 26-year old seamen, being two of the mainly Scottish men buried there. One had accidentally drowned and one had succumbed to sunstroke.

In St. Peter's Church cemetery the civilians buried there included a Surgeon on a mail boat which had sunk off St. Georges in 1846. The Principal Medical Officer on the island had been one of the first victims of a yellow fever epidemic and a nineteen year old had died of "The Prevailing Fever" and another teenager was drowned "by the upsetting of his boat in a terrific squall". More recently Sir Richard Sharples, Governor of Bermuda, was buried after he, his ADC and the ADC's dog, had been killed by an assassin on 10th March, 1973.

I wandered in a very romantic ruin of a church that was never finished and overheard two men avidly discussing their pleasure in the new Harry Potter book while watching the Ipswich/Bolton Football match on television.

The Pollockshields shipwreck is commemorated in the Elbow each Hotel with many photographs. The steamer went on to the rocks in 1915 and a whaleboat owner hauled his own boat overland by horse and cart, making five trips to save the entire crew. Tragically the captain was swept overboard while attempting to rescue the ship's cat and her kittens. They were saved by the whaler on his fifth trip.

My wonderful stay in Bermuda ended at The Swizzle Inn, eating a meal billed as English Fish and Chips, and with the noise of the 'planes on the flight path from Bermuda reminding me of my imminent departure to

England and return to the bosom of my family – there! I have said *that* word without shuddering.

Travelling has reduced my anxieties about my breast cancer and I can make a clean breast (!) of it, to friends and worried soon-to-be patients, with the confidence of experience now. My prescription for both grandmotherhood and survival of bosom bother is: Buy a Ticket and Pack Your Bag and you'll be so glad you to be home, you'll be glad you went!

Remembrance Sunday in Hamilton, Bermuda

Printed in the United Kingdom
by Lightning Source UK Ltd.
116742UKS00001B/121-168